Beethoven's
Chamber Music
in Context

Beethoven's Chamber Music in Context

Angus Watson

THE BOYDELL PRESS

First published 2010
The Boydell Press, Woodbridge
Reprinted in paperback 2012

ISBN 978 1 84383 577 6 hardback
ISBN 978 1 84383 716 9 paperback

The Boydell Press is an imprint of Boydell & Brewer Ltd
PO Box 9, Woodbridge, Suffolk IP12 3DF, UK
and of Boydell & Brewer Inc.
668 Mount Hope Ave, Rochester, NY 14620-2731, USA
website: www.boydellandbrewer.com

A CIP catalogue record for this book is available
from the British Library

The publisher has no responsibility for the continued existence
or accuracy of URLs for external or third-party internet websites
referred to in this book, and does not guarantee that any content
on such websites is, or will remain, accurate or appropriate.

Papers used by Boydell & Brewer Ltd are natural, recyclable products
made from wood grown in sustainable forests

Designed and typeset in Adobe Warnock Pro
by David Roberts, Pershore, Worcestershire

Printed and bound by CPI Group (UK) Ltd, Croydon, CR0 4YY

For Alison

for our family

& for our musical friends

Contents

Foreword

Angus Watson has set himself to survey the entire body of chamber works composed by Beethoven between 1792, when he settled in Vienna, and 1827, the year of his death, and to place each one in the context of Beethoven's life and his relationships with contemporaries, and of the works in other genres that he was writing at the time – a formidable challenge and one that, to my mind, he rises to magnificently.

The story of the thirty-five year journey from the piano trios, op. 1, startling fruit of Beethoven's studies with Haydn, to the visionary beauties of the last string quartets is arguably without parallel in the history of music, and it is told here in absorbing detail: a constantly changing landscape, as Beethoven's 'restlessly and profoundly ranging mind' (Richard Capell's phrase) impels him to strike out new paths and open up unknown worlds of music. But though the author does moving justice to those last transcendent creations, he never falls into the error of patronizing the early works and treating them as mere forerunners. On the contrary, he is equally alive to the energy and extraordinary self-confidence, the sheer originality of those first sonatas, trios and quartets with which the young Beethoven disconcerted the Viennese as much as he dazzled them.

Throughout, the book benefits richly from the fact that its wisdom is grounded in the experience of a professional string player who has played and lived, note by note, the music he writes about with such deep and searching insight.

DAVID CAIRNS

Preface

Beethoven's restlessly and profoundly ranging mind opened up new worlds of music. His significance lay in his sense of an illimitable universe; depth beyond depth and the endlessness of possibility.[1]

Richard Capell (1885–1954)

The aim of this book is to provide professional and amateur musicians and music lovers generally with an outline of the historical context and character of over fifty chamber works composed by Beethoven during his thirty-five years in Vienna.[2] Articles and books on the subject usually focus on specific genres – string quartets, violin sonatas or, more generally, chamber music for strings and piano or strings and wind – and there is much to be said for such an approach in an age of specialists, where such writing can be matched by appropriate boxed sets of compact discs. But something important may be lost in the process.

Although differing in genre, Beethoven's early chamber works, published in the late 1790s and early 1800s, share the same exhilarating context of innovation, excitement and creative energy which he experienced during his earlier years in Vienna. His later chamber music – the three *Razumovsky* quartets, for example, or the A major Cello Sonata, op. 69, and the two op.70 piano trios, were no less affected by the more mature and spacious context created by Beethoven in the aftermath of two of his greatest and truly seminal works, the *Eroica* Symphony and *Fidelio*. The six transcendent late quartets, composed during the last three years of his life, were similarly empowered by the spirituality of the *Missa Solemnis* and the majesty of the Ninth Symphony.

Contemporary audiences expected a mixture of genres at public concerts and private soirées, such as one given by Countess Josephine von Deym on 10 December 1800: 'Beethoven played the sonata with cello. I played the last of the [violin] sonatas, accompanied by Schuppanzigh who, like all the others, played divinely. Then Beethoven, that real angel, let us hear his quartets which have not been engraved yet and are the greatest of their kind. The famous Kraft played the cello, Schuppanzigh first violin. You can imagine what a treat it was for us!'[3] So each work is discussed

---

[1] Capell, *Schubert's Songs*, p. 35.

[2] Beethoven's early chamber music for strings and piano composed in Bonn is discussed briefly in Appendix 1 below; his sets of variations for chamber ensembles in Appendix 2; his wind chamber music not included in Chapter 9 in Appendix 3; and his chamber music arrangements made or approved by him in Appendix 4.

[3] Landon, *Beethoven: A Documentary Study*, p. 130. The programme would therefore have included Beethoven's third Violin Sonata in E flat major, op. 12 no. 3; one of the two op. 5 Cello Sonatas (or possibly the arrangement for cello and piano of the Horn Sonata, op. 17) and one or more of the six op. 18 String Quartets.

here in chronological order regardless of genre – or very broadly so, as approximate dates of composition, noted at the head of each chapter, are not always clear, and publication was frequently delayed for one reason or another, sometimes for two or three years.

Like most professional musicians, I never had time to research the background of this wonderful music in any depth when I performed it myself as a violinist. If I had, I would have played it differently and certainly with greater freshness. Though quoting extensively from a variety of sources, including recent books and articles by contemporary scholars, this does not aim to be a critical or academic book, nor does it include discussion of ever-changing styles of performance. Apart from examining the historical background and character of each work, points of interest in every movement are briefly examined, but do not otherwise stray too far, I hope, from Beethoven's own injunction that if analysis is necessary, 'it should be confined to characterization of the composition in general terms'.[4]

Acknowledgements

Special thanks are due to David Cairns, not only for contributing a Foreword to this book, but also for his many constructive and invaluable suggestions. Few musicians can equal the breadth of his experience and musical insight, whether as chief music critic of the *Sunday Times* (1983–92), author, among other books, of a magisterial two-volume biography of Berlioz or as co-founder of the Chelsea Opera Group and Thorington Players. In recognition of his many achievements he has been honoured as distinguished visiting professor at the University of California, visiting scholar at the Getty Center in Santa Monica, visiting fellow of Merton College, Oxford, Officier de l'Ordre des Arts et des Lettres for services to French music, and CBE.

Thanks are also due to Michael Bonnin for his technical help and to a number of fellow musicians, both professional and amateur, whose comments have been invaluable: William and Gill Agnew, the Alberni Quartet, Levon Chilingirian, John Falconer, Sir David Lumsden, sometime Principal of the Royal Academy of Music, Margaret Lynn, deputy Dean of Music at the Hong Kong Academy for Performing Arts, Frieda Robinson, Jeffrey Sharkey, Director of the Peabody Institute, Johns Hopkins University, Baltimore, Peter Smith, sometime Professor of Music at the University of London, Western Ontario, Clara Taylor, Chief Examiner of the Associated Board of the Royal Schools of Music, Elizabeth Watson and Miranda Wilson. I am also indebted to Dr. Nicole Kämpken of the Beethoven-Haus,

---

[4] Thayer, *The Life of Beethoven*, p. 766. From a letter (now lost) from Beethoven to Wilhelm Müller, organist and director of music in Bremen Cathedral. See also Clive, *Beethoven and his World*, pp. 242–3.

Bonn for her advice on the engraving on the front cover after a painting of Beethoven by Carl Mittag; also to Jacob Franck, a fellow student at the Royal College of Music more than half a century ago. Recently retired as associate conductor at the opera house in Bielefeld, Germany, he volunteered to proof-read the book in its entirety and did so with characteristic thoroughness and enthusiasm. Among the many distinguished past and present Beethoven scholars in Britain, Canada, Germany and the United States, who have provided invaluable insights in articles and books, duly acknowledged in the Bibliography, affectionate mention must be made of the late Philip Radcliffe, my seemingly omniscient supervisor when I was an undergraduate at Cambridge in the 1950s, whose book *Beethoven's String Quartets* (1965) has never strayed too far from my desk.

Finally, I am grateful to members of my immediate family who have helped in a number of ways, among them my brother, John Watson, for his technical help; but most of all, my wife, Alison, who has followed the book through its many stages over a number of years with infinite patience and care, her many suggestions always welcomed and almost always incorporated.

ANGUS WATSON
March 2010

PART ONE ⧆ Context

'I cannot compose anything that is not obbligato, seeing that, as a matter of fact, I came into the world with an obbligato accompaniment.'

Beethoven in a letter to the publisher
Franz Hoffmeister, December 1800

CHAPTER 1

Arrival and Relaunch in Vienna, 1792

A few of Beethoven's earliest compositions were published in Bonn in the 1780s and early 1790s, but when he finally moved to Vienna in November 1792, he decided to delay any further publications until he was satisfied that he could make the greatest possible impact in a variety of genres and styles. Though already celebrated as a virtuoso pianist and master of improvisation, he held back as a composer, spending his first three years there revising the best of his earlier compositions, writing new ones and learning what he could from Haydn and others. In 1794, he was particularly cross with his Bonn friend, the horn player Nikolaus Simrock, for publishing an unrevised version of his Eight Variations for Piano (four hands) on a Theme by Count Waldstein, WoO 67: 'The fact is that I had no desire to publish at the present moment any variations, because I wanted to wait until some more important works of mine, which are due to appear very soon, had been given to the world.'[1]

The musical community in Vienna was much larger than the one Beethoven left behind in Bonn, although several private orchestras had been disbanded in the years following the French Revolution and, at least compared to London, there were surprisingly few public concerts. As a result, opportunities for the promotion of orchestral music were limited while, by contrast, the demand for piano music and chamber music was voracious. Much of the music published at the time was aimed at a modest domestic market – what George Eliot would later describe succinctly as 'airs with variations, a small kind of tinkling, which symbolized the aesthetic part of a young lady's education'.[2] But Beethoven showed little interest in providing such easy fare, reflecting the elevated view of his Bonn teacher Christian Gottlob Neefe that musical forms are closely related to the spiritual life of mankind; so he aimed his 'more important works', as Mozart had done in his later chamber music, at an altogether more cultured and musically literate audience.

The three piano trios, op. 1 (1794–5), were the first of his 'more important works' to be composed and published in Vienna, and three of his five late quartets – op. 130, op. 131 and op. 135, all completed in 1826 would be the last. The journey between them, involving almost fifty significant chamber works, many of them masterpieces and some universally accepted as among the most sublime expressions of genius in art, would be an astonishing one, in which new continents, even new worlds, would be discovered and explored. It would be a mistake to underestimate Beethoven's achievements at the beginning of that journey, or the importance

[1] *Letters of Beethoven*, Letter 10, 18 June 1794: Beethoven to Nikolaus Simrock in Bonn.
[2] George Eliot, *Middlemarch*.

and originality of those early works composed after his arrival in Vienna – a period aptly named 'The First Maturity' by Lewis Lockwood[3] – least of all to regard them as 'imitative', as so many commentators have done over the last two centuries. Beethoven's contemporaries certainly considered them original and, while some found them revelatory, others thought them bewildering and eccentric.

Tension between Beethoven's classical roots and his desire to find new modes of expression lie behind the creative excitement and freshness of his early music. Visionary movements abound: for example, parts of the Largo con espressione in the Piano Trio in G major, op. 1 no. 2 (ex. 5.9), the first two movements in the Violin Sonata in A major, op. 30 no. 1 (ex. 13.1–5), and the astonishing Adagio in the String Quartet in F major, op. 18 no. 1 (ex. 10.4–5), which was inspired by the tomb scene in Shakespeare's *Romeo and Juliet*, could be placed almost unchanged in much later compositions. Long before the *Pastoral* Symphony was conceived, pastoral movements were plentiful in his chamber music: the first movement in the Quartet in D major, op. 18 no. 3 (ex. 10.15–16), for instance, or the *Spring* Sonata, op. 24 (ex. 11.6–10). Powerful, angry music, as in the first movement of the String Trio, op. 9 no. 3 (ex. 8.15), and of the Violin Sonata, op. 30 no. 2 (ex. 13.8–10), both in C minor, appeared several years before the Fifth Symphony; and the heroic *Kreutzer* Sonata, op. 47, large-scale and virtuoso, was completed a few weeks before Beethoven began to sketch the mighty and no less virtuoso *Eroica* Symphony.

Beethoven's piano trios, string trios, violin sonatas and cello sonatas have received much less critical attention than his string quartets and piano sonatas – much less than they deserve. Many of them are masterpieces, including some which are heard surprisingly little. Although each composition is individual, some characteristics are common to all, among them the increasingly 'democratic' balance he achieved between piano and strings, instruments which, in his often expressed view, are entirely different from each other. 'I cannot compose anything that is not obbligato', he explained in a letter to the publisher Franz Anton Hoffmeister in December 1800, 'seeing that, as a matter of fact, I came into the world with an obbligato accompaniment.'[4]

Other shared characteristics include Beethoven's enthusiastic response to contemporary changes in string playing, inspired by Viotti and the influential French School, and to the still greater changes in the construction of pianos, with piano-makers struggling to keep up with his innovations as a pianist and composer. 'Since both his playing and his compositions were in advance of his time', his pupil Carl Czerny wrote many years later, 'so were the pianos of the time often unequal to carrying his gigantic interpretations.'[5]

[3] Lockwood, *Beethoven: The Music and the Life*, p. 169.

[4] *Letters of Beethoven*, Letter 41, 15 December 1800: Beethoven to Franz Hoffmeister.

[5] Carl Czerny, quoted in Landon, *Beethoven: A Documentary Study*, p. 290.

CHAPTER 2

Beethoven, Pianist and String Player

As one of the leading pianists of his generation, Beethoven took it for granted that he would be the first to perform his own violin sonatas, cello sonatas and piano trios with leading string players; this was his personal chamber music, personal in a way that his string trios and string quartets could never be. His brilliance and originality as a pianist owed much to Christian Gottlob Neefe, who, though a Lutheran, became organist at the Catholic court in Bonn in 1782. In addition to piano and organ lessons, Neefe taught him composition and thorough-bass and introduced him to a wide range of music, including Bach's Forty-eight Preludes and Fugues, teaching which Beethoven warmly acknowledged in later years: 'I thank you for the advice you have very often given me about making progress in my divine art. Should I ever become a great man, you will have a share in my success.'[1]

Although he soon wrote himself out of his increasingly difficult string trios and string quartets and had to entrust them to others, Beethoven was a capable violinist and violist in his early years. He had two excellent violin teachers: Franz Rovantini, a relation by marriage of his mother, and Franz Ries, a close family friend and a generous and considerate man, who later became leader of the orchestra. Both of them had been pupils of the violinist, conductor and impresario Johann Peter Salomon, who eventually made his home in England and commissioned Haydn to compose his celebrated 'London' symphonies; so their approach to technical matters is likely to have been similar. After Rovantini's early death, Franz Ries, recently returned from three successful years as a soloist and quartet player in Vienna, took over as his violin teacher. Beethoven never forgot his practical and moral support at the time of his mother's death in 1787 and was able to return Ries's many kindnesses when, later in Vienna, he agreed to teach his son Ferdinand piano and composition. Franz Ries lived long enough to be present when Beethoven's statue was unveiled in Bonn during festivities directed by Liszt in 1845.

Like any small boy starting violin lessons, Beethoven did not always practise what he had been told to practise. A neighbour, Cecilia Fischer, remembered his father reprimanding him for improvising on the violin and the piano. But he continued playing, and in self-defence, said to his father: 'Now isn't that beautiful?' His father replied: 'That is something else, you made it up yourself. You are not to do that yet; apply yourself to piano

---

[1] *Letters of Beethoven*, Letter 6, before 26 October 1793: Beethoven to Christian Gottlob Neefe. Beethoven's first piano teacher was his father, who was followed by Gilles van den Eeden (1708–82), court organist in Bonn, and finally by Christian Gottlob Neefe, whom Beethoven held in high regard.

and violin, strike the notes quickly and correctly. When you have once got so far, then you can and must work enough with your head.'[2]

When the Elector, Maximilian Franz, expanded his musical establishment in 1788, Beethoven was appointed a member of the viola section in the court orchestra 'to serve … for life in the theatre, the church and the concert'.[3] He already held the position of court organist, played keyboard for theatrical rehearsals and was generally considered to be so outstanding a pianist that even his most hardened orchestral colleagues were enthralled whenever he played or improvised. His viola playing was not at that level, but he must have been thoroughly competent, as the orchestra was one of the best in Europe and included several young virtuosos, some of whom are still remembered; among them were the cellist Bernhard Romberg, and his cousin, the violinist Andreas Romberg, the flautist and composer Anton Reicha, the horn player and music publisher Nikolaus Simrock, as well as Franz Ries. One commentator, Carl Junker, was particularly impressed when he heard the orchestra play Mozart and Pleyel symphonies: 'It was not possible to obtain a higher degree of exactness. Such perfection in the pianos, fortes, rinsforzandos; such a swelling and increase in tone and then an almost imperceptible dying away, from the most powerful to the lightest accents – all this was formerly to be heard only in Mannheim. It would be difficult to find another orchestra in which the violins and basses are throughout in such excellent hands.'[4]

It is inconceivable that such an orchestra would have admitted run-of-the-mill players to its ranks, however talented they were. It is also hard to imagine a more thorough musical education for the young Beethoven. Practical experience as a viola player and cembalist in opera, ballet and orchestral performances provided him with invaluable insights into such matters as texture, balance, orchestration and the most effective use of dynamics. As an official court organist, he played for services in the court chapel and at a local monastery and he frequently played chamber music with friends and colleagues – all of this in addition to his principal concerns as pianist, improviser and composer.

Once established in Vienna in the 1790s as a virtuoso pianist, a master of improvisation and composer of such promise that he was already 'commanding extraordinary attention' and 'the undivided applause of connoisseurs and music lovers',[5] some of whom already regarded him as Mozart's heir, Beethoven still insisted on having frequent violin lessons with his close friend Wenzel Krumpholz, and also with a short, tubby teenager, who later became one of the most devoted and authoritative interpreters of his music, Ignaz Schuppanzigh. Beethoven was eager to find out everything he

[2] Gottfried Fischer, quoted in Sonneck, *Beethoven: Impressions by his Contemporaries*, p. 4.

[3] Thayer, *The Life of Beethoven*, p. 95 n. 12.

[4] Thayer, *The Life of Beethoven*, p. 104.

[5] The Fischof Manuscript, quoted in Thayer, *The Life of Beethoven*, p. 164.

could about instruments and instrumental techniques from experts: 'Every day', he noted in his 'Tagebuch' or diary, 'share a meal with someone, such as musicians, where one can discuss this and that, instruments etc., violins, cellos etc.'[6] During his early years in Bonn, for example, he had a few lessons on the oboe and horn and he was lucky to meet and work with some of the finest cellists in Europe as well as with his Bonn colleague, Bernhard Romberg. Among these were Haydn's principal cellist, Anton Kraft, and his son Nikolaus, whom he met in Vienna in the mid-1790s at the palaces of two of his most enthusiastic patrons and friends, Prince Lichnowsky and Prince Lobkowitz. In 1796, during a two-month visit to Berlin arranged for him by Prince Lichnowsky, he met Jean-Louis Duport, the outstanding exponent of the French School of cellists; it was for him that Beethoven composed his first two cello sonatas, op. 5. Many years later he was still 'sharing a meal' and discussing 'this and that' with the cellist in Prince Razumovsky's quartet, Joseph Linke, when sketching his last two cello sonatas, op. 102: 'Do me the favour of breakfasting with me tomorrow morning – as early as you like, but not later than half past seven. Bring a cello bow, for I have something to discuss with you.'[7]

On the face of it, Beethoven's insistence on keeping up frequent violin lessons in Vienna is surprising, as he was much too busy and successful to find time to develop further as a professional string player. But he seems to have found it helpful to improvise on the violin or viola and, according to his piano pupil Ferdinand Ries, who studied with him from 1801 to 1805, he also enjoyed playing the violin in his own sonatas in the privacy of his home, and did so with evident relish:

> When I was there, we occasionally played his sonatas for violin together. But it really was awful … for in his enthusiastic zeal, his ear did not tell him when he had attacked a passage with the wrong fingering (even then Beethoven did not hear well). In his manner Beethoven was very awkward and helpless and his clumsy movements lacked all grace. He seldom picked up anything without dropping or breaking it.[8]

Nonetheless, even as late as 1825, at an open rehearsal of the Quartet in A minor, op. 132, he borrowed Karl Holz's violin and was able to demonstrate the precise articulation he wanted in the last movement, probably, as Clive Brown suggests, the passage marked *col punto d'arco* twenty-eight bars from the end of the finale.[9] His playing, though pretty rough and 'a quarter tone flat', was effective enough for his point to be understood, or at least second-guessed, by members of the quartet, 'who all paid him the greatest

---

[6] Beethoven's *Tagebuch*, no. 36, quoted in Solomon, *Beethoven Essays*, p. 257.

[7] *Letters of Beethoven*, Letter 515, 1814: Beethoven to the cellist Josef Linke.

[8] Ferdinand Ries, *Biographical Notes*, quoted in Sonneck, *Beethoven: Impressions by his Contemporaries*, p. 58.

[9] Brown, 'Ferdinand David's Editions', p. 118, n. 4.

attention.'[10] Perhaps, quite simply, he enjoyed playing the violin, finding that as his hearing gradually deteriorated he could feel the sounds he was producing through the vibrations of the strings and the instrument itself more effectively than when playing the piano.

The French School of string playing

Beethoven also needed to deepen his practical understanding of string playing in general, at a time when important changes were being introduced by Giovanni Battista Viotti and other members of the French School. These led to significant changes in the construction of string instruments: a lengthened fingerboard, a raised bridge and increased string tension. Most radical of all was the growing acceptance in the mid-1780s of the new concave bow designed by François Tourte. The new bow provided Viotti and his followers (among them Rodolphe Kreutzer and Pierre Rode, for whom Beethoven composed respectively his last two violin sonatas, op. 47 and op. 96) with stronger and more varied tonal projection, and with the ability to sustain slow expressive phrases, long *crescendos* and *diminuendos* more effectively, as well as offering more varied forms of articulation. Viotti was known for the nobility and expressiveness of his playing, qualities which Beethoven greatly valued, and his influence spread quickly throughout Europe.

Beethoven was able to experience at first hand the fine qualities of the French Violin School when Kreutzer visited Vienna in 1798 as a member of the entourage of General Bernadotte, the French ambassador, and later wrote that he preferred Kreutzer's 'unassuming and natural manner to that of most virtuosi who are all exterior, with no interior'.[11] All of this surely contributed to his growing conviction that the string quartet was the ideal medium of expression and that consequently he had to develop as profound an understanding of string playing as possible: 'I hear that Count Razumovsky is coming to Baden and bringing with him his quartet', he wrote in a letter to Archduke Rudolph in 1813. 'I know of no greater pleasure ... than music played by a string quartet.'[12]

From fortepiano to pianoforte

Throughout his life Beethoven had reservations about the piano as an instrument. The fortepianos currently popular in Bonn and Vienna suited the clipped manner of playing fashionable in the 1780s and early 1790s. But he increasingly felt that he needed a different kind of instrument, more responsive to the expressive, lyrical, dynamic and dramatic qualities of

---

[10] Sir George Smart, quoted in Sonneck, *Impressions by his Contemporaries*, p. 192.

[11] *Letters of Beethoven*, Letter 99, 4 October 1804: Beethoven to the publisher Nikolaus Simrock.

[12] *Letters of Beethoven*, Letter 429, 24 July 1813: Beethoven to Archduke Rudolph.

his music and of his own playing. Fortunately, Johannes and Nanette Streicher, already known to him and later to be numbered among his staunchest friends and supporters, settled in Vienna in 1794 and under the trading name of Stein (Nanette's family name) established an enviable reputation as one of the two most inventive piano makers in the city; Anton Walter, whose pianos Beethoven also favoured, was the other. The Streichers did their best to respond to Beethoven's specifications and he clearly thought that they understood what he wanted better than most: 'There is no doubt that so far as the manner of piano playing is concerned, the pianoforte is the least studied and developed of all instruments; often one thinks one is listening merely to a harp. I am delighted, my dear fellow, that you are one of the few who realize that, provided one can feel the music, one can also make the piano sing.'[13]

Judging by contemporary descriptions of his playing, Beethoven wanted a piano which mirrored the expressive, sustained qualities of strings, voice or wind. According to Carl Czerny, 'he made considerable use of the pedal, far more than indicated in his [published] works' and his 'interpretation of adagios and his lyric legato style cast an almost magic spell on everyone who heard him, and, to the best of my knowledge, has not been surpassed by anyone.'[14] But if others were impressed by his new style of playing, by his improvisations and by his many fine and original compositions for the piano, he himself remained unconvinced. 'God knows why my piano music still makes the poorest impression on me', he wrote in 1805, perhaps comparing the recent impact of the powerful *Eroica* Symphony, first performed in public on 7 April that year, with the hardly less powerful *Appassionata* Piano Sonata, written in 1804–5, which he must have thought ill-served by even the most advanced pianos of the time. As late as 1826, he still had serious misgivings about the piano, telling his young assistant, Karl Holz, that 'it is and remains an inadequate instrument. In the future I shall write in the manner of my grand-master, Handel, annually composing an oratorio or a concerto for some string or wind instrument.'[15]

Instruments 'utterly different from each other'

There was certainly nothing inadequate in the design of the best stringed instruments, least of all the magnificent quartet presented to Beethoven by his friend and patron, Prince Karl Lichnowsky in 1800 and treasured by him throughout his life: two violins, one by Joseph Guarnerius (1718) and the other by Nicholas Amati (1667); a viola by Vincenzo Ruggieri (1690); and a cello by Andreas Guarnerius (1712), all now preserved in the Beethovenhaus in Bonn. There could surely be no comparison between

---

[13] *Letters of Beethoven*, Letter 18, Vienna, 1796: Beethoven to Johann Streicher.
[14] Carl Czerny, quoted in Landon, *Beethoven: A Documentary Study*, pp. 290–1.
[15] Beethoven in conversation with Karl Holz, quoted in Thayer, *The Life of Beethoven*, p. 984.

these fine instruments created by four of the greatest Italian masters and even the best pianos that Stein, Walter or others could make during that period of evolution and rapid change in piano construction. Thus the challenge for Beethoven when composing chamber music for strings and piano was very different from that of composing for strings alone, in which balanced discourse could be shared naturally between instruments of the same family. It was far harder to achieve a satisfactory balance when faced with 'irreconcilable' differences between piano and violin or piano and cello, instruments which he considered to be 'in all respects ... so utterly different from each other'.[16] His solution was to create a partnership in which the individual characteristics of each instrument were not only acknowledged but positively celebrated: on the one hand, the sustained expressiveness in *crescendo* and *diminuendo* of the strings; the special tone colours in the high, middle and lower registers of a violin, viola or cello; the use of pizzicato, or of sustained chordal string playing; on the other, the piano's variety of texture, tone colour and harmony, its wide-ranging facility and brilliance and inexhaustible forms of ornamentation.

The string quartets of Haydn and Mozart provided Beethoven with awe-inspiring precedents but, apart from Mozart, there were far fewer distinctive examples of chamber music for strings and piano for him to study. Although Haydn composed at least two cello concertos, he wrote no cello sonatas and effectively no violin sonatas. (Those that survive are arrangements.) He composed some fine piano trios, but the piano is dominant in all of them, with the violin generally subordinate and the cello confined for the most part to colouring the piano bass line. Mozart composed no cello sonatas either, but the strings have a much greater share of thematic material in his piano trios than in Haydn's; and his two great piano quartets, K478 and K493, the *Kegelstatt* Trio for piano, clarinet and viola, K498, the Piano and Wind Quintet, K452, and several of his mature violin sonatas are models of integration and balance – models which Beethoven took to heart.

At a superficial level, the piano may sometimes appear to be the first among equals in Beethoven's early piano trios, violin sonatas and cello sonatas; however, at a deeper level, this wonderful music is as truly shared and celebrated as in the string trios and string quartets – not only the melodic material, but also the numerous comments on it, providing as they do musical enlightenment, richness of texture and increasingly varied tone colours. It is intriguing to reflect that, in valuing the individual qualities each instrument could bring to an ensemble, Beethoven was mirroring in purely musical terms what he described in a letter to Nikolaus Simrock as 'these democratic times of ours'.[17]

---

[16] *Letters of Beethoven*, Letter 59, 13 July 1802: Beethoven to Breitkopf & Härtel.
[17] *Letters of Beethoven*, Letter 12, 2 August 1794: Beethoven to Nikolaus Simrock.

CHAPTER 3

Amateurs, Patrons and Professionals

Amateurs

In 1796, four years after Beethoven's arrival in Vienna, the *Jahrbuch der Tonkunst von Wien und Prag* listed 'the names and activities of 210 Viennese musicians under the title *Virtuosen und Dilletante*. According to the descriptions, all these ladies and gentlemen – aristocrats and middle-class people, singers and instrumentalists, professionals and amateurs – were engaged in lively musical activities.'[1] Some aristocrats were capable of playing at the highest professional level, among them two of Beethoven's later pupils, Baroness Dorothea von Ertmann and Archduke Rudolph, the Emperor's youngest brother and future Cardinal Archbishop of Olmütz. Both were sensitive and authentic interpreters of his music. In March 1809, for example, Beethoven asked Dorothea von Ertmann to give the premiere of the A major Cello Sonata, op. 69, with the brilliant young cellist Nikolaus Kraft. The composer and writer Johann Reichardt described her playing enthusiastically: 'A lofty manner and a beautiful face, full of deep feeling. As she performed a great Beethoven Sonata, I was surprised as never before. I have never seen such power and such innermost tenderness combined even in the great virtuosi.'[2] Archduke Rudolph, whose playing also impressed Reichardt as showing 'great skill, accuracy and refinement', was accomplished enough to play with leading professional musicians too, among them the violinist Karl Seidler and the cellist Anton Kraft, in a performance of the two op. 70 piano trios; and later with the visiting French virtuoso, Pierre Rode, in the premiere of the Violin Sonata in G major, op. 96.

Patrons

Beethoven was fortunate in having a number of supportive and enthusiastic patrons. Many years later, his pupil, Carl Czerny recalled that

> far from being neglected and oppressed in Vienna, the truth is that he enjoyed, even as a young man, all possible respect on the part of our high nobility, which has rarely been the portion of a young composer. Later too, when he had alienated many of his well-wishers by his hypochondria, no difficulties were ever put in the way of his often conspicuous idiosyncracies. He was stared at in wonder

---

[1] Komlós, 'The Viennese Keyboard Trio in the 1780s'.

[2] Thayer, *The Life of Beethoven*, pp. 412–13. Beethoven's high opinion of Baroness Dorothea von Ertmann's playing was later confirmed when he dedicated the visionary Piano Sonata in A major, op. 101, to her.

as an exceptional being, and his greatness was also sensed by his opponents.[3]

Among the 'high nobility' supporting Beethoven there were four in particular: Prince Lichnowsky, Prince Lobkowitz, Count (later Prince) Razumovsky, followed in later years by Beethoven's royal pupil, Archduke Rudolph.

Prince Karl Lichnowsky (1756–1814), a former pupil and friend of Mozart, was Beethoven's first patron in Vienna and his wife, Princess Maria Christiane became 'a second mother to [him], acknowledged by himself as such'. She was beautiful, intelligent and able 'to understand any question, as it were in flight and examine it with the greatest clarity',[4] and she was an excellent pianist. According to Baroness du Montet, she was a woman of surprisingly radical views: 'In high Viennese society there were at that time a number of gentlemen and ladies who combined distinction and amiability – Princess Lichnowsky the beautiful, Countess Kinsky and a few others. But as a result of a peculiarity very widespread among the high Austrian nobility, these high-placed persons were nearly all friends of the French Revolution, and hated the émigrés and the [French] aristocrats.'[5] Apart from the quartet of fine Italian string instruments, the Lichnowskys also provided Beethoven with rooms in their palace, gave him an annuity of 600 florins for several years and treated him as an honoured guest. Indeed it was the Princess's over-protective care and concern for Beethoven which eventually led him to leave the Lichnowsky's palace so as to live more independently. Many years later Elizabeth von Bernhard recalled just how completely at home Beethoven was at the palace. As a talented seven-year-old pianist she sometimes played at their soirées and she seems to have been an observant little girl: 'I still remember how both Haydn and Salieri sat on a sofa on one side of the music-room, both most carefully dressed in the old-fashioned style with bag-wig, shoes and silk stockings, while Beethoven used to appear even here in freer ultra-Rhenish garb, almost carelessly dressed.'[6]

The Lichnowskys promoted Beethoven's music enthusiastically at their weekly concerts, including several first performances of his work. One of his closest friends, the Rector of Bonn University, Franz Wegeler, remembered that after the concerts 'the musicians generally stayed to dine [as

---

[3] Carl Czerny, quoted in Landon, *Beethoven: A Documentary Study*, p. 324.

[4] Thayer, *The Life of Beethoven*, p. 389. From a memorable conversation between the singer, Joseph Rockel, and Alexander Thayer at a meeting in Bath in 1861. Rockel had taken part in the celebrated play-through of *Fidelio* at the Lichnowsky palace shortly after the opera's unsuccessful premiere, at which Beethoven's friends, including Princess Christiane Lichnowsky, persuaded him to make several cuts and alterations. See also Sonneck, *Beethoven: Impressions by his Contemporaries*, pp. 60–8.

[5] Baroness Du Montet, quoted in Landon, *Beethoven: A Documentary Study*, p. 68.

[6] Frau von Bernhard, quoted in Sonneck, *Beethoven: Impressions by his Contemporaries*, p. 21.

well as] artists and savants without regard to social position.'[7] Others also invited musicians, artists and intellectuals to their homes; in her memoirs written many years later, for example, Countess Therese von Brunsvik recalled her family's warm friendship with Beethoven, 'a friendship which lasted to the end of his life. He came to Ofen; he came to Martonvasar; he was initiated into our republic of chosen people.'[8] Such soirées – both aristocratic and professional – at which Beethoven's music was played and discussed, provided him, William Kinderman suggests, with an ideal 'laboratory'[9] in which he could develop his radical ideas well away from a musical press that was becoming increasingly hostile, in a creative dialogue with friends and supporters, many of whom remained loyal to him to the end of his life.

Beethoven warmly acknowledged the Prince's generosity in his troubled Heiligenstadt Testament, written in 1802, and also in a letter, written in January 1805, many years after he had moved out of the palace: '[He] is really what is surely a rare specimen in the class to which he belongs, one of the most loyal of friends and promoters of my art.'[10] Although he later quarrelled with the Prince, the Prince's younger brother, Count Moritz Lichnowsky, to whom Beethoven dedicated the *Prometheus* Variations, op. 35, and the Piano Sonata in E minor, op. 90, remained a life-long and much appreciated friend.

Prince Lobkowitz (1772–1816) The Prince was two years younger than Beethoven and one of his most devoted admirers. In addition to providing him, as did Prince Kinsky and Archduke Rudolph, with a substantial annuity for several years, he made his private orchestra available to him whenever he needed it. As Beethoven was always cautious when preparing his compositions for publication, and often revised a score for two or three years before finally sending it to a publisher, the Prince's offer was invaluable. Among major works first tried out by the Lobkowitz orchestra was the radical *Eroica* Symphony, which was played several times privately before its public premiere in April, 1805. Beethoven dedicated some of his finest music to the Prince: the op. 18 quartets, the Triple Concerto, the Third, Fifth and Sixth symphonies, the *Harp* Quartet, op. 74, and the song-cycle, *An die ferne Geliebte*.

Prince Razumovsky (1752–1836) similarly offered Beethoven his professional quartet in which he himself sometimes played second violin, whenever he wanted it. Led by Schuppanzigh, it was a unique ensemble, as three of its members had studied Haydn's quartets with the composer

---

[7] Franz Wegeler, *Notizen*, quoted in Sonneck, *Beethoven: Impressions by his Contemporaries*, p. 18.

[8] Countess Therese von Brunsvik, quoted in Thayer, *The Life of Beethoven*, p. 235. The Countess never married. She became interested in Johann Pestalozzi's school in Switzerland and later founded her own day nurseries in Budapest.

[9] Kinderman, *The String Quartets of Beethoven*, p. 2.

[10] *Letters of Beethoven*, Letter 108, 16 January 1805: Beethoven to Breitkopf & Härtel.

himself and, of course, all four worked with Beethoven; indeed, the three op. 59 quartets were composed with them in mind. Beethoven's friend, the composer and conductor Ignaz von Seyfried, described the situation amusingly: 'Beethoven was, as it were, cock of the walk in the princely establishment; everything that he composed was rehearsed hot from the griddle and performed ... just as he wanted it and not otherwise.'[11] In addition to the three op. 59 quartets, Beethoven later dedicated the Fifth and Sixth symphonies jointly to Prince Razumovsky and Prince Lobkowitz.

Archduke Rudolph (1788–1831), as one of Beethoven's most talented piano and composition students, was more closely involved with him than any of his other patrons, and, perhaps understandably, received a greater share of dedications. As discussed in Chapters 21 and 22, he was not only a reliable patron, tolerant of Beethoven's many foibles, but also a fine pianist. Judging by Beethoven's letters to him, especially after his appointment as Archbishop of Olmütz, he seems to have regarded the Archduke in later years as a valued friend.

The professionals – a quartet of teenagers

Beethoven first met Ignaz Schuppanzigh at the Lichnowsky palace in 1794. Though still only eighteen, Schuppanzigh had formed a string quartet good enough to play regularly at the Prince's weekly soirées and to be coached by Haydn. The other members of the quartet were very young too: Louis Sina, the second violinist, Franz Weiss, the viola player, and Nikolaus Kraft, the brilliant son of Haydn's principal cellist, Anton Kraft, were all only sixteen. Czerny, who knew Schuppanzigh well, believed that his increasingly rotund appearance and jovial manner (Beethoven called him his Falstaff) hid a distinguished and sensitive musical mind: 'As one of the best violinists of that time, he was unrivalled in quartet playing, a very good concert artist and the best conductor of his day. Since he himself was not a composer, he was not swayed by any form of egotism from following Beethoven with unshakeable faithfulness ... no-one knew how to enter into the spirit of this music better than he.'[12] Schuppanzigh's playing was described variously as fiery, piquant, expressive, daring, and his quartet when playing *fortissimo* was said to sound like an orchestra. While Beethoven's long friendship with Schuppanzigh was affectionate and humorous rather than deep, Schuppanzigh's loyalty to Beethoven was unquestioning and unwavering. As one of the first musicians to promote public concerts of chamber music, he included Beethoven's string quartets, piano trios and violin sonatas at every possible opportunity both in Vienna and in Russia, where he lived for a time.

---

[11] Ignaz Seyfried, quoted in Thayer, *The Life of Beethoven*, p. 444.
[12] Carl Czerny, quoted in Landon, *Beethoven: A Documentary Study*, p. 96.

CHAPTER 4

The Spirit of the Composition

Initially, the amateurs and professionals who played and listened to Beethoven's early compositions may have felt reassured by the apparent familiarity of his musical language. But the perceptive ones among them would soon have realized that his was an authentically new and original voice, especially when they heard his early C minor works: the Piano Trio, op. 1 no. 3, the String Trio, op. 9 no. 3, and the *Pathétique* Sonata, op. 13, or the G minor Cello Sonata, op. 5 no. 2, and several movements in the op. 18 string quartets. Some aspects of his originality were clear from the start: the increasingly democratic sharing of significant material between each member of an ensemble, the greater length of many individual movements and the inclusion, in some early sonatas and trios, of four movements in place of Haydn's and Mozart's more usual three; also a reappraisal of key-relationships and formal structures, the prominence given to timbre, to varied and detailed dynamics and other expressive devices, and the frequent recourse to rhythmic distortion and extremes of tempo.

Dynamics, and the 'spirit of the composition'

As a viola player in the Bonn orchestra, with its 'perfection in pianos, fortes, rinsforzandos',[1] Beethoven had experienced at first hand the expressive and dramatic effectiveness of varied dynamics, and this remained for him a vital concern throughout his life. Dismayed by poor orchestral playing at the unsuccessful premiere of *Fidelio*, he complained bitterly that 'all pianissimos and crescendos, all decrescendos and all fortes and fortissimos should have been deleted from my opera! In any case they are not observed. All desire to compose anything more ceases completely if I have to hear my work performed like that!'[2] When he himself conducted, his awkwardly balletic gestures showed how strongly he felt about marks of expression; he would lose all his inhibitions, and cause a good deal of merriment among members of the orchestra, as Louis Spohr later testified: 'So often as a sforzando occurred, he tore his arms, which had previously been crossed upon his breast, with great vehemence asunder. At piano he crouched down lower and lower as he desired the degree of softness. If a crescendo then entered he gradually rose again and at the entrance of the forte jumped into the air.'[3]

---

[1] Karl Junker, quoted in Thayer, *The Life of Beethoven*, p. 104.

[2] *Letters of Beethoven*, Letter 130, April 1806: Beethoven to Friedrich Mayer. Beethoven wanted the opera to be called *Leonore*, but both in 1805 and 1806 it was billed as *Fidelio*.

[3] Louis Spohr, quoted in Thayer, *The Life of Beethoven*, p. 565.

His pupil, Ferdinand Ries, recalled that Beethoven rarely commented if he played a wrong note during a lesson, 'yet when I was at fault with regard to the expression, the crescendi or matters of that kind, or in the character of a piece, he would grow angry.'[4] Many years later, when commending Johann Mälzel and his invention of the metronome, Beethoven stressed that 'words describing the character [as opposed to the tempo] of the composition are another matter. We cannot give those up. Indeed the tempo is more like the body but these [indications of character] certainly refer to the spirit of the composition.'[5] It is not surprising then that he made much greater use of expressive instructions and dynamics – often unexpected and even seemingly perverse ones, which change the whole nature of a passage – than either Haydn or Mozart would have considered desirable or appropriate, in order to underline the drama, the intensity and the colour of his music, or perhaps to emphasize unexpected modulations, chord sequences, changes of texture or rhythmic distortions within a phrase.

Tempo rubato

The expressive quality of Beethoven's own playing, according to Czerny, was distinguished by 'passionate strength, alternating with all the charms of a smooth *cantabile*, strict legato of the chords, a new type of singing tone and many hitherto unimagined effects', characteristics which would be mirrored throughout his creative life, especially in his many profound slow movements. Among these are some of his earlier works, each with words describing their character: the Largo con espressione in the Piano Trio, op. 1 no. 2 (ex. 5.9), for example, or the Adagio affetuoso ed appassionato in the F major Quartet, op. 18 no. 1 (ex. 10.4), and the Largo mesto in the Piano Sonata in D major, op. 10 no. 3, a movement which illustrates a further expressive device which he favoured as a performer: *tempo rubato*. Czerny remembered that when Beethoven played it 'the pace of this rich movement was changed fully ten times, though only so as to be perceptible to the most sensitive ear. The principal theme is always to be repeated in the tempo of its first statement; all the rest is subject to variation in the tempo, each phrase according to its own meaning.'[6] That Beethoven gave his blessing to the sensitive use of *tempo rubato* more generally than is sometimes realized is also suggested by reports of the playing of another of his pupils, Baroness Dorothea von Ertmann.

> She grasped intuitively even the most hidden subtleties of Beethoven's works with as much sureness as if they had been written out before her eyes. This sensitive musician used the same insight with respect to nuances of tempo in a way which cannot be described in

[4] Ferdinand Ries in Sonneck, *Beethoven: Impressions by his Contemporaries*, p. 52.

[5] *Letters of Beethoven*, Letter 845, 1817: Beethoven to the conductor Ignaz Franz.

[6] Carl Czerny, quoted in Landon, *Beethoven: A Documentary Study*, p. 62.

words. She knew how to give each phrase the motion of its particular spirit, how to move artistically from one phrase to the next, so that the whole seemed a motivated unity ... She seemed to have an inborn instinct for playing free tempo correctly.[7]

Intriguingly, when in 1831 the young Mendelssohn met the Baroness and her husband, General Stephen von Ertmann, in Milan, and heard her play some Beethoven sonatas, he felt that she took too many liberties with the tempi. Had her playing changed over the years? Or was Mendelssohn's own style of playing stricter, less 'romantic' than Beethoven's?

Sketchbooks and improvisations

'Playing free tempo correctly' is fundamental to improvisation, so it is not surprising that Beethoven's mastery of improvisation not only affected his piano playing but also influenced his whole approach to composition. In one of her many long and enthusiastic letters to Goethe, Bettina van Arnim, one of Beethoven's most ardent admirers, wrote that 'when he is in a state of exaltation [while improvising], his spirit begets the incomprehensible and his fingers accomplish the impossible';[8] and during his visit to Berlin in 1796, the audience was so affected by his improvisations that they were reduced to tears.

In private, Beethoven continued to improvise on both the piano and the violin and occasionally he was so pleased with the result that he turned it into a finished composition with little further revision. He is said, for example, to have written the horn part of the popular Horn Sonata, op. 17, the night before its premiere at a recital given by the visiting virtuoso, Johann Wenzel Stitch (or Signor Punto, as he preferred to be called); but he had only had time to sketch the piano part, improvising most of it during the performance. His claim that he always remembered his improvisations was fully vindicated when the sonata was encored and performed triumphantly a second time!

On the face of it, it is strange, even puzzling, to find in Beethoven a pianist so much at ease in the spontaneous art of improvisation and, at the same time, a composer whose methods seem anything but spontaneous, relying on the extensive use of sketchbooks, often followed by months and sometimes even years of revision before eventual publication. But for Beethoven there was no inconsistency in such a dual approach. Improvising on paper in his sketchbooks and improvising on the piano were two sides of the same coin: a powerful symbol of the fusion of classical discipline with the subversive spirit of romantic adventure, which typifies so much of his music.

---

[7] Schindler, *Beethoven as I Knew Him*, p. 210.

[8] Thayer, *The Life of Beethoven*, p. 495.

Forms

'Disconnected remarks', wrote Schiller, and 'chance meetings are transformed to incontrovertible proofs in the eyes of a man with imagination,
provided there is a little fire in his heart';[9] similarly improvisation is about
noticing and building on chance thematic and motivic connections. Beethoven's lifelong interest in improvisation's closest relative, variation form,
lies at the heart of his approach to keys and to formal structures generally.
It also accounts, at least in part, for the increasingly varied and unpredictable nature of his music. According to Czerny, 'a few insignificant notes
often sufficed as material for the construction of a whole improvised work';
and a short motive created from 'a few insignificant notes' can also hold
together a complete movement or even a large-scale composition. For
example, each movement in the *Kreutzer* Sonata, discussed in Chapter 14,
is based thematically on a two-note motive (a semitone or tone and their
inversions) and, although the motive's character changes, chameleon-like,
in response to changing moods in the music, and the proportions of formal structures in each movement are varied and unfettered, there is, consciously or not, an overwhelming sense of unity throughout. Beethoven
put the same two-note motive to creative use in other compositions too,
and with totally different results, among them, the Violin Sonata in A
major, op. 12 no. 2 (ex. 7.10), and the Quartet in A minor, op. 132 (ex. 26.1a).
Indeed, whatever material they share in common, not one of Beethoven's
compositions is like another.

The principal drawback of sonata form and variation form, as then
understood, was that too much interest was concentrated at the beginning
of a movement. However, Beethoven the improviser instinctively preferred
to draw his listeners away from the opening and into the heart of his music,
or to resolve the thematic issues raised in an extended coda, as in the first
movement of the Fifth Symphony. It is not unusual for later material to be
more significant than his opening ideas: the third theme (ex. 14.6) in the
first movement of the *Kreutzer* Sonata, for example, is much more powerful musically than the busy, almost petulant first subject (ex. 14.4a).

The opposite can also occur, however, especially when a composition
begins with an extended lyrical melody, as in the opening movement of
the *Spring* Sonata (ex. 11.6), or in the *Archduke* Trio (ex. 21.1). Alternatively,
contrasting thematic material can be balanced and of equal importance,
like the first and second subjects (ex. 17.1a, 17.3) in the first movement of
the A major Cello Sonata, op. 69. Beethoven sometimes extends the same
principle to movements within a work, focusing attention and giving extra
weight, like Mozart in the *Jupiter* Symphony, to the finale of the Piano
Trio in C minor, op. 1 no. 3 (ex. 5.14–15), for example, or the third *Razumovsky* Quartet, op. 59 no. 3 (ex. 16.18b, 16.19), and the Ninth Symphony.
Less commonly, a slow movement can provide the centre of gravity at the

---

[9] Friedrich Schiller, quoted in Stendhal, *Scarlet and Black*.

heart of a work, as in the Quartet in F major, op. 18 no. 1 (ex. 10.4–5), or the Quartet in E flat major, op. 127 (ex. 25.5–8).

Quiet beginnings and introspective moments

Another way of drawing the listener from the opening of a movement into its heart – and a further example of the importance Beethoven attached to dynamics – is to start quietly, whatever dramatic events are to follow later, as in the intensely emotional Violin Sonata in C minor, op. 30 no. 2 (ex. 13.8). Of course, there are many examples of powerful openings: the Fifth Symphony, the *Emperor* Concerto, the *Hammerklavier* Sonata and the F minor String Quartet, op. 95, to name only a few; and their effect is so overwhelming that it is easy to think of them as somehow defining the 'essential' Beethoven. On closer examination, however, it is clear that such openings, at least so far as Beethoven's chamber music and piano sonatas are concerned, are far from typical. Among approximately 270 movements in his chamber music and piano sonatas, more than 220 start quietly. In addition, from his earliest works onwards, he often included quiet, intro-spective moments in the middle of otherwise cheerful or powerful move-ments, such as the Allegro ma non tanto in the A major Cello Sonata, op. 69 (ex. 17.4).

So the impulsive creativity of Beethoven's improvisations, tempered by his habit of revising almost all of his compositions at length, with constant recourse to his sketchbooks, seems to hover and resonate in the back-ground of many of his most original works. The Abbé Maximilian Stadler appears to have sensed this when, in conversation with the English music publisher Vincent Novello in 1829, he compared Mozart's and Beethoven's music. While recognizing Beethoven's 'extraordinary genius, though irreg-ular, extravagant', Stadler confessed that he had never really come to terms with the unpredictability of his compositions, the very quality Beethoven's supporters most admired: 'Beethoven often began before he knew his mind and altered the passages backwards and forwards, placing them in different places as mere fancy or whim directed. But Mozart [whom the Abbé venerated] never began to write anything till he had arranged the whole design in his mind.'[10] To which Beethoven might well have replied, as in a letter to his pupil Ferdinand Ries: 'Between ourselves, the best thing of all is a combination of the surprising and the beautiful!'[11]

---

[10] Novello, *A Mozart Pilgrimage*, pp. 168–9. Stadler's claim that Mozart 'never began to write anything till he had arranged the whole design in his mind' was not true. Mozart had also to resort to sketches at times – for example, when experimenting with new ideas for his *Prussian* quartets.

[11] *Letters of Beethoven*, Letter 1209, 16 July 1823: Beethoven to Ferdinand Ries in London.

PART TWO ⁓ 1793–9

'Some more important works of mine'

Beethoven, in a letter to the
publisher Nikolaus Simrock, 1794

Three Piano Trios, op. 1

Beethoven's decision to delay for three years the publication of his 'more important works', until he was satisfied that they would make an impact in Viennese musical circles, was a shrewd one. Prince Lichnowsky was determined to do what he could to help, and is thought to have paid for three advertisements (9, 13, 16 May 1795) in the *Wiener Zeitung* announcing the publication by Mathias Artaria of the three piano trios, op. 1. Subscriptions were invited and the response was so enthusiastic that the contract between Beethoven and Artaria was signed soon afterwards and the first printed copies appeared in late August.

The Lichnowskys must have been busy lobbying their relations and friends, because the final list of 123 subscribers included a number of people from their circle who had actively supported Haydn and Mozart in the past, and would support Beethoven no less actively in the years to come, and receive dedications from him. Several ordered more than one copy of the trios, the Thun family of Prague (Princess Lichnowsky's relations) took twenty-five copies between them and the Prince's brothers and their respective wives an enthusiastic twenty-seven; a remarkable tribute to the young Beethoven and the powerful impression he had already created in Viennese musical circles. Further copies were made available on general sale and the trios became so popular that several other publishers decided to print them, with twenty new editions appearing over the next thirty years. Never was an opus 1 more eagerly awaited or more warmly welcomed at its premiere.

The trios were probably composed, or at least extensively revised, between 1793 and early 1795 and were dedicated to Prince Lichnowsky. Some subscribers, especially those who were regularly invited to concerts at the Lichnowsky's palace, would have heard them played long before they were published and word must have got around that, for all his eccentricities, the brilliant improviser and pianist from Bonn was an exciting composer as well – perhaps even Mozart's spiritual heir, as the Lichnowskys firmly believed, and as Beethoven's teacher in Bonn, Christian Gottlob Neefe, and his early patron, Count Waldstein, had already predicted.

Haydn at the premiere

'Most of Vienna's artists and music lovers' were at the official premiere of all three trios in August 1795, at the Lichnowsky palace, among them Joseph Haydn, who had just returned from a visit to London. Great care had been taken at rehearsals, with Beethoven happy to accept practical suggestions from his colleagues, and 'the trios were played and at once made an extraordinary impression. Haydn, too, said many fine things about them', but he was surprised that the third Trio in C minor had been included in the publication 'as he had not imagined that it would be so rapidly and easily grasped, and so favourably taken up by the public'.[1] On the face of it, this does not seem to be an unreasonable comment from Haydn, Beethoven's principal teacher in Vienna, nor was it necessarily a critical one. However, Beethoven was hurt, not least because he regarded the C minor Trio as the best of the three. Haydn's feathers may have been ruffled too, because Beethoven had not added 'Pupil of Haydn' to the title page of the new publication, as his other pupils dutifully did. So for a time relations between the two may have been strained, though probably not as seriously as some have suggested. In any case, things soon calmed down; Haydn invited Beethoven to play one of his first two piano concertos at a concert he was to conduct at the Kleine Redoutensaal, and three months later Beethoven dedicated his second opus to Haydn – the three piano sonatas, op. 2.

More important than these genuine or imagined personal difficulties was the way in which the three piano trios, those 'pearls of all sonatas', and subsequent early publications were received by those who first heard them: 'Connoisseurs and music lovers bestowed upon them undivided applause, which grew with succeeding works as the hearers not only accustomed themselves to the striking and original qualities of the master but grasped his spirit and strove for the high privilege of understanding him.'[2]

Although contemporary audiences found these wonderful trios 'striking and original', many later critics have underestimated their originality, stressing their presumed debt to Haydn and Mozart, instead of focusing, as Nigel Fortune urges, on their novelty and individual qualities: 'It is difficult, but important, for us to try to hear this music with the ears of its first attentive listeners and to try to forget the great masterpieces to come, and thus determine which elements must have sounded new and arresting, and even disconcerting.'[3]

All the characteristics of Beethoven's style discussed in the previous chapter are to be found in the op. 1 piano trios, sometimes in embryo and sometimes already developed: the focus on dynamics and expressive devices; the significance of rhythmic and melodic motives as a unifying device within and between movements; the sharing of significant material between each member of the ensemble and, in particular, the growing independence of the cello; the expansive scale of each work; and a freer and less predictable approach to form and key relationships, enriched by startling moments of improvisatory genius.

---

[1] Ferdinand Ries, *Notizen*, quoted in Sonneck, *Beethoven: Impressions by his Contemporaries*, pp. 48–9.

[2] The Fischof Manuscript, quoted in Thayer, *The Life of Beethoven*, p. 164.

[3] Fortune, 'The Chamber Music with Piano', p. 202.

Trio no. 1 in E flat major for piano, violin and cello, op. 1 no. 1

Allegro
Adagio cantabile
Scherzo & Trio: Allegro assai
Finale: Presto

Allegro Appropriately, Beethoven's first official publication in Vienna opens with a celebratory 'Mannheim Rocket' (*x* in ex. 5.1), the brilliant arpeggio 'signature' of the renowned Mannheim Orchestra, familiar to eighteenth century audiences. 'Connoisseurs and music lovers' might also have noticed two comparative novelties in the first subject: the independence of the cellist, who proposes a toast before the violinist gets a chance to do so, and the uncertain tonality – is the key E flat major, or is it, as the insistent D flats in bars 3–5 appear to suggest, the subdominant, A flat major, as in Mozart's Piano Quartet in E flat major, K493, where a similar modulation occurs in the first two bars?

Ex. 5.1

There are two linked themes in the second subject. The first (ex. 5.1b), in turn serious and lyrical, plays no part in the development section, but reappears in the recapitulation and, perhaps by way of compensation, in the coda as well, while the second is more fluent and wide-ranging. The development, with its focus on the 'rocket' motive would have offered the audience few further surprises, but there *is* a surprise in the recapitulation; a false, though thoroughly convincing 'final' cadence, followed by further discussion of elements from both subjects in an extended coda, initially secretive, but later uninhibited.

Adagio cantabile The Adagio is a fairly unusual example of a slow movement in rondo form (A–B–A–C–A+coda). The principal theme (ex. 5.2), introduced by the piano, takes the opening bars of the second subject in the previous movement (*y*) as its unassuming, even casual starting point. The same trick of tonality is also repeated, with the G flat in the first bar suggesting an early shift from the tonic (A flat major) to the subdominant (D flat major).

Ex. 5.2

Tentative questions are then raised by the violin (*z*) and the strings dominate the two episodes that follow. The first is an expressive conversation shared between them, and the second, introduced by the piano, is repeated with increasing intensity by the violin in E flat minor and finally taken up by the cello in F minor, one of Beethoven's darkest keys. Further tensions arising from such remoteness of key are eventually resolved, and agreement is reached in a triumphant C major proclamation – a precursor of a similar passage in the Romance in F major for violin and orchestra, op. 50, composed in 1798. The rondo theme reappears, though now in more varied form, and the movement ends with a meditative coda.

Scherzo & Trio: Allegro assai   Four crotchets and an appoggiatura are developed at length in the fleet-footed Scherzo. The general dynamic level is soft and the *ritardando* in the coda is quite magical. But there are robust moments too and even a hurdy-gurdy for good measure. In the Trio, the audience at the premiere might well have found the piano's flowing commentary, accompanied by sustained three-part chords for the strings, particularly original (ex. 5.3), an early example of Beethoven celebrating the 'irreconcilable' differences between strings and piano, discussed in Chapter 2.

Ex. 5.3

Finale: Presto   Opening with four bars of cheeky questions (high-kicking quavers) and four bars of busy cross-rhythms in reply (ex. 5.4), the finale is among Beethoven's most engaging movements.

Ex. 5.4

The questions become more insistent but, after an energetic bridge passage, the second subject (ex. 5.5) emerges quietly: a march, thematically developed from part of the first subject (*u*), above a sustained, and then a 'toy soldier' bass (*v*).

Ex. 5.5

What follows is a complete surprise – a brilliant parody of Mozart's chromaticisms (ex. 5.6, bars 84–7) and Haydn's 'Gypsy Rondo' mood (ex. 5.6, bars 92–6), each a variant of *u*.

Ex. 5.6

Both subjects are discussed energetically in the development section, but nothing prepares us for what is to come: a complete change of mood with forty-three contemplative bars created from the most unlikely of sources, the four sustained bars (*v*) played by the cello in ex. 5.5. Such unexpected moments of introspection are among Beethoven's most attractive characteristics. The recapitulation is greatly extended (263 bars in place of the exposition's 121) and contains further variants of thematic material, as well as many swashbuckling modulations, notably the sudden drop from E major to E flat major. So it is hardly surprising that such audacious, even hilarious music should receive the original audience's 'undivided applause'.

Trio no. 2 in D major for piano, violin and cello, op. 1 no. 2

Adagio – Allegro vivace
Largo con espressione
Scherzo & Trio: Allegro
Finale: Presto

Adagio   Beethoven was determined to offer as much variety as possible in his first official opus, as Haydn and Mozart had done in their published sets of chamber music, so clearly it was time now for something more serious. The third bar of the multi-layered Adagio anticipates the first subject in the ensuing Allegro vivace (ex. 5.7), but for most of the introduction, the piano is in an improvisatory world of its own, seemingly unaware of the expressive duet shared by the strings.

Allegro vivace   As in the first Piano Trio, tonality is again uncertain, and
it is some time before the tonic, G major, is finally established in an assertive statement of the first subject (ex. 5.7), played by the violin, accompanied by busy semiquavers on the cello and cheerful 'oom-pahs' on the
piano.

Ex. 5.7

The poised second subject takes its rhythmic cue from *x*, but is more
light-hearted in mood and structurally more self-contained. The same
motive also provides enough material for much of the contrapuntal development section (ex. 5.8), though a new *cantus firmus* (*y*), similar to a fugue
subject Beethoven would return to twenty years later in the finale of his
last cello sonata, op. 102 no. 2 (ex. 23.13), introduces a degree of seriousness into the discussion.

Ex. 5.8

Further development takes place in the extended and increasingly brilliant recapitulation and coda, with its cheerful variants of the first subject.

Largo con espressione   If the piano is the dominant partner in the first
movement, each instrument is fully engaged in the astonishing Largo in E
major that follows – the first of Beethoven's sublime slow movements and
an early masterpiece. Though improvisatory and meditative in character, in
form it is a set of double variations (A–B–A–B–A+coda), the first theme
(ex. 5.9a) expressive, the second (ex. 5.9b) searching and at times anguished.
Both are enriched by colourful textures and increasingly adventurous
modulations.

Ex. 5.9

Beethoven based part of the first theme (*z*) on his Allemande for piano, WoO 81, composed in 1793, and returned to it three decades later in the second movement of his A minor String Quartet, op. 132, discussed in Chapter 26.

Scherzo & Trio: Allegro The Scherzo, thematically an offspring of the opening theme in the Largo, is another jewel in the crown of the G major Trio. The scale motive on which it is based is passed softly from one instrument to the other, turned upside down and teased by off-beat *sforzandi*. In the midst of all this hurly-burly the instruments unite to play a folk-dance of great charm (ex. 5.10), only to go their separate ways, all too soon and before the dance can be properly grasped, or perhaps even noticed.

Ex. 5.10

This innocent world is further explored in the Trio with its lively quavers, trills and gentle, foot-tapping bass; and, as in the Scherzo of the E flat trio, this delightful movement ends reluctantly with a six-bar *calando*.

Finale: Presto Good-natured rivalries dominate the finale. Pianists can do many things that string players cannot do, but when it comes to playing very fast semiquavers on a single note, only a virtuoso capable of playing Liszt's *La Campanella* faultlessly can face them with equanimity. For string players on the other hand, nothing could be simpler nor, as an added bonus, more effective. Two face-saving alternatives are provided for the pianist: alternating semiquavers a semitone apart and an octave apart. There are a few gentle moments: the serene closing theme, for example. But surely the audience at the Lichnowsky palace would have particularly enjoyed the second subject (ex. 5.11), a charming 'galop' and also the mood of high comedy, so different from the solemn Adagio with which the Trio opened and the sublime Largo at its heart.

Ex. 5.11

Trio no. 3 in C minor for piano, violin and cello, op. 1 no. 3

Allegro con brio
Andante cantabile con Variazioni
Menuetto & Trio: Quasi Allegro
Finale: Prestissimo

Beethoven's C minor moods are unpredictable. Sometimes, as in the first movement of the *Pathétique* Sonata, the mood is one of unresolved anger. At other times, most famously in the finale of the Fifth Symphony, hope triumphs over adversity in a heroic C major blaze of glory. No less effectively, the extreme violence in the first movement of the final piano sonata, op. 111, is purged in the beautiful C major Arietta and its subsequent variations. Expressions of hope appear timidly, even poignantly, at the end of other C minor compositions, among them this early masterpiece. Haydn, whose comments at the premiere upset Beethoven, would soon undertake his own C minor/C major journey in Part One of *The Creation*. But for him the keys would be of universal, not personal, significance, with 'The Representation of Chaos' in C minor at the beginning, and God's creation of Earth and Heaven – 'The Heavens are telling the Glory of God' – acclaimed in C major at the end. So he may have found the overtly personal emotions expressed by Beethoven in the outer movements of this trio uncomfortable and perhaps even inappropriate. Beethoven too would address universal themes later in *Fidelio* and the Ninth Symphony, but he seems to have retained a special affection for this trio, and returned to it many years later when he arranged it in 1817 for string quintet, as op. 104.[4]

Allegro con brio Opening with anxious questions (ex. 5.12a) and tentative answers (ex. 5.12b), the Allegro is deeply troubled – dramatic contrasts, abrupt off-beat accents, ambiguous tonality, obsessive rhythmic motives and swirling climaxes. As if this were not enough, tensions are explored still further and in clinical detail in the development and recapitulation. Although the second group offers some relief for a time – a tender duet in E flat major, with the two 'voices' (piano and violin) mirroring each other (ex. 5.12c) – the closing theme (ex. 5.12d) is almost Schubertian in its longing and despair.

Ex. 5.12

Andante cantabile con Variazioni   The Andante – a gentle theme and five variations followed by an introspective though richly chromatic coda – comes as a relief after so much tension and violence. Played alternately by piano and strings, the theme is disarmingly simple and, though suggested harmonically in the texture, retires into the background in the first and third variations, both of which are dominated by the piano. In the three string variations and the coda, the theme's contours are clear: a contrapuntal duet for violin and cello, a variation of sad intensity played high on cello and violin, and an exquisitely textured variation in three string parts (the violin playing two of them), decorated on the piano by fluent and delicately imagined patterns, as in a medieval Book of Hours (ex. 5.13).

Ex. 5.13

Menuetto & Trio: Quasi Allegro   Contrasts are again extreme in the unusually swift Minuet, the first of many examples of thematic motives based on minor and major seconds and their inversions. While the Menuetto is as troubled and obsessive as much of the first movement, the Trio is ardent and warm, the cello exploring its tenor register, high above the violin.

Finale: Prestissimo   With its angry interjections, the ferocious introduction to the finale is as unsettling as its whirlwind tempo (ex. 5.14, bars 1–8), and the first subject (ex. 5.14, bars 9–17), developed from an inversion of the second bar (*x*) of the introduction, is as obsessive in its way as the Menuetto.

Ex. 5.14

The entry of the second subject (ex. 5.15a), however, is one of the great moments in Beethoven's earlier compositions: a spacious and noble aria, which would not be out of place in his post-*Fidelio* chamber music. This fine extended melody, particularly its opening two-bar motive (*y*), is developed at length, visiting a number of different keys before reaching a heroic

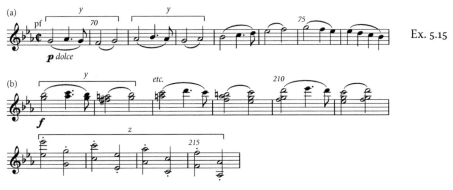

Ex. 5.15

climax of striding minims (ex. 5.15b) that can claim kinship with the climax in Handel's Hallelujah Chorus (*z*).

Not surprisingly the recapitulation sounds subdued after so much fervour and, as the general dynamic level subsides, even the occasional angry outbursts seem to lack conviction. Several of Beethoven's piano sonatas end softly, but quiet endings are rare in his chamber music – the Violin Sonata in A minor, op. 23, and the *Harp* Quartet, op. 74, are among the exceptions. The end of the C minor Piano Trio, however, is unique: ninety bars of quiet, subdued music during which all hope of a positive outcome seems doomed by persistent, stabbing D flats – an effect to which Beethoven would soon return in his two cello sonatas, op. 5, discussed in the next chapter. Schubert too would use the same D flat/C motive with desolate effect three decades later in the last bar of his String Quintet in C major, D956. But finally, with eleven bars quietly settled in the tonic major, a troubled peace somehow prevails, though one which seems strangely inconclusive.

Dedicatees

Among the 123 subscribers to the op. 1 piano trios several later received dedications from Beethoven:

Baroness Josephine Braun: Two piano sonatas, op. 14; Horn Sonata, op. 17.

Count and Countess Browne: Between them – three string trios, op. 9; three piano sonatas, op. 10; the Piano Sonata in B flat major, op. 22; several sets of variations.

Countess Brunsvik: Piano Sonata in F sharp major, op. 78; **Count Brunsvik**: Piano Sonata, op. 57 (*Appassionata*).

Count and Countess von Fries: Two violin sonatas, op. 23 and op. 24 (*Spring*); String Quintet, op. 29; and the Seventh Symphony, op. 92.

Prince & Princess Kinsky: Two sets of songs, op. 75 and op. 83; and the Mass in C major, op. 86.

Princess 'Babette' Odescalchi: One of Beethoven's pupils whose father, **Count Keglevics**, subscribed: Piano Sonata, op. 7; Six Variations on an Original Theme, op. 34; the First Piano Concerto, op. 15.

Prince Karl Lichnowsky: Three piano trios, op. 1; two piano sonatas, op. 13 (*Pathetique*) and op. 26; the Second Symphony, op. 36.

Princess Maria Christiane Lichnowsky: Variations on a theme from *Judas Maccabaeus*, WoO 45; piano arrangement of the *Prometheus* ballet music, op. 43.

Count Moritz Lichnowsky: Prince Karl's younger brother and one of Beethoven's lifelong friends: *Prometheus* Variations, op. 35, and the Piano Sonata in E minor, op. 90.

Princess Josephine of Liechtenstein: Piano sonata in E flat major, *Quasi una fantasia*, op. 27, no. 1.

Prince Lobkowitz: Six string quartets, op. 18; Triple Concerto, op. 56; Third Symphony, op. 55 (*Eroica*); Quartet in E flat major, op. 74 (*Harp*); song cycle, *An die Ferne Geliebte*, op. 98; and, jointly with Prince Razumovsky, the Fifth and Sixth symphonies, op. 67 and op. 68.

Prince Razumovsky: Three string quartets, op. 59 (*Razumovsky*); and, jointly with Prince Lobkowitz, the Fifth and Sixth symphonies, op. 67 and op. 68.

Prince and Princess Schwartzenberg: Piano and Wind Quintet/Piano Quartet, op. 16.

Baron van Swieten: First Symphony, op. 21.

Countess Wilhelmine Thun-Hohnstein: Clarinet Trio, op. 11.

Two Cello Sonatas, op. 5

Beethoven's first two cello sonatas are extraordinary. Although treasured by cellists, their ground-breaking originality has too often been underestimated and their many beauties overlooked by music-lovers more generally – so much so that Nigel Fortune found it necessary to make a special plea for them as 'among the finest of Beethoven's early works ... and still too little recognized as such', describing the first movement of the G minor sonata in particular as 'arguably [Beethoven's] most notable achievement to date'.[1] Historically, they are important because they are the first true cello and piano duo sonatas to be composed by anyone. Although Haydn wrote at least two concertos for Anton Kraft, the leading cellist in his orchestra at Eisenstadt, he wrote no cello sonatas, and Mozart composed no solo music for cello, though he wrote fine, idiomatic cello parts in his chamber music. Even the cellist-composer Boccherini, who greatly extended the late-eighteenth-century repertoire for the instrument in his concertos and chamber music, was content to fall back on traditional continuo accompaniments in his sonatas. The only possible precedents for Beethoven, which he may or may not have known, were Bach's three sonatas for harpsichord and viola da gamba, BWV1027–9, precedents in the important sense that they represent a true partnership between the two instruments, instead of the unequal relationship between soloist and accompanying continuo customary in Baroque music.[2]

Prague and Berlin

Beethoven composed the sonatas quickly during a two-month visit to the Prussian capital, Berlin, at the end of a successful concert tour organized by Prince Lichnowsky. The tour, like an earlier one the Prince had arranged for Mozart, included several weeks in Prague, and was of both symbolic and practical importance to Beethoven. Princess Lichnowsky's family, the Thuns, lived in Prague and had subscribed enthusiastically to the op. 1 piano trios, so his reputation had preceded him: 'First of all, I am well, very well', he told his brother Johann.[3] 'My art is winning me friends and renown, and what more do I want? And this time I shall make a good deal of money. I shall remain here for a few weeks longer and then travel to Dresden, Leipzig and Berlin.'

---

[1] Fortune, 'The Chamber Music with Piano', p. 210.

[2] Bach wrote several other duo sonatas with fully composed keyboard parts: six for violin and harpsichord, BWV1014–19, and two for flute and harpsichord, BWV1030 and 1032.

[3] *Letters of Beethoven*, Letter 16, February 1796: Beethoven in Prague to his brother, Johann, in Vienna.

Beethoven would have few periods of unalloyed happiness in his life, but this tour seems to have been a triumph from start to finish, with the best and most productive weeks saved for the end. In later years he was fond of recalling his time in Berlin. In 1810, for example, he told Bettina Brentano that after he had finished an improvisation at a Berlin Sing-akademie concert the audience 'did not applaud, but came crowding round him weeping', adding jokingly: 'that is not what we artists wish for; we want applause!'[4] Ferdinand Ries too remembered Beethoven's delight that the gold snuff-box filled with *louis d'ors*, presented to him by the King when he left Berlin, was not an ordinary one 'but such a one as it might have been customary to give to an ambassador'.[5] Berlin was one of the most cultured cities in Europe at the time, with a varied and lively concert life both in the city and at court. The King of Prussia, Friedrich Wilhelm II, who commissioned the two cello sonatas which Beethoven dedicated to him, was a devoted musician, with more serious tastes than his uncle, Frederick the Great. He loved chamber music and, as an accomplished cellist, he was not above joining the cello section in his own orchestra at rehearsals. Both Haydn and Mozart had dedicated string quartets with prominent cello parts to him, and 'the gentle, patient and polite' Boc-cherini, for some years his official, though non-resident, court chamber composer, regularly sent him charming compositions, also with prominent cello parts, from his home in Madrid.[6]

Jean-Louis Duport

Beethoven was particularly busy during his short stay in Berlin, continuing to work on the op. 16 Quintet for Piano and Wind and the First Symphony, as well as completing the two cello sonatas, while somehow finding time to perform at court and at public Singakademie concerts in the city. As if this were not enough, he added two sets of variations for cello and piano: WoO 45, on 'See, the conqu'ring hero comes' from Handel's *Judas Macca-baeus*, dedicated to Princess Christiane von Lichnowsky; and op. 66, on Mozart's 'Ein Mädchen oder Weibchen' from *Die Zauberflöte*, dedicated to Count von Browne. Artistically, however, the most rewarding aspect of the visit was his meeting with the King's principal cellist, Jean-Louis Duport (1749–1819). Always ready to learn what he could from instrumen-talists of every kind, Beethoven had already benefited from the experience of two other leading cellists, Bernard Romberg in Bonn and Anton Kraft

---

[4] The wife of the poet and novelist, Achim von Arnim, Bettina Brentano, was a fervent admirer of Goethe and quickly became a no less fervent admirer of Beethoven. She corresponded regularly with both of them. 'Dear Bettina Brentano ... speaks of you with delight and affection' Goethe told Beethoven in a letter, dated 25 June 1811, 'and counts the hours she spent with you among the happiest of her life.' Quoted in Clive, *Beethoven and his World*, p. 8.

[5] Ferdinand Ries, quoted in Thayer, *The Life of Beethoven*, p. 184.

[6] Alexander Boucher, quoted in Sadie, 'Boccherini, Luigi'.

in Vienna. However, Jean-Louis Duport was generally regarded as the finest exponent among cellists of the increasingly dominant French or Viotti School of string playing, and seems to have been in a class of his own. He was not only a masterly performer, but he was also an intelligent man with a keen, analytical mind. A few years later Duport would summarize his ideas on cello technique in his influential *Essai sur le doigté du violoncelle et sur la conduite de l'archet*, published in Paris, in which he interpreted for cellists Viotti's far-reaching technical innovations for violinists; he included, among other examples, solutions to technical problems arising specifically in the op. 5 cello sonatas. Beethoven would have agreed wholeheartedly with the aims of Duport's book: a singing, expressive and resonant tone, clear articulation and the importance of varied dynamics; also his insistence on 'variety in the manner of playing, gradations of sound and ... expression [which] depend on the bow, and are matters of taste and feeling'.[7]

Great performers can inspire great composers. The late Mstislav Rostropovich, for example, inspired several composers to write some of their finest music for cello, among them Shostakovich and Britten. Listening to the new, varied and original combinations of sound and texture created by Beethoven in these sonatas during his short visit, it is not hard to sense the excitement he must have felt working with such a talented and intelligent cellist as Duport. Boccherini might compose cello sonatas with continuo accompaniment for the King of Prussia if he wanted to, but for Beethoven, a virtuoso pianist second to none, it was a matter of course that he would share the honours with Duport on equal terms; and so the modern duo sonata for cello and piano was born.

The formal layout of both sonatas – an extended introduction, an Allegro in sonata form and finally a Rondo – is unusual, though not without precedent. Beethoven probably knew Mozart's violin sonatas in C major, K303, and in G major, K379, which are planned in much the same way; he would return to a similar layout nineteen years later in his Cello Sonata, op. 102 no. 1, and later still (though replacing the rondo with variations) in his final, titanic Piano Sonata in C minor, op. 111.

Sonata no. 1 in F major for piano and cello, op. 5 no. 1

Adagio sostenuto
Allegro
Allegro vivace

Adagio sostenuto   The sonata opens quietly, with the two instruments in companionable, perhaps symbolic, unison. Various topics are briefly discussed – a sustained melody, for example, high in the cello's most expressive register, repeated by the piano in the minor with rich harmonies and

---

[7] Jean-Louis Duport's *Essai*, quoted in Watkin, 'Beethoven's Sonatas for Cello and Piano', pp. 106–7.

still greater intensity. Ascending and descending variants of a triad become increasingly intricate and culminate in a short piano cadenza, a habit of Beethoven's which some later critics deplored. Donald Tovey, for instance, regarded his miniature cadenzas as 'illustrations of a licence which was beneath the dignity of Haydn and Mozart',[8] while others, the violinist Mark Kaplan among them, have taken a more positive view: 'Virtuosity and cadenzas are appropriate, because Beethoven was one of the supreme virtuosi of the time. The trip to Berlin was part of a concert tour and it would have been unnatural for Beethoven not to have displayed his gifts as a performer – gifts not easily separable at this stage of his career from his composing gifts.'[9] Beethoven continued to include miniature cadenzas from time to time – in the *Kreutzer* Sonata, op. 47, for example, or the A major Cello Sonata, op. 69, and the A minor String Quartet, op. 132.

Allegro   There are six distinct themes in the Allegro, and a strong sense of forward momentum. The opening theme, shared in turn by each instrument, is unusually long and wide ranging – the piano version ornamental over the plainest of accompaniments; the cello sweet-toned (ex. 6.1) and increasingly fervent. Two motives (*x, y*) are put to extensive use later.

Ex. 6.1

Both themes in the second group are introduced by the cello. The first, with its minor/major tonality is alternately passionate and flirtatious, while the second is more assured. The extensive material linking the themes in the second group is as exuberant as the cadenza in the introduction, with brilliant, competitive scales and an invigorating sequence of hemiolas (ex. 6.2a). But there are gentler moments too, notably the tender closing theme (ex. 6.2b).

Ex. 6.2

There are also some novel textural ideas, among them one which Beethoven would later put to dramatic use in the A major Cello Sonata, op. 69: a cello solo on the G and C strings, well below the accompanying piano. Among the many surprises in the varied and inventive recapitulation is

---

[8] Tovey, *Beethoven*, p. 89. However, as David Cairns has suggested, Haydn and Mozart would also have expected performers to improvise similar cadenzas.

[9] Kaplan, 'Beethoven's Chamber Music with Piano', p. 133.

yet another new theme (ex. 6.3), an expressive descant above an incisive accompaniment based on the third bar of the first subject (*y*).

Ex. 6.3

The coda, in four sections, is full of colour and interest, including contrapuntal discussion of the opening theme, an expressive reminder of the Adagio, an impetuous presto and finally, parts of the opening theme proclaimed in triumphant octaves.

Allegro vivace   Textures are especially colourful in the finale: a sequence of high-spirited dances in freely constructed sonata-rondo form. The rondo theme is in two sections: a poised *pas de deux* and an energetic galop, followed by a robust transition. The first episode is conversational – initially polite, but increasingly animated; while the second is a swirling round dance with off-beat *sforzandi* and cheerful pizzicatos over a lively semiquaver accompaniment, each eight-bar section scrupulously shared. But most original of all is the quiet second episode (ex. 6.4) with the piano fluent and the cello at rest on a sustained two-part pedal; a moment of magic after such an expenditure of energy.

Ex. 6.4

Waking up from such a dream-like interlude understandably takes a little time, but eventually the dance returns with renewed energy for a full recapitulation, and the sonata ends after further reflection with the piano sparkling and the cello occupying heights normally reserved for violinists.

The Second Cello Sonata and Handel's *Judas Maccabaeus*

With the powerful and highly original G minor Cello Sonata, Beethoven completed the emancipation of the cello as a distinctive voice and equal partner in chamber music. Although formal outlines are much the same as in the F major Sonata and the search for new colours and textures continues with unabated enthusiasm, the G minor Sonata is very different in mood, style and organic structure. What is more, with its strongly Handelian flavour and prophetic signs of Beethoven's future voice, it sounds quite different too. Brought up on Bach when studying with Christian Gottlob Neefe in Bonn, Beethoven only came to appreciate Handel fully after his arrival in Vienna, where he sometimes attended concerts of early music promoted by another subscriber to the op. 1 piano trios, Baron Gottfried von Swieten (1733–1803), to whom he later dedicated the First Symphony. A performance of Handel's oratorio *Judas Maccabaeus* in 1794 made a strong impression on him and he soon came to regard Handel as among the greatest of all composers, admiring in particular his ability to create a mood or a drama from the simplest of materials, something which Beethoven would become very good at himself.

Friedrich Wilhelm II, like his uncle, Frederick the Great, was also an enthusiastic Handelian, and performances of Handel's oratorios were a regular feature at Berlin Singakademie concerts. As it happens, *Judas Mac-cabaeus* was the main choral attraction during Beethoven's visit to Berlin and, after the performance, he responded appropriately by composing a set of variations for cello and piano based on the oratorio's most popular movement, 'See! the conqu'ring hero comes', WoO 45.

However, at a deeper level Beethoven cannot have failed to notice the strong sense of thematic unity in the oratorio and the economy of Handel's melodic invention. A three-note motive (*x*) provides basic material for at least fifteen movements in *Judas Maccabaeus* (ex. 6.5).

Ex. 6.5

Among them are two very different arias: the serene 'Oh lovely peace!' (ex. 6.5a) and the tragic 'Ah! wretched, wretched Israel'. Significantly, and most unusually, the despairing introduction to 'Ah! wretched Israel' is played unaccompanied as a cello solo (ex. 6.5b) and if, as seems likely, the solo was performed by Jean-Louis Duport at the Berlin Singakademie concert, it can hardly have failed to make a profound impression on Beethoven. Indeed, the three-note motive *x* appears in varied form throughout the G minor Cello Sonata, leaving its imprint on almost every thematic idea in the Adagio and the Allegro molto and, as if that were not enough, introducing the rondo theme as well. The tragic overture to *Judas Maccabaeus*, with its minor tonality, crisp dotted rhythms and powerful motives (ex. 6.5c), seems also to have made a strong impression on Beethoven, as the Adagio, with which the G minor Cello Sonata begins, shares not only the same key with the overture, but similar rhythmic figures and descending scale patterns as well.

Sonata no. 2 in G minor for cello and piano, op. 5 no. 2

Adagio sostenuto e espressivo
Allegro molto più tosto presto
Rondo: Allegro

Adagio sostenuto e espressivo   There are two contrasting ideas in the Adagio: first, an elegiac dialogue based on a variant of the three-note motive *x* and shared in turn with increasing fervour by the cello and piano (ex. 6.6a); secondly, a 'Handelian' scale motive (ex. 6.6b), which frames the dialogue and at times dominates the movement, reaching an anguished climax on the cello's lowest, most resonant open string. The final three-note version of the motive with its characteristic augmented second would provide Beethoven with inspiration for a number of later works, among them the String Trio, op. 9 no. 3 (ex. 8.15a), and, thirty years later, the finale of the Quartet in C sharp minor, op. 131 (ex. 29.1).

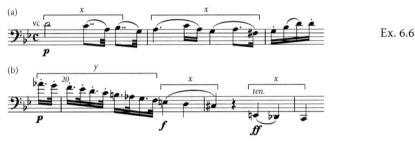

Ex. 6.6

Beethoven must also have sensed the dramatic and emotional power of silence in Handel's music, as he creates a high degree of tension at the end of the Adagio by leaving short, questioning phrases in the air, tension further increased by suspending resolution of the tonic key until the fourth bar of the following movement (ex. 6.7a).

Allegro molto più tosto presto   Melodic ideas in the Allegro are musically strong, and, although clearly defined and individual in character, all are developed in one way or another from the three-note motive *x* in the Adagio. As a result, one of Beethoven's longest movements, with a span of 509 bars excluding repeats, remains coherent and unified throughout. The first group is in two sections: a quiet fourteen-bar conversation-piece (ex. 6.7a), followed by a wide-ranging and emphatic theme (ex. 6.7b).

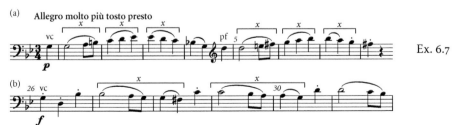

Ex. 6.7

There are two themes in the second group as well: the first, a gentle inversion of *y* and the second, poised and tender. The mood soon changes, however, engulfed by a series of wild, off-beat distortions of the three-note motive (ex. 6.8).

Ex. 6.8

The development section is also extremely violent; not so much an argument between the two instruments as a full-blooded duel. Further extensive development of *x* leads to the recapitulation and what appears to be a decisive conclusion in G minor. However, Beethoven has still more to say, returning to the first group for quiet reflection and further drama, while the key-note (high G), sustained for eighteen bars by the cello, proves eventually to be a calming influence, as threatening gestures from the piano finally dissipate. There is only one further matter to be resolved: will G major prevail or G minor, as that earlier cadence had misleadingly asserted? The last three triumphant and robust bars leave no room for doubt – G major it is!

Rondo: Allegro   There are no fewer than seven themes and motives in the cheerful and inventive rondo. The principal rondo theme, an inversion of *x*, accounts for three of them. The first is carefree, the second provides material for later contrapuntal development, and the third, a commanding two-bar phrase developed with increasing intensity, doubles as a transition. The first episode is alternately charming and aspirational, while the long second episode in C major (ex. 6.9), effectively the heart of the rondo's underlying ternary structure, is expansive and gallant.

Ex. 6.9

As if there were not already enough melodic ideas in this masterly fusion of rondo, ternary and variation forms, Beethoven allows himself one more at the start of the coda – a quiet, though fervent melody (ex. 6.10), anticipating the serene contours and mood of the final bars in the *Pastoral* Symphony.

Ex. 6.10

Postscript

When the two cello sonatas were eventually published as op. 5 in Vienna in 1797, Beethoven sent a copy to Jean-Louis Duport with a personal inscription confirming that, although dedicated to the King of Prussia as a matter of form, the sonatas had really been composed for him. Duport replied with a warm letter of thanks in September 1798, and expressed the hope that one day they would play the sonatas together again. There is no evidence that they did so but, as mentioned earlier, Duport quoted examples from the sonatas in his influential *Essai sur le doigté du violoncelle et sur la conduite de l'archet* published in Paris a few years later.

Beethoven was justifiably proud of his first two cello sonatas and he is known to have played them in Vienna with other cellists, including Bernard Romberg and Anton Kraft. He also played the second sonata with the legendary double bass virtuoso, Domenico Dragonetti, in 1799 – an occasion recalled many years later in an eye-witness account by an Englishman, Samuel Appleby, in conversation with Alexander Thayer:

> Beethoven had been told that his new friend could execute violoncello music upon his huge instrument, and one morning, when Dragonetti called at his rooms, he [Dragonetti] expressed his desire to hear a sonata. The contrabass was sent for, and the Sonata, op. 5 no. 2, was selected. Beethoven played his part, with his eyes immovably fixed on his companion, and, in the finale, where the arpeggios occur, was so delighted and excited that at the close he sprang up and threw his arms around both player and instrument ... The unlucky contrabassists of orchestras had frequent occasion during the next few years to know that this new revelation of the powers and possibilities of their instrument to Beethoven, was not forgotten.[10]

---

[10] Thayer, *The Life of Beethoven*, p. 208.

CHAPTER 7 ❧ 1797–8

Three Violin Sonatas, op. 12

Eighteen years before Beethoven wrote the first duo sonatas for cello and piano, discussed in the previous chapter, Mozart had composed his first real duos for violin and piano: six sonatas, K301–6, written in 1778, partly in Mannheim and partly in Paris and published the same year. In a letter to his father and sister, dated 6 October 1777, he described 'six duets for clavicembalo and violin by Schuster, which I have often played here. They are not bad. If I stay on, I shall write six myself, as they are very popular here.'[1] Mozart, who like Beethoven was both a pianist and a violinist, took his new violin sonatas seriously, composing several more over the next eleven years. Among them are some of his most beautiful chamber works, with independent parts for each instrument – a point noted by a perceptive critic, who described the Mannheim sonatas as 'the only ones of their kind ... the accompaniment of the violin is so artfully combined with the clavier part that both instruments are kept constantly on the alert so that these sonatas require just as skilful a player on the violin as on the clavier.'[2]

Other composers were working along similar lines, among them Beethoven's teacher in Bonn, Christian Gottlob Neefe, who published six violin sonatas in 1776, and the Bonn Kapellmeister, Andrea Lucchesi, who wrote a *Sonata facile* in the mid-1780s – 'good evidence', Sieghard Brandenburg suggests, 'that dialogue writing for piano and obbligato violin had become generally accepted outside Vienna.'[3] There is persuasive evidence too that Beethoven knew several of Mozart's violin sonatas. For example, a phrase in the first movement of the Sonata in E flat major, op. 12 no. 3 (ex. 7.1a) almost exactly mirrors part of the first subject in Mozart's Violin Sonata in E minor, K304 (ex. 7.1b).

Ex. 7.1

Moreover, the thoughtful Adagio in the same Beethoven sonata, with its long elegiac melody (ex. 7.2a), is similar in mood and contour to another of Mozart's violin sonatas (ex. 7.2b).

Important though Mozart's influence was, Beethoven was aware from the start of the complementary role of each instrument in matters

---

[1] Einstein, *Mozart*, p. 253.

[2] An anonymous comment in *Cramer's Magazine*, quoted in Einstein, *Mozart*, p. 256.

[3] Brandenburg, 'Beethoven's opus 12 Violin Sonatas', p. 5.

Ex. 7.2

of timbre and balance. For example, he was angry and frustrated when his popular set of Variations on 'Se vuol ballare' from Mozart's *The Marriage of Figaro* for violin and piano, WoO 40, was published in 1793 with numerous mistakes: 'First of all', he complained, 'there is a mistake on the title-page where it is stated "avec un violon ad libitum". Since the violin is inseparably connected with the pianoforte part and since it is not possible to perform the v[ariations] without the violin, this should be worded "avec un violon obligate" exactly as I corrected it, moreover, in one copy!'[4]

Beethoven's first three violin sonatas are as individual in structure as they are varied in mood. But their originality shocked a writer in the *Allgemeine musikalische Zeitung*:

> The critic, who heretofore has been unfamiliar with the pianoforte pieces of the author, must admit, having looked through these strange sonatas, overladen with difficulties, that after diligent and strenuous labour he felt like a man who had hoped to [take a walk] with a genial friend through a tempting forest and found himself barred every minute by inimical barriers, returning at last exhausted and without having had any pleasure. Learned, learned and always learned – and nothing natural, no song … a striving for strange modulations … a heaping up of difficulties.[5]

Although a violinist's involvement may be implied by the reference to 'a genial friend', the sonatas are referred to throughout as 'pianoforte pieces' and, to add insult to injury, no mention is made in the review of a violin part or of a violinist; so presumably the critic expected to find the substance of each sonata in the piano part alone. At the time, separate parts were provided for each instrument, but as the violinist had been expected to offer little more than additional colouring in 'accompanied sonatas', it was not thought necessary nor economic to go to the additional expense of engraving a full score. In the interests of balance, however, Beethoven's piano writing is generally lighter in texture in his violin sonatas than in his solo piano music, and the violin contributes at least as much to the character and impact of each sonata as the piano. So it is hardly surprising that the critic was bewildered if he devoted 'his diligent and strenuous labour' to the piano part alone.

Publishers and music lovers proved to be more discerning; it was not

---

[4] *Letters of Beethoven*, Letter 5, August 1793: Beethoven to (?) Nikolaus Zmeskall.
[5] *Allgemeine musikalische Zeitung*, 5 June 1799; Thayer, *The Life of Beethoven*, pp. 277–8.

long before the op. 12 violin sonatas were in such demand that Mathias Artaria decided to print eight further editions, and publishers in Bonn, Paris, London, Mainz, Leipzig and Hamburg soon followed his lead.[6] 'My compositions bring me in a good deal and I may say that I am offered more commissions than it is possible for me to carry out', Beethoven wrote in a long letter to his friend Franz Wegeler. 'Moreover, for every composition, I can count on six or seven publishers, and even more if I want them; people no longer come to an arrangement with me; I state my price and they pay. So you can see how pleasantly situated I am.'[7]

It is thought that Beethoven completed the op. 12 sonatas early in 1798, as at least one of the set was performed by him, perhaps with Schuppanzigh, at a public concert on 29 March 1798, given for the benefit of Mozart's friend, the singer Josefa Dušek.[8] A week later, Beethoven is known to have played in a private concert at Prince Lobkowitz's palace with Rodolphe Kreutzer, the distinguished French violinist whose name he would later immortalize.[9] Again, details of the concert are not known, but it seems likely that one or more of the op. 12 set were included in the programme.

Antonio Salieri

Beethoven usually took great care over his dedications so, on the face of it, his decision to dedicate his first three violin sonatas to the popular opera composer Antonio Salieri (1750–1825), is surprising. However, as court composer, Kapellmeister and sometime president of the Tonkünstler-Societät, Salieri was the most influential musician in Vienna at the time, and Beethoven no doubt thought that dedicating significant instrumental music to him would not go amiss, with the added advantage that it was unlikely to provoke criticism from a composer who specialized in opera.

Beethoven had met Salieri at the Lichnowskys soon after his arrival in Vienna and may have taken advantage of his kindly offer of free tuition at regular tutorials three times a week, open to any composition student who needed advice; he is known to have had more formal lessons later. For some time at least they were on particularly good terms, and Beethoven composed a set of piano variations on a duet from Salieri's most recent

---

[6] Brandenburg, 'Beethoven's opus 12 Violin Sonatas', p. 21. Sieghard Brandenburg's list of early publications of the three op. 12 violin sonatas is remarkable: Artaria with eight further editions in Vienna; Simrock (1800) in Bonn; Imbault (1800–1), Pleyel (1801) and Sieber (1804) in Paris; Broderip & Wilkinson (1800–1) and Clementi (1802) in London; Zulehner (1806) in Mainz; Böhme (1808) in Hamburg, followed by fourteen further editions published during Beethoven's lifetime, including Peters and Breitkopf & Härtel in Leipzig.

[7] *Letters of Beethoven*, Letter 51, 29 June 1801: Beethoven to Franz Wegeler in Bonn.

[8] Josefa Dušek had given the first performance of Beethoven's concert aria, *Ah! Perfido*, op. 65, in Prague two years earlier.

[9] Rodolphe Kreutzer visited Vienna in 1798 as a member of the entourage of the French ambassador, General Bernadotte. See also Chapter 14 below.

opera, *Falstaff*.[10] As with his other teachers and friends, there were misunderstandings later, including his rejection of Salieri's suggested changes
in *Fidelio*. There were times of reconciliation too: in December 1813, for
example, Salieri agreed, as did many other leading musicians in Vienna,
to take part in the two premieres of the *Battle* Symphony (*Wellingtons
Sieg*, op. 91), with responsibility for the all-important percussion section
of drums and cannons; and five years later, Beethoven and Salieri issued
a joint statement in support of Johann Mälzel and his new invention, the
metronome.

Sonata no. 1 in D major for violin and piano, op. 12 no. 1

Allegro con brio
Tema con Variazioni: Andante con moto
Rondo: Allegro

Allegro con brio   In fairness to the unfortunate critic of the *Allgemeine
musikalische Zeitung*, it must be conceded that, uniquely in Beethoven's
violin sonatas, there is little 'song' in the first movement, though 'songs'
abound in the other two. Nonetheless, Beethoven's first violin sonata, like
his first piano trio, opens in celebratory style; not with a rocket this time,
but with a fanfare (ex. 7.3) and one which will leave its imprint, a rising
major sixth (*x*), on the opening bars of the other two movements as well.

Ex. 7.3

A crowded stage is revealed, filled with interrelated phrases linked
together by a seamless, sequential motive (ex. 7.4, lower stave). Yet for all
its wealth of material, its many contrasts in texture, dynamics and mood,
the first movement is as coherent as it is energetic, held together by balanced dialogue and a strong sense of forward momentum. There are two
motives in the first group: an expressive phrase (ex. 7.4, upper stave) which
takes its cue from the fanfare, and a question-and-answer dialogue which
fulfills a number of other significant roles later – both played above the
sequential motive (ex. 7.4 lower stave).

Ex. 7.4

---

[10] Twelve Variations for piano on 'La stessa, la stessissima' from Salieri's opera *Falstaff*,
WoO73, dedicated to Countess Barbara Keglevics.

The second group remoulds the sequential motive, giving it clearer melodic outlines and, in a lighter, more delicate vein, finds in it further topics for discussion. The monumental closing theme provides the perfect foil to the fanfare at the beginning of the movement and serves also to introduce the development section, now played softly in the unexpected key of F major; and a lively variant of the fanfare (ex. 7.3), now played in the bass (ex. 7.5), provides an exhilarating return to the foreshortened recapitulation.

Ex. 7.5

Andante con moto   Beethoven always maintained that 'the artist must be able to assume all humours',[11] and as, according to several of his friends, he was often in love, he would not have needed to imagine romantic emotions when composing this beguiling set of variations. The character of the song-like theme (ex. 7.6), a lyrical extension of the major sixth 'signature' (*x*) with which the sonata opens (ex. 7.3), changes subtly from expressive to tentative and finally ardent.

Ex. 7.6

The first two variations are highly decorative: the first for piano and the second for violin, each clearly designed to impress the other. The third variation, in A minor, is as turbulent as a lovers' quarrel: triplets battling with quadruplets, extreme dynamic contrasts, off-beat *sforzandi* and violent chords from each instrument in turn. But all is forgiven in the beautifully crafted fourth variation, marked *dolce*, with the theme almost hidden in flowing piano textures and tenderly suggested in the violin descant. Most magical of all is the *pianissimo* coda, an additional variation in its own right (ex. 7.7). The opening phrase (*x*) is similar in outline to the fanfare with which the sonata began (ex. 7.3) and also to the principal subject in the Rondo (ex. 7.8), while the delicate triplet semiquavers, which accompany it, anticipate the compound time of the finale. No *segue* is marked, but perhaps it can be felt?

---

[11] *Letters of Beethoven*, Letter 351, February 1812: Beethoven to Breitkopf & Härtel.

Ex. 7.7

Rondo: Allegro   The major sixth 'signature' (*x*) and a new rhythmic cell (short-long) created by off-beat *sforzandi* (*z*) punctuate the cheerful rondo theme (ex. 7.8) and give it its special athletic character.

Ex. 7.8

The first episode is four times as long as the principal theme and con- sists of three distinct ideas: the first an exuberant flourish, the second alternately charming and energetic, and the third gently expressive. But often the simplest ideas are the best, and when the rondo theme eventu- ally returns as expected in D major on the piano, only to be repeated by the violin without warning in D *minor*, it never fails to surprise us. The second, central episode (ex. 7.9a), a not too distant relative of the sequential motive in the first movement (ex. 7.4, lower stave), has its own key signature (the 'pastoral' key of F major) and its own development section and includes a three-note figure (*u*) which will play a prominent part in the eventual return to D major (ex. 7.9b) and the recapitulation.

Ex. 7.9

However, the real genius of the movement is again to be found in the coda, which combines parts of the pastoral melody in the second episode with the short-long rhythmic motive (*z*) so characteristic of the rondo theme. At the same time it teases us with ever stranger modulations through unrelated keys (the rondo theme in E flat major, for example); bril- liant and audacious, and just the thing to upset that Leipzig music critic!

Sonata no. 2 in A major for violin and piano, op. 12 no. 2

Allegro vivace
Andante, più tosto Allegretto
Allegro piacevole

Allegro vivace   The opening bars of Beethoven's second violin sonata could hardly be more different from those of the first. Boisterous fanfares are here replaced by grace, even fragility, in the first group (ex. 7.10), created from the simplest of materials (*x* – a rising semitone and its inversion), and kept airborne by the simplest of dancing accompaniments. There is no hint of sentimentality; the word 'vivace' and the scurrying semi-quavers see to that.

Ex. 7.10

The second group, with its adventurous modulations (F sharp minor, G major, E minor, F major, E major) contains three ideas: the first, purposeful, the second as carefree as a nursery 'round', while the third is uncertain and questioning. The exposition ends with a mysterious closing theme, played by both instruments in haunting octaves, and the short development section opens with a restatement of the first group, now unexpectedly in C major. A full recapitulation follows; the two-note figure (*x*), on which the opening theme is based, is then shared equally between all three parts in the tangled and witty coda, with one part a quaver ahead of, or behind, the other two, causing wonderfully piquant discords on the second and fifth quavers of each bar (ex. 7.11).

Ex. 7.11

The movement ends in complete silence as Beethoven adds a full bar's rest (with pause) after the music stops, to ensure that the spell is not broken too soon; a comparatively rare device which he used from time to time as, for example, at the end of the Piano Sonata in G major, op. 31 no. 1.

Andante, più tosto Allegretto   An aura of romantic longing pervades the Andante, a mood which the infant Schubert, born on 31 January 1797 (more or less at the same time as the op. 12 sonatas were composed), would make his own two decades later. Structurally, the movement is a model of classical symmetry: simple ternary form with an extended coda, in which thematic and accompanying material is precisely balanced and shared. The principal theme, played in turn by each instrument as if serenading one another, is in two eight-bar sections, the first, wistful in A minor; the second, more hopeful and persistent in C major, though eventually ending crestfallen in A minor. Introduced by the violin and again shared equally by both instruments, the central theme (ex. 7.12) is also in two eight-bar sections, although the mood is more conversational than before, and the textures are enriched by closely imitative counterpoint.

Ex. 7.12

In the recapitulation, the principal theme is decorated by expressive descants and its last two bars provide the text for the coda, its reflective mood increasingly forlorn.

Allegro piacevole   The last movement is among Beethoven's most serene and engaging rondos. The pastoral opening theme (ex. 7.13), introduced by the piano and completed by the violin, seems simple enough, but its many subtle qualities are to be found in the detail: suspended cross-rhythms, expressive descants and colourful, wayward modulations (A major, B minor, D major, A major, all visited within a sixteen-bar span). It is typical of Beethoven that its least significant phrase (z), the final two-bar cadence, is put to extensive use later.

Ex. 7.13

The transition, a sparkling variant of (ex. 7.13), frames the first episode, while in the second (ex. 7.14) Beethoven provides separate expressive and dynamic instructions for each part: *dolce* for the violin, *piano* for the pianist's right hand and threatening *sforzandi* for the 'cadence figure' z in the bass.

Not surprisingly feelings run high at such disruptive behaviour in an ostensibly peaceful (*piacevole*) movement. When all else has been tried – retaliatory second-beat *sforzandi* in the melody, for instance, or quiet pleading – battle is joined with surprising ferocity, and peace only restored after the intervention of material from the transition. After a full recapitulation, the movement ends as delightfully as it began with parts of the rondo theme and the transition combined, and with more than a hint of duple cross-rhythms in the final flourishes.

Ex. 7.14

Sonata no. 3 in E flat major for violin and piano, op. 12 no. 3

Allegro con spirito
Adagio con molt' espressione
Rondo: Allegro molto

Allegro con spirito   Technically and musically the most challenging of the three op. 12 violin sonatas, the first movement begins with lively, virtuoso gestures which frame the opening subject, and perhaps suggest that Beethoven is about to embark on one of his more dramatic improvisations. The second subject (ex. 7.15) is much less complicated; a jaunty tune that asks to be whistled, first introduced by the violin and repeated an octave higher by the piano, followed by yet more competitive flourishes and off-beat dance steps.

Ex. 7.15

But the closing section, a descendant of the first subject in Mozart's Violin Sonata in E minor, K304 (see ex. 7.1 above), is altogether more serious and, after focusing again on virtuoso elements at the start of the development, Beethoven reflects on it at some length. Tension mounts as keys and moods darken, all the more effective because the music is soft, heralding an expressive new melody (ex. 7.16) in the remotest of all major keys, C flat major, played only once in octaves by both violin and piano, over a mysterious, shimmering accompaniment – surely a moment of deep significance to Beethoven, as he would return to a similar theme later in his Third Piano Concerto.

Ex. 7.16

Adagio con molt' espressione   As suggested earlier (ex. 7.2), the Adagio in Mozart's Violin Sonata in E flat major, K481, may have been in his mind when he wrote this early example of the many sublime slow movements he would compose in years to come. There are similarities in melodic shape, in the mood of quiet intensity and in the use of remote modulations. But there are significant differences too; for example, while Mozart's slow rondo is rich in melodic material, Beethoven improvises meditatively on one extended idea only – a long melody, which spans an almost continuous forty-six bars, and reflects on several mutually dependent phrases, variants and inversions (*x* in ex. 7.17) played in turn by each instrument. Accompanying textures remain simple in piano solos, but are increasingly florid in the long violin solo, as its expressive central phrases venture into darker keys to reach the emotional heart of the Adagio (ex. 7.17). That Beethoven cared deeply for this movement and for these spellbinding bars in particular, is suggested by his detailed instructions: *con molt'espressione* for the movement as a whole, and *perdendosi* at its two most significant moments.

Ex. 7.17

Rondo: Allegro molto   The principal theme (ex. 7.18) is forty carefree bars long and in three sections – the first two introduced by the piano and repeated by the violin, the third (a restatement of the first) played by both instruments together.

Ex. 7.18

Throughout the movement, the rhythmic cell *y*, formed by the first three notes of the theme, is especially productive, both as a unifying agent and also as a topic for thematic discussion, not least when introducing the cheerful first episode. The second, central episode is altogether more serious, however, with its exploration of increasingly remote flat keys and its forceful contrapuntal phrases in an uneasy antiphonal relationship with gently lyrical gestures. The recapitulation, involving only the rondo theme and the first episode, brings back happier memories, but seriousness returns at the start of the impetuous coda, a fugato with inversions, diminutions, dominant and later tonic pedals and its own stretto, based on the rondo theme. Also based on the theme is a seemingly new, beguiling melody, accompanied by the rhythmic motive (*y*) which introduced the movement and with which it so triumphantly ends.

CHAPTER 8 ※ *1794?–1798*

Five String Trios, op. 3, op. 8, op. 9

Count Anton Apponyi, to whom Haydn dedicated six string quartets, cannot have been alone among Beethoven's early patrons and friends in finding the composer's apparent refusal to write string quartets thoroughly mystifying.[1] After all, Beethoven was a pupil of Haydn, the creator of the classical Viennese string quartet, so what was the problem? Even when, at a soirée in the Lichnowsky palace in 1795, the Count specifically 'asked Beethoven to compose a quartet for him for a given compensation',[2] nothing came of it. Two other chamber works for strings were published the following year: op. 3, the first of Beethoven's five string trios, and the String Quintet in E flat major, op. 4, an arrangement of the earlier Wind Octet in the same key, composed in Bonn and published posthumously as op. 103. But there would be no sign of any string quartets for some time to come.

Beethoven's tight control of his launch as a composer in Vienna was probably the reason for the delay. As a virtuoso pianist and an experienced viola player, he would naturally feel most at home writing chamber music for piano and strings. His op. 1 piano trios had already stood favourable comparison with Haydn's and Mozart's trios, and his two cello sonatas, op. 5, the first real duos for cello and piano, were unique. Haydn had composed no significant violin sonatas, so Beethoven's op. 12 set, which could confidently be compared with all but Mozart's greatest violin sonatas, had no contemporary rivals. However, to compete with Haydn's and Mozart's string quartets was a much tougher proposition, and Beethoven must have realized that he needed more time for study and experiment if his 'more important works' were to include quartets of a high enough standard to justify his growing reputation as 'Mozart's heir'.

His solution was a challenging one; he would learn how to compose string quartets the hard way by focusing, for a time at least, on a rare and difficult genre, the trio for violin, viola and cello; difficult because, with three instruments rather than four, it is harder to create enough variety in texture, contrapuntal line and harmony, and to share melodic and accompanying material in an interesting way. Harmonic possibilities can be, and often are, extended by the use of double stopping and, although the balance of two-part chords can be adjusted on string instruments, with bow contact given more or less weight on either the upper or lower string, contrapuntal lines are, for the most part, limited to a maximum of three. Beethoven clearly relished the challenge presented by such restrictions, and sometimes returned to similarly lean textures in his later music. The outer

---

[1] Count Apponyi was Haydn's sponsor when he became a Freemason. In return Haydn dedicated the three op. 71 quartets and the three op. 74 quartets to him.

[2] Thayer, *The Life of Beethoven*, p. 262.

movements of the A minor Violin Sonata, op. 23, for example, are largely dependent on three-part textures, and the march-like second subject in the first movement of the C minor Violin Sonata, op. 30 no. 2, is confined to two. Beethoven certainly appreciated the distinctive qualities of a string trio and as, in his own words, he 'came into the world with an obbligato accompaniment',[3] he made sure that the characteristics of each instrument were used to the full.

As with many of his contemporaries, Haydn's numerous trios and three-part divertimenti were mostly written, as were Baroque trio sonatas, for two violins or two flutes and cello, so the only precedents for Beethoven to study were Boccherini's string trios for violin, viola and cello, some of which he may have heard during his visit to Berlin, and Mozart's Divertimento in E flat major, K563, one of his later masterpieces,[4] composed in 1788 three years before he died and four years before Beethoven finally settled in Vienna. Not surprisingly, Beethoven chose Mozart's divertimento as the model for his first string trio. Both share the same key, and the same number of movements; both include two minuets, and the slow movement in both is in the subdominant, Mozart's usual choice for slow movements. More significantly perhaps, much of the music in both is serious rather than entertaining, as the word 'Divertimento' normally implies – a title, like 'Serenade', which Mozart rather oddly gave to some of his most serious chamber works, among them the great serenades for wind instruments in E flat major, K375 and in C minor, K388.

Beethoven's exploration of the genre would include four more string trios, composed over a period of four or five years, so it cannot be compared to the much longer voyage of discovery which he undertook later with his sixteen string quartets, from the relative security of op. 18 to the new worlds he would explore in his late quartets. Nonetheless, his string trios provided him with invaluable technical experience and the last three, op. 9, published in 1798, were so rewarding musically that he himself judged them to be the best of his compositions to date.

Beethoven's music heard in England for the first time

Many critics have been dismissive of the first two string trios, perhaps, as Robert Simpson warns, because we sometimes 'underestimate Beethoven's earlier works in the light of his later achievements'.[5] Hopefully, studying his music in context and broadly in chronological order may encourage us to play and listen to his early music with some of the excitement and freshness experienced by his contemporaries; music lovers like William Gardiner (1770–1853), for instance, who found the op. 3 String Trio revelatory: 'How great was my surprise', he wrote, 'on playing the viola part to

---

[3] *Letters of Beethoven*, Letter 41, 15 December 1800: Beethoven to Hoffmeister.

[4] There are also significant passages for strings alone in Mozart's two piano quartets.

[5] Simpson, 'The Chamber Music for Strings', p. 241.

[Beethoven's] Trio in E flat, so unlike anything I had ever heard. It was a new sense to me, an intellectual pleasure which I had never received from sounds … It was a language that so powerfully excited my imagination, that all other music appeared tame and spiritless.'[6] William Gardiner, a hosiery manufacturer from Leicester, was an enthusiastic amateur viola player, conductor, composer and writer and a good enough singer to take part in Queen Victoria's coronation in 1838 as a member of the semi-chorus. His proudest claim to fame, however, was that he was the first to introduce Beethoven's music to England, performing the E flat major String Trio, op. 3, 'with surprise and delight in a room in the town [of Leicester], in 1794, several years before the works of Beethoven were introduced in London'.[7] The cellist on this historic, though modest, occasion was a local amateur musician with whom Gardiner regularly played quartets and the excellent violinist was the chaplain to the Archbishop of Cologne, the Abbé Dobler, whom Gardiner had met in Bonn when on business. As Napoleon's armies approached the city, the Abbé left Bonn in company with an English aristocrat, the Hon. Mrs Bowater, who lived near Leicester, and brought a copy of the Trio and other music with him.

As Beethoven's reputation in England grew, William Gardiner became something of a celebrity, and was invited to the unveiling of Beethoven's statue in Bonn in 1845, where he enjoyed the additional distinction of signing his name on the inaugural parchment just below the signatures of Queen Victoria and Prince Albert.

String Trio no. 1 in E flat major for violin, viola and cello, op. 3

Allegro con brio
Andante
Menuetto & Trio: Allegretto
Adagio
Menuetto & Trio: Moderato
Finale: Allegro

Allegro con brio   Although Beethoven's first string trio owes much structurally to κ563, Mozart's musical fingerprints can be detected only rarely. Perhaps significantly, however, they appear in the very first bar, with its dramatic cross-rhythms recalling similar unsettling introductions to the D minor Piano Concerto, κ466, and the Queen of the Night's first recitative in *Die Zauberflöte*. The context is still, of course, a classical one, but the musical language is sufficiently individual to explain William Gardiner's excitement at its English premiere in Leicester.

There are four motives in descending order of importance in the first group. The powerful, cross-rhythmic figure (ex. 8.1a) is by far the most

[6] Thayer, *The Life of Beethoven*, p. 166.

[7] Mrs T. Fielding-Johnson, *Glimpses of Ancient Leicester*, quoted in Thayer, *The Life of Beethoven*, p. 168.

productive one, reappearing in the transition and in the second group (ex. 8.1b), and adding spice and buoyancy to the development section and coda as well.

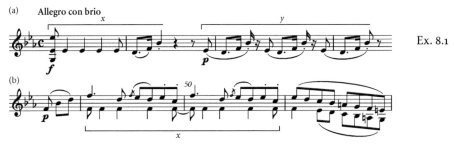

Ex. 8.1

The repeated four-note reply (*y*) has to wait a long time for its moment of glory, reappearing in the recapitulation but, most delightfully, in the coda, where it is combined with the first motive (*x*) in closely imitative dialogue. A third motive provides an oasis of calm in all the excitement both here and in the recapitulation. Introduced by a short and lively transition, there are two themes in the second group; the first (bars 41–68), an elegant example of classical lyricism, later provides the Adagio with its principal motive, while the second (ex. 8.1b), is enlivened by the cross-rhythmic figure from the opening bars of the movement (*x*). If turns of phrase are firmly classical, there are signs of things to come, however, among them the use of unexpected dynamics. In spite of the Trio's dramatic opening and its *concertante* finale, for example, most of it is quiet and unassertive, and includes several examples of those haunting moments of quiet introspection (ex. 8.2) that would remain one of Beethoven's most appealing characteristics throughout his creative life.

Ex. 8.2

Andante   Haunting too is the fragile Andante, an early example of Beethoven's light-weight slow movements which appear later in such masterpieces as the first *Razumovsky* quartet and the Eighth Symphony. The movement is in simplified sonata form, with the repeated four-note motive in the delicate first subject providing material also for both the closing section and coda. The second subject, though more ornamental and expressive, is no less delicate than the first, and shares similar dynamics and accompanying patterns. Apart from a four-bar outburst in the short development section and some unexpected *sforzandi* in the recapitulation, the mood is generally restrained throughout.

Menuetto & Trio: Allegretto   If the Andante is quiet, silence has the most significant role in the Menuetto, with its missing first beats and intriguing syncopations. However, in the Trio the melody flows expressively above the cello's buoyant pizzicatos, and the movement ends with an introspective coda.

Adagio   Beethoven would return later to the principal theme of this simple rondo (A–B–A–B–A) when composing the first movement of the Quartet in F major, op. 18 no. 1 (ex. 10.1a). A light-textured transition leads to an expressive second theme, developed with great intensity in a declamatory manner. Both subjects are differently scored and more varied the second time round – the principal theme, for example, is now awarded to the cello high above the accompanying viola and, as in the first movement, there are more of those magical, introspective moments framing the final statement of the theme as the Adagio draws to a close.

Menuetto & Trio: Moderato   William Gardiner would have found himself on more familiar ground in the stately second Menuetto and the rustic musette which follows, characterized by second-beat *sforzandi* and played high above a four-part drone. Unusually, the second section of the Trio is not repeated.

Finale: Allegro   The principal theme in this rondo, an early *tour de force*, looks ahead (though in embryo) to later *concertante* movements. It is in two sections, one witty (ex. 8.3a) and the other almost obsessive (ex. 8.3b), with its repeated phrases and its emphasis on the second beat of each bar.

Ex. 8.3

In the lyrical first episode, the violin is teased *rinsforzando* by the viola (z); not, as is perhaps more usual, the other way round (ex. 8.4).

Ex. 8.4

More virtuoso opportunities follow, shared or played competitively by each instrument in turn. The powerful central episode is combative in mood while, in the recapitulation, motives from the rondo theme and first episode jostle for attention and finally merge happily in a short Adagio – another magical moment, just before the end.

Serenade in D major for violin, viola and cello, op. 8

Marcia: Allegro – Adagio
Menuetto & Trio: Allegretto
Adagio – Scherzo: Allegro molto
Allegretto alla Polacca
Andante quasi Allegretto (Varationen) – Marcia: Allegro

Beethoven was not above writing a certain amount of light music during his early years in Vienna. Haydn, Kozeluch, Dittersdorf and Süssmayer had all been invited to compose orchestral dances in the early 1790s for the annual St Cecilia's Day ball given by the Gesellschaft der bildenden Künstler, and it was clearly advantageous for him in his turn to accept an invitation to compose Twelve Minuets, WoO 7, and Twelve German Dances, WoO 8, for the 1795 ball – not least because arrangements of the dances would be widely circulated after the event.

In later years too, as Napoleon's armies became ever more menacing, Beethoven was amused to be asked by his pupil and patron, Archduke Rudolph, to compose morale-boosting marches for the cavalry's military band:

> I see that Your Imperial Highness wants to have the effects of my music tried on horses as well. Alright! But I must see whether the riders will thereby be enabled to make a few skilful somersaults. Well, well, I cannot help laughing at the idea of Your Imperial Highness's thinking of me on this occasion.[8]

Of course, Beethoven was fully aware of the dividing line between such music and his aspirations as a serious composer and, although he rarely crossed the line in his 'more important works', he was prepared to balance on it, if a little precariously at times, in some of his most endearing chamber works, among them the Serenade in D major, op. 8.

Nothing seems to be known about the origins of the Serenade, but it was first mentioned in an advertisement in the *Wiener Zeitung* on the 7 October 1797. Like the op. 3 String Trio, it was published without dedication but, judging by the numerous arrangements that followed, it was an instant success. A piano version of the Polacca, for example, was soon in every young Viennese lady's repertoire under the beguiling title, 'Favorite Polonoise', and an arrangement of the complete Serenade for viola and piano, made by the Viennese composer F. X. Kleinheinz, was published in 1804 as a 'Notturno pour Fortepiano et Alto', op. 42, prompting a particularly cross letter from Beethoven to the publisher Franz Anton Hoffmeister: 'The arrangements were not made by me, but I have gone through them and made drastic corrections in some passages. So do not state in writing that I have arranged them. If you do, you will be telling a lie.'[9]

---

[8] *Letters of Beethoven*, Letter 274, August 1810: Beethoven to Archduke Rudolph.

[9] *Letters of Beethoven*, Letter 82, September 1803: Beethoven to Hoffmeister & Kühnel, Leipzig.

It is not hard to understand the Serenade's enduring popularity. The movements are short, the tunes catchy, the rhythms in the dances lively and the music not too demanding technically. But there is a price to pay for such simplicity and appeal; a melody with accompaniment is easier for many listeners to follow than more complex textures and, as a result, the Serenade is far more soloistic in manner than the other four string trios, with the violin given most of the melodic material, the cello a few important solos and the viola even fewer – justification, if that were needed, for Kleinheinz's arrangement of the complete Serenade for viola and piano only!

Marcia: Allegro – Adagio   Apart from the variations, little attempt is made to develop thematic material in any of the movements; but the simple device of opening and closing the Serenade with the incisive rhythms of the march (ex. 8.6c), and with all flags flying, provides even the least attentive listener with satisfying feelings of well-being and symmetry. Moreover, the fact that Beethoven accepted Kleinheinz's title 'Notturno' as an alternative to his original title, Serenade, suggests that each movement is intended to evoke colourful and romantic emotions with which every listener can identify, laced with humour and a touch of irony here and there for the more sophisticated. Certainly the Adagio is romantic enough, starting shyly but increasingly ardent with expressive double-stopping in both the cello and violin to reach an anguished *fortissimo* climax in the dramatic development section.

Menuetto & Trio: Allegretto   Though melodically simple, based as it is on scale patterns, the Minuet is intriguingly asymmetrical. In place of the usual eight-bar (or multiples of eight-bar) sections, the first section is six bars long, the second sixteen and the coda ten. There are two other surprises: the *fortissimo* hammering of the dominant seventh of A major, which stoutly refuses to resolve itself, and a frisky dance played in canon by the violin and viola. In the Trio, each instrument is given a different form of articulation, the viola providing a buoyant, staccato accompaniment below the cello's sustained descant, and far below the violin's delicately swaying melody – magical!

Adagio – Scherzo: Allegro molto   Beethoven surely had his tongue in his cheek in what appears to be a miniature operatic scene here (ex. 8.5). If that is indeed what he intended – and he is known to have had a programme in mind on occasion – it is not hard to imagine the alternating D minor Adagio and D major Scherzo as a dialogue between a fervent lover singing his heart out, only to be forcefully rejected in no uncertain terms (cello chord) by the object of his passion, a role which would become all too familiar to Beethoven in later years. His second, more ardent proposal is even less successful – her refusal, a sustained and seething *fortissimo*, unquestionably final, leaving the lover no alternative but to retire, crestfallen in the final Adagio.

Ex. 8.5

Allegretto alla Polacca   However, with its foot-tapping pulse and lively syncopations, this polka would surely have cheered him up again: a simple rondo in which all four episodes, though melodically different from each other (A–B–A–C–A–D–A–E–A–coda), share some off-beat accompanying patterns with the theme. The subtle dynamic marks are anything but simple, however, reflecting perhaps the thoughts of the dancers rather than the dance itself. The violin is dominant in the first two episodes, but the cello takes over in the third episode and in the ensuing rondo theme, challengingly high in register, joined by the violin later in the closely imitative coda.

Andante quasi Allegretto (Variazionen) – Marcia: Allegro   The theme (ex. 8.6b), a parody perhaps of Gluck's most celebrated tragic aria, 'Che farò senz' Euridice' from *Orfeo ed Euridice* (ex. 8.6a),[10] is warmly romantic but, apart from the dramatic third variation in D minor, the overall mood is anything but tragic. There may be some darker colours in the coda and feelings of suspense too, but they are soon replaced by a brilliant *coup de théâtre*: the cheerful return of the March (ex. 8.6c), its opening bars so closely modelled on the opening theme in the *first* movement that it could easily be mistaken for a final variation.

Ex. 8.6

Concertante elements in the three string trios, op. 9

Beethoven was firmly back on serious ground in his three remarkable string trios, op. 9, composed in 1797–8 and published soon afterwards. His music was in such demand by then that he was able to negotiate an

[10] Beethoven would have heard Gluck's opera *Orfeo ed Euridice* when it was performed in Bonn in 1785.

impressively high fee with the publisher, Johann Traeg: 'fifty ducats for the whole opus … about the value of a grand piano … under the circumstances not a bad price for works by a composer at the beginning of his career.'[11] Unfortunately for generations of amateur string players, however, Beethoven had Schuppanzigh and his brilliant young professional colleagues in mind when he composed them. Unlike the Serenade, op. 8, melodic material, accompanying textures and virtuoso passages are shared equally between all three instruments in op. 9, creating what is, in effect, *concertante* chamber music. Then as now, there were many amateur string players well able to overcome such technical challenges, among them the cellist civil servant Baron Zmeskall von Domanovecz and the viola-playing hosiery manufacturer, William Gardiner, who found no insuperable technical difficulties when he performed op. 3 in Leicester. But the first performance of the three op. 9 trios was given by professionals: Schuppanzigh, and probably two of his string quartet colleagues, the violist Franz Weiss and the cellist Nikolaus Kraft or his father, Anton. Schuppanzigh later included the trios in his concert programmes, together with Beethoven's string quartets and, in doing so, became one of the first musicians to create a public audience for chamber music.

The trios were dedicated to Count Johann Browne-Camus (1767–1827), a general in the Russian army then living in Vienna, and one of the original subscribers to the op. 1 piano trios. Judging by the number of compositions in a variety of genres that Beethoven dedicated to the Count and his wife, he must have regarded them not only as generous patrons and hosts but also as discerning music lovers.[12] The Count seems to have been eccentric as well as charming – he famously gave Beethoven a horse in return for the *Wranitzsky* Variations for piano, WoO 71, which had been dedicated to his wife. However, Johannes Büel, tutor to the Brownes' son, a man, according to Peter Clive, who was 'blessed with a character and manner which opened all doors to him and won him friends wherever he went',[13] including Beethoven, viewed his employer with mixed feelings: 'I live with one of the strangest men, full of excellent talents and beautiful qualities of heart and spirit on the one hand and, on the other, full of weakness and depravity.'[14]

In the published dedication Beethoven described the op. 9 trios as the 'best of my works', suggesting that he thought more highly of them than, for example, his three recent piano sonatas, op. 10, dedicated to the Count's wife, Anna Margaretha. Certainly, the best movements in the three

[11] Platen, 'The String Trios', p. 116.

[12] Beethoven dedicated several compositions to Count von Browne: the three string trios, op. 9 (1798); Variations for Cello and Piano on Mozart's 'Bei Männern' from *The Magic Flute*, WoO46 (1802); Piano Sonata in B flat, op. 22 (1803); and Six Gellert Songs, op. 48 (1803). To the Countess he dedicated two sets of variations for piano and the three piano sonatas, op. 10 (1798).

[13] Clive, *Beethoven and his World*, p. 64.

[14] Thayer, *The Life of Beethoven*, p. 212.

op. 9 trios can stand comparison with the best in the six op. 18 quartets, which Beethoven was already sketching, and a few are among his early masterpieces.

String Trio no. 3 in G major for violin, viola and cello, op. 9 no. 1

Adagio – Allegro con brio
Adagio ma non tanto e cantabile
Scherzo: Allegro
Presto

Adagio   The short, though imposing, introduction indicates that this is to be a serious movement and one of extreme contrasts. Two motives, the first monumental, played *fortissimo* and the second mysterious and searching, played *pianissimo*, underline these contrasts and also provide thematic templates for much of the material that follows.

Allegro con brio   The Allegro opens quietly and off key with a four-note fragment (*x*) borrowed from the introduction, an apparently insignificant phrase which, as so often with Beethoven, plays an important part later in the development and the coda. The first group proper (ex. 8.7) consists of a highly charged theme (*y*), played *fortissimo* and punctuated by *sforzandi*, its striding minims and crotchets recalling the muscular power of the opening bars of the Adagio.

Ex. 8.7

There are two themes in the second group as well; in deference, perhaps, to the general's profession as a soldier, the first is a crisp march in the dominant minor, D minor, repeated with a charming fife-like descant, and secondly, a carefree theme, resilient enough to shrug off a series of threatening *sforzandi*. There is further development in the brilliant coda, all the more dramatic for the viola's twelve bars of tremolo, a technique fairly unusual in Beethoven's earlier chamber music, but one to which he would return in the slow movement of the *Ghost* Trio, op. 70 no. 1, for example, or the recitative leading into the finale of the Quartet in A minor, op. 132.

Adagio ma non tanto e cantabile   Beethoven's mastery of the string trio as a genre is illustrated by the emergence of different thematic layers in the opening bars of this beautifully crafted movement (ex. 8.8) – rich textures indeed from only three instruments. A spacious melody in E major, first introduced by the violin, is repeated in exquisite thirds and sixths by the viola and cello.

Ex. 8.8

The mood changes gradually, however, as superimposed above these flowing textures two new voices (violin and viola) engage in anxious dialogue, leading to the limpid transitional theme and the troubled second subject. The opening melody appears once more in its entirety, but it is crushed by violent forces unleashed in the central episode and left out of an otherwise complete recapitulation; a fragment survives, however, to add poignancy to the coda.

Scherzo: Allegro   Although each scherzo in the three op. 9 trios has an independent central section, the title 'trio' is omitted in all of them, as Beethoven increasingly distanced himself from traditional conventions in his scherzos and minuets. The outer movement in G major is in two sections, the second a mini-development of the first, and both return unchanged later. The central 'trio' in C major, also in two sections, is most unusual, however. It opens robustly enough, but becomes unstable, as each phrase runs out of steam (*calando*) and fades into silence (G.P.). The addition of a silent bar at the end of each of the three phrases induces feelings of insecurity. Beethoven may have had some doubts about this particular passage, effective though it is, as he composed an alternative version, which he eventually decided not to use. Clara Schumann owned the manuscript (Hess 28) for a time, and her daughter later presented it to the Beethovenhaus in Bonn.

Presto   The finale is as sparkling as an *opera buffa* overture, an early example of Beethoven's *moto perpetuo* finales in such masterpieces as the *Kreutzer* Sonata and the third *Razumovsky* quartet. Textures are lean throughout, often restricted to only two parts, as in the chattering first subject. The movement is in sonata form, with the first group and transition enlivened by a continuous stream of melodic or accompanying quavers and, in the development, venturing dangerously into exposed flat keys. The rainbow-shaped second subject (ex. 8.9a) provides a few moments of wonder and mystery in the exposition and recapitulation, and space is found in the development section for an extended meditation on its inversion (ex. 8.9b).

Ex. 8.9

The closing section, based almost entirely on a four-note motive borrowed from the first two bars of the movement is particularly engaging, with all three instruments chattering away in quavers for all they are worth, finally making way for the coda – a comic stretto, with the first subject picked out in crotchets over a dominant pedal and those irrepressible quavers as busy as ever. Like the other two op. 9 string trios an extra bar's rest is added at the end of the movement; it is certainly needed here.

String Trio no. 4 in D major for violin, viola and cello, op. 9 no. 2

Allegretto
Andante quasi Allegretto
Menuetto: Allegro
Rondo: Allegro

Allegretto   Beethoven's fourth string trio, the first of his chamber works to start *pianissimo*, is one of his more elusive compositions and among the least often played – a pity, as it is full of imaginative and experimental ideas. There are two very different themes in the first group: one wide-ranging but questioning (ex. 8.10), the other created from short and repetitive cells. The transition also depends on similarly obsessive motives of the assertive kind that will become familiar later in Beethoven's heroic orchestral music.

Ex. 8.10

The second group is also in two sections – a gentle duet for violin and viola, followed, most unusually, by the return of the repetitive cells from the first group. All three instruments take the lead at one time or another – the delicate closing section, for example, is introduced by the viola and further embellishment of thematic material continues throughout the movement with the first subject almost extravagantly varied at the start of the recapitulation (ex. 8.11).

Ex. 8.11

Andante quasi Allegretto Between 1797 and 1801, Beethoven had some lessons in vocal composition with Salieri – twenty settings of Italian texts which he submitted to Salieri survive – and judging by the sequence of expressive 'arias' in this beautiful rondo, the lessons had a wholly beneficial effect on his instrumental music. The principal theme (ex. 8.12) is in two short, though productive, sections and is full of surprises.

Ex. 8.12

The first (*x*) is rhythmic, its point of balance realigned in the second bar to give weight to the weaker beat, and it appears in more than half of the movement in either a solo or an accompanying (pizzicato) role. The second (*y*) is lyrical, and later becomes a source of melodic inspiration for two distinctly operatic episodes. As if this were not enough, there are no fewer than three modulations within its ten-bar span (D minor – F major – G minor – D minor). The first episode, also in two sections, is an ardent dialogue between the violin and viola and receives a no less expressive response from the cello. Feelings run high in the coda, only to dissolve into a mood of quiet resignation.

Menuetto: Allegro The Minuet is a particularly strong and inventive one, long enough to include a contrapuntal middle section, a recapitulation and coda. It owes much of its vitality to its unusually quick tempo and such rhythmic uncertainties as the fortepiano on the third beat of the opening bar or the violin's unaccompanied solo in the second section (ex. 8.13), forced into duple time by off-beat *sforzandi*, and ending with yet further rhythmic ambiguities (*z*).

Ex. 8.13

The central section of the movement could hardly be more different, however, anticipating as it does the innocent romantic world of Mendelssohn's Shakespearian fairies, or even of Grieg's dances. Marked *pianissimo* throughout, it consists of six restatements of a fragile theme, accompanied simply or danced as a round in a flurry of diminished fifths and sevenths.

Rondo: Allegro Beethoven's mastery of the dual arts of improvisation and variation form, in which a single theme can lead to wholly different, even conflicting, outcomes, is yet again illustrated in this spacious Rondo. The principal theme (ex. 8.14), for example, is shared with the opening bars of the Romance in F major, op. 50, for violin and orchestra (also a rondo) which, in spite of its later opus number, was composed at much the same time. But the Romance, with its expressive melodies, dramatic gestures and trumpet calls, is implicitly narrative, while this movement, brimming with creative ideas and innovative structures, is concerned with purely musical matters. The principal theme, with its sustained tonic pedal, is pastoral in character and ternary in structure.

Ex. 8.14

The outer sections include two melodic motives (*u, v*), which are developed extensively later in the movement. The short central motive, a two-bar question followed by a two-bar answer, is much less substantial and, although it appears twice more, it is not developed further. The first episode has more melodic ideas than many complete movements can boast: the first extrovert, the second mysterious, and the third open and warmhearted. The second episode introduces no new material, but focuses on an extended development of motives in the rondo theme (*u, v*), exploring a dizzying array of flat keys on its way to a dramatic climax. After a few moments of quiet reflection on a dominant pedal, a full recapitulation follows, making way eventually for yet more drama – the focus again on the principal theme enlivened by buoyant rhythms and yet further celebrated in the cheerful coda.

String Trio no. 5 in C minor for violin, viola and cello, op. 9 no. 3

Allegro con spirito
Adagio con espressione
Scherzo: Allegro molto e vivace
Finale: Presto

As every string player knows, the resonance of an open G or C string is a powerful force capable, in the right context, of expressing the deepest emotions; a contributory factor, perhaps, to Beethoven's choice of C minor for this magnificent Trio and for several of his most challenging works. For example, the three-note motive, marked *fortissimo/tenuto* in the introduction to the G minor Cello Sonata (ex. 6.6b), is overwhelming, not only because of its anguished augmented second (E–D♭) and its forceful dynamics, but also because of the powerful resonance of its third note: an open C. An almost identical four-note motive (*x* in ex. 8.15a) dominates the first movement of this groundbreaking and visionary masterpiece, composed a year or two later in 1797–8 – an early example of Beethoven's use of a 'motto theme', intended to unify a movement, or even a complete work as in the Fifth Symphony (also in C minor). Here, however, it is an open G (*fp*), played in unison by all three instruments, that unleashes the turbulence that follows – *fortissimo* is saved up for the masterly return of the recapitulation. Twenty-nine years later, the same motive would reappear in the finale of the String Quartet in C sharp minor, op. 131 (ex. 29.9), and after a small shake of the kaleidoscope, would also provide the fugue subject in the opening movement as well (ex. 29.2).

Allegro con spirito　The first group (ex. 8.15), consists of three elements, each structurally important: the motto theme (*x*), a wide-ranging melody (*y*), and finally a series of explosive, off-beat chords (*z*). The energy and intensity of the first movement, the Scherzo and the finale is yet further enhanced by the involvement of all three players equally as principals in the drama, so that the listener's ears and eyes have to be constantly on the alert as each subject is discussed in turn.

Ex. 8.15

Though quiet, the transitional theme is no less energetic, urged on by continuous semiquavers to reach the seemingly innocent, though complex, second group – a combined inverted and retrograde variant of the motto theme – a light-hearted, if nuanced, tribute, perhaps, to Beethoven's old teacher, Albrechtsberger, who liked the C minor Trio so much that he arranged it for orchestra. It is not known what Beethoven thought of the arrangement when it was performed at one of Count von Browne's soirées, but he was fond of Albrechtsberger and sorely missed him after he died. When asked by Cipriani Potter in 1817 to recommend a teacher, he replied: 'I have lost my Albrechtsberger and I have no confidence in anyone else.'[15] The motto theme *x* hovers over the closing section as well as the development and recapitulation – sometimes mystical and withdrawn, though assertive in the extended coda.

15 Clive, *Beethoven and his World*, p. 4.

Adagio con espressione The opening of the Adagio, however, is any-thing but assertive. The first subject is ternary in shape, fragmentary in character and consists of a series of two bar phrases (tentative questions and no less tentative answers) (ex. 8.16). Beethoven would later remem-ber the second phrase (*u*) in 1802 when he included it in the exquisite slow movement of the A major Violin Sonata, op. 30 no. 1.

Ex. 8.16

The short transition appears only once, but the violin's aspiring scales provide a foretaste of more complex textures to come. The second group, a duet for violin and viola, is relaxed and comfortable, though its more expressive central motive will be put to serious and extended use later. Both themes are developed at some length – the first, as expected, in the development section; the second unexpectedly in the recapitulation – and the accompanying textures which enfold, and sometimes overwhelm them, are not only improvisatory and decorative in character, but profoundly expressive too, qualities illustrated also in the coda, with its tender, poetic descant.

Scherzo: Allegro molto e vivace There is no looking back in this mag-nificent movement – one of Beethoven's most compelling scherzos. The underlying ternary structure is as usual, but the sounds and language are quite new – sounds which E. T. A. Hoffmann would describe so vividly several years later,[16] and language which both Schumann and Mendelssohn in their more impetuous moods would speak with such conviction. The middle section, with its graceful dances (C major) and hunting horns (E flat major) is heard as from a great distance (*pianissimo* throughout). But in the outer sections, the forward momentum, the unexpected stresses, the dramatic use of dynamics and the unsettled tonality (C minor – B flat major – D major – G minor – E flat major – C minor – all within the first fourteen bars) are deeply unnerving. But nothing prepares us for the sheer ferocity of the second section where compound duple time is thrown forci-bly into the melting pot by all three instruments together in violent unison.

Finale: Presto The opening flourishes here (ex. 8.17a) and in the last movement of the F major String Quartet, op. 18 no. 1, probably written a few months later, are similar in shape, but very different in emphasis,

---

[16] E. T. A. Hoffmann, quoted in Strunk, *Source Readings in Music History*, p. 777.

character and outcome. While the first motive in the quartet is carefree, the opening bars here are moody, even curt. The first five notes in particular (*v*) play an important part rhythmically, structurally and emotionally throughout the movement – sometimes purely creative, as when shaping the poignant closing section, but more often confrontational.

Ex. 8.17

Even the lyrical second theme (ex. 8.17b) seems anxious in this unsettled environment, although it provides some moments of gentle polyphony in the development section. Violence as ferocious as anything in the first movement and Scherzo, however, returns in the later bars of the development and in the recapitulation. But like the finale of the C minor Piano Trio, op. 1 no. 3, the movement ends in C major, enigmatically and softly, as if emotionally drained.

Chamber Music for Wind, Strings and Piano

Piano and Wind Quintet/Piano Quartet in E flat major, op. 16 – 1796
Trio for Clarinet/Violin, Cello and Piano, op. 11 – 1798
Septet for Wind and Strings, op. 20 – 1799
Serenade for Flute, Violin and Viola, op. 25 – 1801

Before Beethoven finally left Bonn for Vienna in November 1792, he had presented the Elector, Archduke Maximilian Franz, with his latest composition, a wind Octet. It was a particularly apt choice, as the Archduke enjoyed listening to wind-band *Tafelmusik* when he ate his supper, a habit which Mozart caricatured with such dramatic effect in the last act of *Don Giovanni*, where the Don, entertained by an on-stage wind-band, awaits the fateful arrival of the Commendatore's statue. Once settled in Vienna, Beethoven made an arrangement of the Octet for String Quintet and it was published in 1796 as op. 4. He also revised the original version for wind, but seems to have forgotten that he had done so, as it was found among his papers after he died and published posthumously as op. 103.

The history of the Octet perfectly illustrates Beethoven's ambivalent attitude to wind chamber music. He continued to compose delightful *Tafelmusik* from time to time in the early to mid 1790s,[1] but he did not include such *pièces d'occasion* among his 'more important works', and usually put them aside, often for several years. When he was particularly short of funds, he would send them rather apologetically to publishers and, as a result, they tend to re-emerge with misleadingly mature opus numbers.

However, three compositions involving wind and strings were unquestionably as important as any of Beethoven's early chamber works: the Quintet for piano and wind, published simultaneously as the Quartet for piano and strings (both op. 16); the Trio for piano, clarinet (or violin) and cello, op. 11, and the ever popular Septet for clarinet, bassoon, horn, violin, viola, cello and bass, op. 20. The Serenade for flute, violin and viola, op. 25, is not in that class, but it is included in this chapter because it is unique and especially beguiling, and also because it is the only chamber work that Beethoven composed during his years in Vienna to include a flute, apart from an optional appearance in two sets of National Airs with Variations, op. 105 and op. 107.[2] His other wind chamber music is discussed in Appendix 3.

---

[1] See Appendix 3 below.

[2] For Beethoven's chamber music involving a flute, see pp. 288–9.

Mozart's Piano and Wind Quintet, K452, as a model

A comparison between the op. 16 Quintet, one of Beethoven's most appealing 'classical' works, and the G minor Cello Sonata, op. 5 no. 2, both composed, if not completed, during his three-month visit to Berlin in 1796, illustrates a significant parting of the ways in his style in the mid to late 1790s. In the Cello Sonata, discussed in Chapter 6, he was beginning to experiment with a new tonal and dynamic language suited to the extreme emotions he increasingly wanted to express. In the Quintet, on the other hand, he seems to have made a conscious decision to work within the classical constraints of the recent past, using Mozart's Piano and Wind Quintet, K452, composed thirteen years earlier, as his model. Mozart, the great teacher that Beethoven never had,[3] was the acknowledged master of wind music, so he could hardly do better than study a work which Mozart himself had regarded as 'the best … I have ever composed'.[4]

Both begin with a slow introduction and share the same key and the same number of movements; both are scored for oboe, clarinet, horn, bassoon and piano, and both are written in a *concertante/obbligato* style. It is clear from the start, however, that Beethoven was not to be intimidated by his celebrated model, as there are significant differences between his quintet and Mozart's. Thematic material, for example, is more extensive, less focused than in K452 and, as the clarinet rather than the oboe takes the leading part among the wind, the overall sound is quite different too. According to Mozart's widow Constanze, Baron Nikolaus Zmeskall von Domanovecz,[5] the gifted amateur cellist and loyal member of Beethoven's inner circle of friends, owned the autograph of Mozart's Quintet, and although it is not known when he first acquired it – Constanze's letter to a music publisher referring to his ownership of the manuscript was written on 30 May 1800 – he may well have had it in his possession for several years. If so, it is inconceivable that Beethoven would not have been given every opportunity to study it thoroughly, and he would certainly have been able to do so before the two versions of op. 16 were finally published in 1801.

Alternative versions, both listed as op. 16

It is not known when Beethoven arranged the piano and string version of op. 16, but the quality and character of the changes he made suggest a

---

[3] Beethoven visited Vienna in 1787, hoping to study with Mozart, but he had to return to Bonn when his mother became seriously ill. She died soon afterwards. Mozart died on 5 December 1791, almost a year before Beethoven finally returned to Vienna.

[4] Mozart, in a letter to his father, dated 10 April 1784.

[5] Nikolaus Zmeskall (1759–1833) was a lifelong admirer of Beethoven's music and a frequent dining companion. Beethoven dedicated the String Quartet in F minor, op. 95, *Quartetto Serioso*, to Zmeskall, and Haydn dedicated a new edition of his op. 20 String Quartets to him.

later rather than an earlier date, and imply that his publisher, reassuringly named Tranquillo Mollo, whose business included the sale of maps, globes and views of Vienna as well as music publication, convinced Beethoven that he would sell more copies if an alternative version for strings was also on offer. Both versions were published as op. 16 in 1801 and dedicated to Prince Joseph Johann zu Schwarzenburg, one of the original subscribers to the op. 1 piano trios and a highly regarded promoter of large-scale concerts; these included the historic premieres in his palace of Haydn's two great oratorios, *The Creation* in 1798 and *The Seasons* in 1801.

The piano part is identical in both versions and, as it was not customary at the time for full scores to be printed, Beethoven only had to write parts for violin, viola and cello to complete the double set for publication. Nonetheless, as Myron Schwager has shown, the changes he made in the string version are 'so effective that one can only wonder why [he] did not incorporate them into the original work.'[6] Schwager explores three kinds of change: more florid and idiomatic parts for the strings in solo passages than the technically less demanding wind parts; the use of 'filler' material for the strings when accompanying long piano solos, where the wind are given frequent and often long rests; and the use of off-beat accents to break the symmetry of the phrasing. 'It is precisely such a concern with musical momentum', Schwager continues, 'which has been found to be a guiding influence in all these arrangements.' Nonetheless, when compared with the adventurous spirit of Beethoven's duo sonatas, trios and quartets, the string version of op. 16 feels constrained by the limited range of keys available to contemporary wind instruments, constraints which Beethoven found increasingly frustrating; so much so that, shortly afterwards, he gave up composing chamber music involving wind instruments altogether.

Each instrument is given two roles in op. 16: the wind (or strings) as members of an ensemble and as obbligato soloists; the piano as accompanist and as *concertante* soloist, a role which caused both irritation and merriment at a performance given in Prince Lobkowitz's palace in December 1804:

> In the last Allegro there are several holds before the theme is resumed. At one of these Beethoven suddenly began to improvise ... and entertained himself and the others for a considerable time – but not the other players. They were displeased and [Friedrich] Ramm [the distinguished visiting oboist], even very angry. It was really very comical to see them, momentarily expecting the performance to be resumed, [putting] their instruments to their mouths, only to put them down again. At length, Beethoven was satisfied and dropped [back] into the Rondo. The whole company was transported with delight.[7]

---

[6] Schwager, 'A Fresh Look at Beethoven's Arrangements'.

[7] Ferdinand Ries, quoted in Thayer, *The Life of Beethoven*, p. 350.

Perhaps those wind players would have been more forgiving if they had known the reason for Beethoven's behaviour, and understood the significance of the event which had taken place earlier that day in the Lobkowitz palace: an event which would come to be regarded as one of the greatest turning points in the history of music, the first rehearsal of the *Eroica* Symphony.

Quintet in E flat major for piano, oboe, clarinet, bassoon and horn, op. 16

Quartet in E flat major for piano, violin, viola and cello, op. 16

Grave – Allegro, ma non troppo
Andante cantabile
Rondo: Allegro ma non troppo

Grave   Seemingly insignificant intervals and motives in the introduction (ex. 9.1) reappear later in different guises and provide the listener, consciously or not, with a sense of the work's overall shape – an approach which would give Beethoven the formal and structural freedom he increasingly sought in his later music. There are three examples – the rising major sixth at the start (*x*), an interval which also introduces the first two themes in the Allegro (ex. 9.2); the descending cadential scale (*y*), its expressive contours anticipating the principal theme in the Andante (ex. 9.4); and the obbligato arpeggios that follow (*z*) which take on an important accompanying role later (ex. 9.2a).

Allegro, ma non troppo   At first, the formal outlines of the Allegro seem conventional enough, though melodic material in both the first and second subject is lyrical and does not offer the usual contrasts in mood; that important role is assigned to the brilliant transition which links them together. The opening theme, introduced by the piano, is in two sections: a gentle melody (ex. 9.2a), evolved from thematic contours in the opening bars of the Grave (*x*), over crisp, ascending arpeggios based on the horn solo in the ninth bar (*z*); then a four-bar variant of (*x*, *y*), played by each instrument in turn (ex. 9.2b) and colourful enough to provide inspiration for the transition and coda as well.

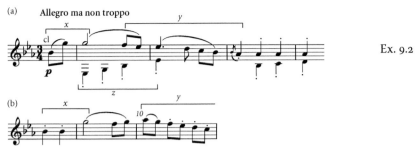

Ex. 9.2

The second subject, a further variant of *y*, is also introduced by the piano, and then repeated by the wind (ex. 9.3) in gently flowing counterpoint.

Ex. 9.3

In the closing section assertive statements (*z*) and lyrical responses (*y*) recall similar contrasts in the Grave, and the final bars of the exposition provide the impetus for the dramatic opening bars of the development section. Quieter counsels soon prevail, however, and a variant of the first subject, together with its crisp arpeggios (*z*), inspires more gentle discussion. The end of the development is especially magical – sustained, shifting wind chords, accompanied by crisp crotchets, precisely marked *p queste note ben marcato*.

There are two potential cadenzas for the piano – pauses in bars 355 and 396 – and the other instruments are given a chance to shine in the coda – not least the horn, with some brilliant arpeggio passages.

Andante cantabile The tender principal melody (ex. 9.4) in this slow rondo (A–B–A–C–A+coda), a further extension of *y* in the Grave, is quietly introduced by the piano and repeated by the wind over a richly expressive accompaniment.

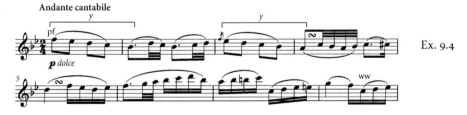

Ex. 9.4

The mood changes to one of gentle pathos in the two episodes – the first, a duet for oboe and bassoon and the second, an expressive solo for horn, rounded off by further variants of the opening melody. However, as so often with Beethoven, the loveliest moments are saved for the coda – a quiet meditation on the first five notes of the theme (*y*) and its inversion.

Rondo: Allegro ma non troppo   According to Carl Czerny, Beethoven 'got many of his ideas from chance occurrences and impressions', claiming, for example, that the finale of the Piano Trio in E flat major, op. 70 no. 2, was inspired by a galloping horse.[8] This Rondo, however, opens in a more leisurely way (ex. 9.5) – a canter, perhaps, rather than a gallop.

Ex. 9.5

The mood becomes more assertive and brilliant in the transition while, by contrast, the two themes in the first episode are respectively carefree (ex. 9.6a) and energetic (ex. 9.6b).

Ex. 9.6

There is no new material in the second episode, which doubles as a development section, and after a full recapitulation, distant horn calls proclaim the end of the movement – and presumably the end of the hunt as well – in a short but cheerful coda.

Trio no. 4 in B flat major for piano, clarinet (or violin) and cello, op. 11

Allegro con brio
Adagio
Thema: 'Pria ch'io l'impegno' & Variations

In spite of its earlier publication date (1798) and opus number, the genial Clarinet Trio, op. 11, was composed more than two years later than the op. 16 Quintet. It is more compact, if less innovative, than the first three piano trios, but it is not without sophistication: Beethoven's witty solutions to problems of tonality, for example, when writing for the late-eighteenth-century clarinet with its limited range of available keys; the 'democratic'

[8] Carl Czerny, quoted in Cooper, *Beethoven and the Creative Process*, p. 43.

distribution of melodic material, shared with almost unprecedented fairness between all three instruments, clear from the start and consistent throughout; the subtle use of rhythmic motives, the rich textures and beguiling melodic invention. The alternative clarinet and violin parts are almost identical: a few three-part chords for the violin at cadences, two short flourishes in the Allegro and, in the finale, some more three-part chords in the fifth variation.

Beethoven dedicated the Trio to the elderly Countess Maria von Thun, the mother-in-law of two of his leading patrons, Prince Lichnowsky and Count (later Prince) Razumovsky; an appropriate choice, as the Trio's classical qualities would surely have appealed to someone of her generation who had personally known and supported Gluck, Haydn and Mozart. Perhaps it was a peace offering as, according to Frau von Bernhard, Beethoven had not always been sensitive in his relations with the Countess: 'I have seen Countess Thun, the mother of Princess Lichnowsky, on her knees before him – he was seated on the sofa – and begging him to play something – and Beethoven would not do it. But then, Countess Thun was a very eccentric woman.'[9]

Beethoven was uncomfortable whenever his music (notably the Septet) became too popular, and when he realized that Joseph Weigl's song, which the clarinettist Josef Berr had suggested as the theme for variations, was wildly popular, he toyed with the idea of replacing it with a theme of his own. His discomfort must have increased still further when he read an equivocal review in the *Allgemeine musikalische Zeitung*: 'This Trio flows more smoothly than some other works of its composer. [With] his uncommon understanding of harmony and his love of profound expression [he] would give us a great deal of value if he would only write always in a more natural than far-fetched manner.'[10]

The first two performances in Count von Fries' house were as comic in their way as Weigl's song. Daniel Steibelt, a gifted though eccentric pianist and composer, was present on both occasions. His eccentricities included the frequent use of tremolo and, after his marriage, the addition of tambourine parts so that his wife, a tambourine virtuoso, could join him on stage. He was patronizing in his comments at the premiere of op. 11 and, much given to 'contests' with other musicians, he considered himself victorious after performing an improvisation and a quintet of his own. On the second occasion, according to Ferdinand Ries, he

> had prepared (and this was quite evident) a brilliant improvisation, choosing as a theme the subject of the variations of Beethoven's Trio. This outraged not only Beethoven's supporters but also the composer himself. He went in his usual, I must say ungracious, manner to the instrument as if half lunging towards it, grabbing as he passed the

---

[9] Frau von Bernhard in Sonneck, *Beethoven: Impressions by his Contemporaries*, p. 21.

[10] *Allgemeine musikalische Zeitung*, May 1799, quoted in Schmit-Görg and Schmidt, *Beethoven Bicentenniel*, p. 133.

violoncello part of Steibelt's quintet, placed it (intentionally?) upside-down on the music stand and from the opening notes drummed out a theme with one finger. Offended and stimulated at the same time, he improvised in such a manner that Steibelt left the room before Beethoven had finished.[11]

Allegro con brio   There are two themes in the first group, one assertive (ex. 9.7a) and the other polite and elegant (ex. 9.7b). The opening five-note motive (x) is put to immediate use and extended, step by chromatic step, to six bars, while the second motive (y) is saved up for high drama later in the development section.

Ex. 9.7

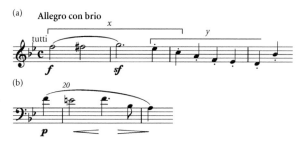

After the triumphant conclusion of the first group in F major, the transition for solo piano, played on both occasions by Beethoven himself, enters mysteriously and without warning in the unrelated key of D major – then an uncomfortable key for a B flat clarinet – returning deftly to F major just in time for the clarinet to introduce the lyrical second group of themes. There are two further ideas, both characterized by a cheerful off-beat cell (z), which inspire some lively contrapuntal exchanges later in the movement (ex. 9.8), and anticipate both rhythmically and melodically Weigl's cheery song in the finale (ex. 9.9).

Ex. 9.8

The development opens with the mysterious transition, again introduced by the piano in a remote key – D flat major this time – but the mood soon changes as the six-crotchet motive from the opening bars of the movement (y) is thrown vigorously from one instrument to another, urged on by energetic semiquavers.

Adagio   The melody with which the expressive Adagio opens, shared in turn by the cello and clarinet, recalls not only the previous movement (z), but also one of Beethoven's most popular tunes – the Tempo di Menuetto in the Septet and the Piano Sonata in G major, op. 49 no. 2. The extended middle section is full of pathos, as the piano and cello venture into keys too remote for the clarinet – E flat minor, C flat major/B major to reach E

[11] Ferdinand Ries, quoted in Landon, *Beethoven: A Documentary Study*, p. 135.

major – but all three instruments are reunited in time for the rich-textured recapitulation and the short, withdrawn coda.

Thema: 'Pria ch'io l'impegno' & Variations ('Before I begin work I must have something to eat!')   The nine variations on Weigl's song (ex. 9.9), with its cheeky melodic and rhythmic references to the motive (*z*) in the first two movements, explore a colourful range of moods and textures.

Ex. 9.9

The piano keeps the first variation to itself, and the clarinet and cello share an unaccompanied, contrapuntal duet in the second. Thereafter honours are even, as the mood swings from forceful (III) to sombre (IV), then dramatic (V), charming (VI), smart and soldierly with plenty of 'spit and polish' in the form of crisp dotted rhythms (VII), quietly confident and heroic (VIII), and finally schoolmasterly – canonic discipline severely enforced.

Then, in an attempt to escape from his self-imposed straightjacket if only for a moment, Beethoven flies off at a tangent with carefree abandon in the unrelated key of G major to create a syncopated dance variation in compound time (ex. 9.10).

Ex. 9.10

It is not long, however, before the tonic key is re-established so that the clarinet and cello can join in the fun, only to be called to order (all too soon, as is the way when everyone is enjoying themselves) so that formal farewells in staid old common time can be made with due propriety.

Septet in E flat major for clarinet, bassoon, horn, violin, viola, cello and bass, op. 20

Adagio – Allegro con brio
Adagio cantabile
Tempo di Menuetto & Trio
Tema con Variazioni: Andante
Scherzo & Trio: Allegro molto e vivace
Andante con moto alla Marcia – Presto

For musicians, a chance to play Beethoven's Septet is like being invited to a wonderful party – the best sort, where each guest is welcomed individually for who they are, and are listened to for what they have to say, whether it is serious or amusing. Each instrument is given a chance to shine, sometimes in a group, sometimes as a soloist, in line with Beethoven's own instructions: 'violin, viola, violoncello, double bass, clarinet, horn, bassoon – tutti obbligati'.[12] Of course, technical challenges have to be faced in the process; Beethoven's friend Baron Zmeskall, for example, was not the only cellist to be sent his part in advance so that he could practise that high cello solo in the Scherzo, as generations of cellists have anxiously done ever since. In spite of Beethoven's celebrated meeting with Dragonetti earlier in the year, daring feats of virtuosity are not asked of the double bass player; but his or her all-important role is to provide depth, tonal resonance and firm rhythmic direction.

The Septet was first performed informally on 20 December 1799, in Prince Schwarzenburg's palace, and a few weeks later the First Symphony was completed in time for the official premieres of both compositions on 2 April 1800, at the first of Beethoven's benefit concerts in the Imperial National Court Theatre. In spite of poor orchestral playing, the concert was well received – 'truly the most interesting concert in a long time', wrote a correspondent of the *Allgemeine musikalische Zeitung*.[13] The orchestra's poor showing in the symphony seems to have been caused by a disagreement over conductors for the occasion, but the Septet, played by Schuppanzigh, Schreiber, Schindlecker, Bär, Nickel, Matauschek and Dietzel would, no doubt, have received a much more polished performance.

Beethoven took particular care over his choice of dedications for this important occasion, dedicating the First Symphony to Baron Swieten, a subscriber to the op. 1 piano trios and an influential advocate of Baroque music in Vienna; and the Septet to the Empress of Austria, Maria Theresa, a keen musician and a trained singer. He was careful to include in the programme a Mozart symphony, together with an aria and duet from Haydn's *Creation* – a graceful acknowledgment of his debt to both of them, but also perhaps a subtle message to his audience that he was indeed the heir to Mozart and a worthy companion for Haydn. This was not, after all, an occasion for modesty.

History has been much kinder to the Septet than to the First Symphony, overshadowed as it is by the sheer magnitude of its successors. Berlioz, one of Beethoven's most influential advocates in the nineteenth century, probably reflected and still reflects the views of many others when he wrote: 'The poetic idea is completely absent [in the First Symphony], even though it is so grand and rich in the greater part of the works that followed ... Beethoven is not here.'[14]

By contrast, the Septet was hugely popular from the start and has

[12] *Letters of Beethoven*, Letter 41, 15 December 1800: Beethoven to Franz Anton Hoffmeister.

[13] Thayer, *The Life of Beethoven*, p. 255.

[14] Berlioz, *A Critical Study of Beethoven's Ninth Symphony*, quoted in Lockwood, *Beethoven: The Music and the Life*, p. 149.

been treasured by chamber musicians and music lovers ever since. Gratifying though this was, Beethoven became increasingly frustrated by his many critics who regarded the Septet and his other 'classical' compositions as templates by which all his later, more challenging music should be measured. An article on the *Eroica* Symphony in the periodical *Der Freimüthige*, dated 26 April 1805, was fairly typical: 'One wishes that H[err] v[an] B[eethoven] would use his recognized great talent to present us with works similar to his first two Symphonies ... [and] to his agreeable Septet in E flat.'[15] Eventually, visitors were advised not to mention the work when they met him. Those who were not forewarned, such as Cipriani Potter, the Principal of the Royal Academy of Music in London, got a frosty answer: 'In those days, I did not know how to compose. Now I believe I do.'[16]

Nonetheless, the Septet remained as much a favourite among Beethoven's inner circle of friends as it does among musicians and music lovers to this day, and he was forced to revisit it from time to time over the next two decades. He arranged it in 1802 for clarinet, cello and piano (op. 38), for example, as a thank-offering to his doctor, Johann Schmidt. In 1816 he was asked to decide on metronome marks for a new edition of the Septet and heard a performance later the same year at Schuppanzigh's farewell concert, together with the third *Razumovsky* Quartet, op. 59 no. 3, and the Quintet for Piano and Wind, op. 16 – an emotional occasion at which Beethoven shared with Schuppanzigh, the most loyal of his many loyal supporters, 'the deafening applause of the crowded audience'.[17]

Adagio – Allegro con brio   Two factors contribute (perhaps subconsciously) to the Septet's undying popularity: first, the symmetry of the outer movements, each with its own imposing introduction leading into a quick movement, and the alternating symmetry of the inner movements – the Adagio and Andante followed respectively by the Menuetto and Scherzo; secondly, the thematic evolution, as in Beethoven's many improvisations, of a three- or four-note motive (x) which provides inspiration for principal and accompanying material in five of the Septet's six movements. The motive appears mysteriously in many different guises; in the Adagio (ex. 9.11a–b), for example – an introduction awe-inspiring enough to unnerve any latter-day Tamino; then in the Allegro the same motive introducing both the first subject (ex. 9.11c) and the closing section (ex. 9.11d) with the insouciance of a Papageno. As if that were not enough, the same motive (x) provides in inverted form a companionable accompaniment for the second subject (ex. 9.12).

[15] Landon, *Beethoven: A Documentary Study*, p. 153.

[16] Stich, 'String Quartets', p. 81.

[17] Thayer, *The Life of Beethoven*, p. 640. In 1816 Schuppanzigh left Vienna for Russia, where he promoted Beethoven's music with his customary enthusiasm. He returned to Vienna in 1823.

Ex. 9.11

Ex. 9.12

There are two development sections – the first mostly concerned with material in the transition and closing section, and the second a dramatic intervention by the cello and double bass in the recapitulation (ex. 9.13), calmed by a serene descant for horn.

Ex. 9.13

Adagio cantabile   Like the slow movement in the F major Quartet, op. 18 no. 1, composed a little later and discussed in Chapter 10, the Adagio is an exquisite example of instrumental *bel canto* and shows how much Beethoven had benefited from his recent (and perhaps current) studies in vocal composition with Salieri. There are rich rewards for each instrument, as Weber's friend, the great clarinettist Heinrich Baermann, discovered in its opening bars: 'The artist, who manages to perform this beautiful motif (ex. 9.14) with the same intimacy and warmth which Beethoven thought and felt, should grip and inspire every listener.'[18] Baermann's 'beautiful motif', shared alternately between the clarinet, violin and bassoon over a light-textured accompaniment, is extended with an increasing sense of

[18] Pamela Weston, *Clarinet Virtuosi of the Past*, quoted in Lawson, 'The Development of Wind Instruments', p. 77.

Ex. 9.14

wonder to twenty-eight bars. There are two shorter, conversational ideas in the second subject – the first played in turn by the string and wind trios, the second tenderly expressive – while in the development the violin, cello and horn explore new ways of expressing the opening melody.

Tempo di Menuetto & Trio   Beethoven's decision to borrow the first few bars from his little Piano Sonata in G major, op. 49 no. 2, was an appealing one. The Sonata, composed in 1795–6 but not published until 1805, was originally written for children, and the childlike innocence of this Minuet is almost without parallel in Beethoven's chamber music, although the gentle Allegretto in B flat for piano trio, WoO 39, composed for the ten-year old Maximiliane Brentano in 1812, runs it close. Gentle too is the Trio (ex. 9.15) with its soft exchanges between strings and horn and its teasing hemiolas (*y*).

Ex. 9.15

Tema con variazioni: Andante   Beethoven gives each member of both string and wind groups a chance to shine above the benevolent (though perhaps envious) gaze of the double bass in this unassuming march with five variations and coda. Most of the variations are light-textured: duets for viola and cello, for example, or for clarinet and bassoon; delicate, understated virtuosity for the violin; an impassioned Minore, initiated by the horn; an expressive tutti and a surprisingly sinister coda.

Scherzo & Trio: Allegro molto e vivace   Contemporary horn virtuosos were not limited to hunting calls, but had a 'wonderful array of melting, floating and dying away effects'[19] at their command, and could also play 'as softly as a flute or gamba', as in the earlier Trio (ex. 9.15) or in the fourth variation – qualities which Beethoven explored to the full and with great subtlety in the Septet and had earlier done in his beguiling Sextet, op. 81b, which is effectively a concerto for two horns with string quartet accompaniment.[20] In the Scherzo, however, with its galloping pulse and cheerful

[19] Ernst Gerber and Horace Fitzpatrick, quoted in Lawson, 'The Development of Wind Instruments', pp. 74–5.

[20] See Appendix 3 below.

exchanges between riders, the horn does what is traditionally expected of it, tally-hoing with the best of them, while in the Trio the cello is the unexpected leader of an eager and energetic dance, clearly invigorated by this open-air music and high above its normal range.

Andante con moto alla Marcia – Presto The horn dominates the majestic introduction to the finale, and does so with great solemnity and decorum. But solemn thoughts are soon thrust aside by the lively opening theme of the Presto (ex. 9.16a) with its off-beat accents and busy accompaniment – characteristics which later lend themselves to contrapuntal development, sometimes in association with a new motive (z in ex. 9.16c), in the gallant second subject (ex. 9.16b).

Ex. 9.16

Perhaps as a tribute to Schuppanzigh, the violin is the unquestioned first among equals throughout the finale, with frequent virtuoso passages and even a substantial cadenza for good measure (bar 135). However, the most surprising moment in the Septet appears near the end of the development section as Beethoven withdraws for a few moments of introspection. The principal motive in the first movement (x in ex. 9.11b) is recalled, though now transformed into ancient plainsong, accompanied by pizzicato footsteps (ex. 9.17) – a moment to treasure and one which Mendelssohn may have remembered when he composed the Pilgrims' March in the *Italian Symphony*.

Ex. 9.17

Serenade in D major for flute, violin and viola, op. 25

Entrata: Allegro
Tempo ordinario d'un Menuetto – Trio I – Trio II
Allegro molto
Andante con Variazioni
Allegro scherzando e vivace
Adagio – Allegro vivace e disinvolto – Presto

Although Beethoven gave important orchestral solos to the flute – including one of the most exhilarating moments in symphonic music when the principal flute portrays excitement, freedom, joy and ecstasy following those off-stage trumpet fanfares in *Leonore* Overture no. 3 – he wrote little chamber music for the flute, excluding it from most of his wind ensembles in favour of the oboe and clarinet. There are a few exceptions, noted in Appendix 3, which were composed in Bonn and published posthumously: the Trio in G major, WoO 37, for flute, bassoon and clavicembalo, dated 1786; the Duo in G major, WoO 26, for two flutes; also perhaps, a Sonata for piano and flute in B flat major, Anh. 4, which was found among Beethoven's papers after he died, but which may be spurious.[21] So far as his later chamber music is concerned, flautists have to make the best they can of Six National Airs with Variations, op. 105, Ten National Airs with Variations, op. 107, both sets arranged for voice(s) and piano with flute or violin obbligato and, of course, this Serenade, a cheerful and colourful companion to the op. 8 Serenade for String Trio, which Beethoven also composed in Vienna.

It is not known when op. 25 was written, as no sketches have survived, but it was published in 1802 by Giovanni Cappi in two sets, each containing three movements and, like the D major Serenade for String Trio, op. 8, it was later arranged by Franz Kleinheinz for piano and flute or violin, an arrangement grudgingly revised by Beethoven and published the following year by Hoffmeister & Kühnel as op. 41. Few commentators mention it and those who do are generally dismissive, though Philip Radcliffe stoutly defends it as having 'very great charm' and for being 'extremely effective in performance'.[22]

Thematically and structurally the Serenade is simple – a miniature ballet, perhaps, with its theatrical title, 'Entrata', and its sequence of varied dances. Indeed, if it were technically not quite so difficult it could have been composed, like the two op. 49 piano sonatas, for children. Though stylistically conventional, it is beautifully written throughout, with melodic material carefully shared between all three instruments. It is a joy to play and its high tessitura and unique choice of instruments offer an unusual experience in tone colour and texture – an ideal curtain-raiser.

---

[21] See Cooper, *The Beethoven Compendium*, p. 226.
[22] Radcliffe, *Beethoven's String Quartets*, p. 22.

Entrata: Allegro   The Entrata, like three of the five later dances, is in simple ternary form (A1+A2 – B1+B2 – A1+A2) and is distinctly mischievous in character. As the curtain rises, the dancers are already on the stage, summoned by a spritely fanfare (ex. 9.18), eager and energetic enough for them to dance their way through the next five movements.

Ex. 9.18

Tempo ordinario d'un Menuetto – Trio I – Trio II   With a nice touch of irony, the poise of this seemingly conventional minuet is upset in the second section by ill-mannered string chords, and later attempts to introduce a little fervour into the music are laughed out of court. Though not named as such, two trios are included, allowing each instrument a chance to shine in a series of virtuoso displays – the first shared in turn by the violin and viola, the second a brilliant solo for flute.

Allegro molto   The outer sections of this dance, with its minor key, third-beat *sforzandi* and manly leaps, is focused and energetic while, by contrast, the central section in D major is distinctly flirtatious, and the coda hilarious.

Andante con Variazioni   The hymn-like theme, played in four parts by the strings, introduces a touch of solemnity, both at the start and in the thoughtful coda. But dancing is resumed in three beautiful variations – a solo for each instrument in turn, the accompanying textures increasingly intricate.

Allegro scherzando e vivace   Dotted rhythms and unexpected dynamics characterize the outer sections of this taut and controlled scherzo, but the expressive and contrapuntal Minore is a welcome surprise.

Adagio – Allegro vivace disinvolto – Presto   This Serenade knows its place; there is to be no grand introduction to the final movement as in the Septet. Aware of the modest pretensions of the Adagio, Beethoven provides a simple folk-song (ex. 9.19) as the principal rondo theme, instructing the performers to play the Allegro in an assured, easy manner (*disinvolto*); encouragement certainly needed in this crisp and (in the second episode) highly competitive rondo, in which only the robust first episode stills the onward rush of semiquavers.

Ex. 9.19

Six String Quartets, op. 18

Where the serious Count Apponyi had failed in 1795 to persuade Beethoven to compose even a single string quartet, the young and enthusiastic Prince Franz Joseph Lobkowitz (1772–1816), not a man for half measures where music was concerned, succeeded triumphantly three years later when he commissioned no fewer than six quartets from Beethoven and a further six from Haydn. To be fair, the Prince was luckier than the Count in matters of timing; Beethoven was so pleased with his op. 9 string trios – 'the best of my works' – completed earlier in 1798 and published the same year, that he seems to have felt ready at last to face the ultimate challenge in chamber music – composing string quartets.

His sketchbooks show that he started with the D major Quartet (later published as op. 18 no. 3) in the autumn of 1798, followed chronologically over the next two years by numbers 1, 2, 5, 4, and 6. However, when the quartets were published by Tranquillo Mollo in two instalments in June and October 1801, duly dedicated to Prince Lobkowitz, Beethoven rearranged the order to ensure that each instalment was framed by the more obviously appealing quartets. To avoid confusion, however, they are discussed here in their published order. It is known that the first version (Hess 32) of the F major Quartet, op. 18 no. 1, was completed in the early summer of 1799, as Beethoven sent a copy to Karl Amenda on 25 June that year 'as a small memorial of our friendship',[1] only to withdraw it two years later because he had revised it extensively in the meantime: 'Be sure not to hand on to anybody your quartet, in which I have made some drastic alterations. For only now have I learnt how to write quartets; and this you will notice, I fancy, when you receive them.'[2]

In addition to his studies with Haydn, Beethoven is known to have made copies of two Mozart quartets, K387 and K464, at much the same time as he began work on the op. 18 quartets. His warm friendship with the composer Emanuel Aloys Förster (1748–1823) may also have been significant. Förster, whom he first met at the Lichnowskys, composed more than sixty string quartets and, judging by a review in the *Allgemeine musikalische Zeitung*, his music was of the adventurous kind that would appeal to Beethoven: Förster's 'Quatuors will cause more sensation through their bizarre, humoristic and wilful nature than through agreeableness and naturalness.'[3] Beethoven was a regular visitor at Förster's home, 'a favourite resort of the principal composers and dilettanti where,

---

[1] Thayer, *The Life of Beethoven*, p. 224.

[2] *Letters of Beethoven*, Letter 53, 1 July 1801: Beethoven to Karl Amenda in Courland.

[3] Stich, 'String Quartets', p. 87.

after regular quartet meetings on Thursday evenings and Sundays at noon, the conversation usually turned upon musical theory and composition'.[4]

Prince Lobkowitz authorized the payment of 200 florins to Beethoven on 14 October 1799, and a further payment on 18 October 1800, so it can be assumed that draft versions of each set of three quartets were in circulation well before they were published. They would have been played by Schuppanzigh's quartet in revised or unrevised form at Prince Lobkowitz's palace, at Prince Lichnowsky's regular Friday morning concerts or at such informal gatherings as the soirée at Countess Josephine von Deym's house on 10 December 1800, recalled in the Preface, 'when Beethoven, that real angel, let us hear his quartets [op. 18] which have not been engraved yet … the best of their kind'.[5] However, unlike the Countess's soirée, an exclusively Beethoven evening, most programmes would also have included music by other composers, so Beethoven was well aware that everything he wrote would be measured against the finest music composed by Haydn and Mozart in one of the noblest and most demanding of art-forms.

Haydn for his part was no less aware that comparisons would be made between him and his erstwhile pupil and, fearing that at least some of his younger listeners would share Josephine von Deym's view that the op. 18 quartets were 'the best of their kind', he seems to have backed away from the possibility of a 'direct confrontation between Beethoven's op. 18 and his own op. 77 [quartets] at the Palais Lobkowitz'.[6] Robbins Landon has suggested that this was not out of character. Haydn composed no more piano concertos after 1782 and no more complete operas after 1784 in the face of Mozart's 'supreme achievements' in those genres, and whether or not the success of Beethoven's op. 18 quartets was indeed the cause, Haydn completed only two of the six quartets commissioned by the Prince (op. 77, nos. 1 and 2) and, apart from two movements in the unfinished Quartet in D minor, op. 103, wrote no more quartets thereafter.

String Quartet no. 1 in F major, op. 18 no. 1

Allegro con brio
Adagio affettuoso ed appassionato
Scherzo & Trio: Allegro molto
Allegro

Allegro con brio   Beethoven sketched several versions of the six-note motive (*x* in ex. 10.1b), which dominates the first movement, before finally coming up with a brisk version of one which he had already used in the Adagio of his String Trio, op. 3 (ex. 10.1a). The motive's rhythmic thrust ensures that momentum is never lost. In addition, its catchy melodic shape makes for clarity in the many contrapuntal episodes – then regarded as the

---

[4] Thayer, *The Life of Beethoven*, p. 262.

[5] Landon, *Beethoven: A Documentary Study*, p. 130.

[6] Landon, *Haydn: Chronicle and Works: The Years of the 'Creation'*, p. 505.

Ex. 10.1

hallmark of serious purpose in string quartet writing – which appear unexpectedly (often in remote keys) in the exposition, the development and the
adventurous recapitulation. Some ideas, however, are unaffected by the
motive: celebratory scales, for example, leading into the recapitulation and,
with slower steps, to the coda; also, in complete contrast, the gentle, flowing second subject (ex. 10.2).

Ex. 10.2

Although for much of the movement the first violin leads the debate, there
is plenty of general discussion too, with each member of the ensemble asking and answering questions in conversational polyphony, as in the central
development section (ex. 10.3); or reaching agreement in dramatic unison
passages which, according to contemporaries, would have sounded like a
full orchestra when played by Schuppanzigh and his colleagues.

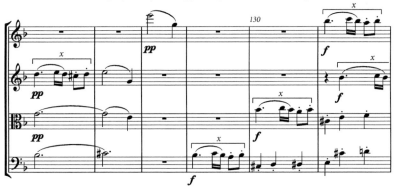

Ex. 10.3

Adagio affettuoso ed appassionato   Beethoven was sometimes inspired
by events or people when composing; but with a few exceptions – one-
word titles such as *Pathétique* and *Eroica*, for example, or the *Pastoral*
Symphony, with its descriptive programme – he avoided giving his listeners too precise an explanation of what he 'meant' in his music. As it happens, however, there is well-documented evidence that he was inspired to
compose this wonderful Adagio by one of the most romantic moments in

literature, the vault scene in Shakespeare's *Romeo and Juliet*. His sketches include specific references to the scene at various points in the movement, rather oddly written in French: 'il prend le tombeau – désespoir – il se tuer – les derniers soupirs.'[7] When, after hearing the movement, Karl Amenda told him that 'he pictured [in it] the parting of two lovers', Beethoven was delighted: 'Good!' he replied. 'I thought of the scene in the burial vault in Romeo and Juliet'.[8] The op. 18 quartets were written at much the same time as Beethoven's studies in vocal composition with Salieri, and the long, sustained opening melody (ex. 10.4), one of his most beautiful (and one to which Fauré would return eight decades later in his song *Après un rêve*) shows how fruitful those lessons were.

It is possible that Salieri, whose primary interest was opera, suggested the use of references to events in the tomb scene as a practical guide to constructing an emotional narrative in a movement, and this may be why Beethoven noted them in his sketches. Although he deleted all reference to Shakespeare's play in the published edition of the quartet, the depth of feeling in this desolate, intensely romantic music, underlined by Beethoven's use of both affettuoso and appassionato, is never in doubt. The general level of dynamics is soft as the Adagio unfolds and, as a result, the *forte/fortissimo* outpourings of raw despair later in the development section and recapitulation are all the more overwhelming. The flowing second theme, introduced by the second violin and later shared by all four instruments, is gentler; but the heart of the movement is to be found in the closing section (ex. 10.5): four bars of profound sadness and one of those visionary moments in Beethoven's earlier music when he looks far ahead to the spiritual landscape of his late quartets.

Scherzo & Trio: Allegro molto   Beethoven did not have to travel too far in mind from the Montagues and Capulets in Verona when composing these two extraordinary dances, both of which seem to evoke the sinister world of the *commedia dell'arte*, a milieu particularly associated with Venice and its masked balls. With its frequent modulations and asymmetric phrasing – 6+2+2; 3+3+9 – the Scherzo (ex. 10.6), a miniature rondo in form, is strangely unsettling.

---

[7] Cooper, *Beethoven and the Creative Process*, p. 43.
[8] Thayer, *The Life of Beethoven*, p. 261.

Ex. 10.5

Ex. 10.6

The Trio (ex. 10.7) also creates feelings of extreme tension with its gro-tesque leaps, mysterious, harlequinesque whisperings, explosive outbursts and sliding tonality.

Ex. 10.7

Allegro There is nothing miniature about the last movement, however. The light-hearted principal theme (ex. 10.8) – an extension of the opening bars in the last movement of the C minor String Trio, op. 9 no. 3 (ex. 8.17a) – is another catchy, easy-to-recognize figure like the six-note motive in the first movement (ex. 10.1) and almost as ubiquitous.

Ex. 10.8

This extended sonata-rondo is planned on the grandest scale, and is of such contrapuntal complexity that Beethoven originally marked it 'Alle-gretto' to ensure that each part could be clearly heard and savoured. But Allegretto is not only an indication of tempo; it suggests a gentle, unhur-ried mood as well. So Beethoven eventually decided to live danger-ously and settle on Allegro; rightly so, though performers would be wise to heed Robert Simpson's advice that 'the finale should not be taken too fast … there is no excuse for rushing it (as is often done) and trivializing it.'[9] Episodes include a gentle canonic dialogue between the two violins over a flowing accompaniment which, in inverted form (*y*), becomes a disciplined, thrusting countersubject to the opening theme (ex. 10.9a). A sequence of dramatic fugal events and adventurous modulations follows in the central episode, alternating with a thoughtful version of the closing theme (ex. 10.9b) – a preview, incidentally, of the *Prometheus* theme in the finale of the *Eroica* Symphony. The quartet ends with a brilliant display of polyphonic invention and dramatic surprise.

Ex. 10.9

String Quartet no. 2 in G major, op. 18 no. 2

Allegro
Adagio cantabile – Allegro – Tempo I
Scherzo & Trio: Allegro
Allegro molto quasi Presto

Beethoven was determined to ensure that his first six string quartets were individuals rather than too obviously members of the same family. Preliminary ideas for the G major Quartet appear in two sketchbooks, the first dated early 1799 to August the same year, and the second, May to August 1800. It is clear from Beethoven's comments in the earlier sketchbook, 'Le seconde quatuor dans un style bien léger excepté le dernier',[10] that in character and mood the second quartet was to be completely different from the dramatic and intense first. The extensive changes Beethoven made when revising the G major Quartet later in the 1800 sketchbook, particularly the insertion of an Allegro section in the middle of the slow movement, add still more to its effervescent wit and lightness of touch.[11]

Allegro   All the principal themes in the two outer movements are introduced by a three-crotchet motive, sometimes with an additional flourish (*x*), sometimes plain (*z*). Elegant questions are asked in the first subject

[9] Simpson, 'The Chamber Music for Strings', p. 249.

[10] Quoted in Lockwood, *Beethoven: The Music and the Life*, p. 165. 'The second quartet in a light style, except the finale.'

[11] For dates of Beethoven's sketches of op. 18 no. 2, see Cooper, *Beethoven and the Creative Process*, p. 88.

(ex. 10.10a) and answered with wit and charm; a parody, perhaps, of conversations at the many soirées Beethoven attended during his early years in Vienna. By contrast, the sturdy, march-like rhythms (*z*) in the second subject (ex. 10.10b) suggest more purposeful and serious discussion.

Ex. 10.10

It is not long before conversation becomes more general, however, sometimes light-hearted as in the closing section; sometimes mystical, as in the strangely beautiful development (ex. 10.11), expressed in thoughtful, sustained polyphony accompanied on the cello by a delicate rhythmic figure (*y*) borrowed from the third bar of the movement.

Ex. 10.11

High spirits and laughter return when the cello, high in the treble clef, impatiently anticipates the recapitulation (bars 141–8) with those opening flourishes (*x*) and martial rhythms (*z*). Each topic in the exposition is further developed in the recapitulation and, after the guests have finally departed, the movement ends as charmingly as it began, the candles snuffed out pizzicato in the final cadence.

Adagio cantabile – Allegro – Tempo I   The Adagio is a noble aria (ex. 10.12a) which Beethoven may have remembered later when composing the fourth of his Six Gellert Songs, op. 48: 'Die Ehre Gottes aus der Natur' ('The Praise of God in Nature') (ex. 10.12b).[12] Contrapuntal exchanges follow, shared by all four instruments (ex. 10.12c) in the secretive Allegro; its characteristic shape, marked with an asterisk (*), reveals its thematic connection to the opening bar of the Adagio (motive *w*). The cello, soon joined by the first violin, then introduces an elaborate variation of the aria – a variation so 'full of *fioriture*', wrote Daniel Mason, that 'we may wonder whether the luxuriance of the vegetation is not overdone. But as we listen

---

12 Radcliffe, *Beethoven's String Quartets*, pp. 30–1.

Ex. 10.12

it all falls into place, partly because the *fioriture* are so beautifully imagined, partly because the essential melody that carries and subordinates
them all is so pure and noble.'[13] In striking contrast to such elaboration,
the five-note figure (*v*) with which the Allegro was first introduced is gently
recalled by each instrument in turn in the exquisite coda.

Scherzo & Trio: Allegro   Outlines of the complete opening theme in the
Adagio (ex. 10.12a), are clear in the Scherzo as well – its mischievous offspring (ex. 10.13a), again marked with a star (*), skipping this way and that
throughout the movement, chased by determined scales and purposeful
counterpoint; hiding successfully during the Trio, but managing to wriggle
free whenever caught, most cheekily in the *pianissimo* bridge passage leading back to the Scherzo (ex. 10.13b).

Ex. 10.13

Allegro molto quasi Presto   Although Beethoven decided that the finale
would not be 'dans un style bien léger' like the other three movements,
he borrowed the march-like motives (*z*) from the transition and second
subject in the first movement to introduce the opening theme, and again
adopted the same four-bar question-and-answer phrase-lengths. Once
launched, however, there is a greater sense of momentum here than in the
first movement, with one idea suggesting and often merging into another.
Although in sonata form, much of the musical interest is to be found in
insignificant-seeming ideas in both subjects. The three-note march motive

[13] Mason, *The Quartets of Beethoven*, pp. 35–6.

(*m*), together with its inversion (ex. 10.14) – each a variant of the march motive (*z*) in the first movement – appear throughout the finale, sometimes introspective in mood and sometimes forceful. But there is much else besides, including adventurous modulations and bold, contrapuntal, sometimes canonic, passages in the development, with each part chasing or competing with the other, up hill and down dale; proud, exuberant and conclusive.

Ex. 10.14

String Quartet no. 3 in D major, op. 18 no. 3

Allegro
Andante con moto
Allegro [Maggiore] & Minore
Presto

Allegro   Perhaps aware of the solemnity of the occasion, Beethoven purchased a bound manuscript book (now known as Grasnick 1 and dated August 1798 to early 1799), in which he planned to sketch this, the earliest of his string quartets. From then on he continued to use such books, when possible, in preference to the single sheets of manuscript paper he had previously favoured. First to appear in the book are extensive sketches for this quartet, completed in January 1799, and published in 1801 as op. 18 no. 3. Apart from the last movement, it is a gentle, introspective work, so the decision to place it third is understandable, though symbolically a pity, as there is an unmistakable sense of dawn, of new beginnings, in its opening bars (ex. 10.15a) and also in the frisky motive with which the first subject ends (ex. 10.15b).

This is the earliest example, incidentally, of several unaccompanied openings which occur in some of Beethoven's finest and most thoughtful chamber works, among them the *Kreutzer* Sonata, op. 47, the Cello Sonata, op. 69, the Piano Trio, op. 70 no. 2, the Violin Sonata, op. 96, the Cello Sonata, op. 102 no. 1, and the String Quartet in C sharp minor, op. 131. The transitional theme suggests that Beethoven was fully aware of the quartet's symbolic importance when, accompanied by a celebratory peal of bells (ex. 10.16a), he remembered, consciously or not, Haydn's setting of

Ex. 10.15

particularly apt words in *The Creation*, which had received its premiere
in Vienna only a few months earlier: the Aria and Chorus, 'A new created
world' (ex. 10.16b).

Ex. 10.16

There are other delights to savour in Beethoven's own 'new created world',
notably the pastoral second subject (ex. 10.17) – perhaps the most touching
music in any of the quartets. Clearly he was pleased with it, as it is played
twice more: first *piano* in the recapitulation and finally *pianissimo* in the
coda in distant E flat major, an especially remote key with D major as tonic.

Ex. 10.17

Andante con moto With the last of Beethoven's five string trios successfully completed, there is symbolism of a more practical kind in the
Andante. Clearly the addition of a second violin to the ensemble in the
first quartet that Beethoven composed, calls for celebration! From the start,
accompanying harmonies and contrapuntal textures are notably richer and
more varied than in the string trios, and the principal subject (ex. 10.18),
created from two contrasting sequences (*x*, *y*), is appropriately introduced
by the welcome newcomer, played sul G to ensure that when the first violin

Ex. 10.18

enters with the principal subject in the fifth bar the individual tone of the second violin remains focused.

In outline, the Andante is a closely woven rondo, with a principal theme and two episodes. The first episode, introduced by the concluding phrase of the principal theme, is very different from it in character and texture, with short phrase-lengths and delicate tracery. But it too ends in a similar way to the rondo theme, though now in a mood of extreme intensity. The second episode, introduced hauntingly by the cello, low on the C string in D flat major, is an extended development of both sequences *x* and *y* in the principal theme. But the loveliest music, heralded by unexpectedly assertive *sforzandi* triplets, is saved for the introspective coda, where fragments of the principal theme are softly remembered.

Allegro [Maggiore] & Minore   With its cross-rhythms and frequent offbeat *sforzandi*, the Allegro is another of Beethoven's quiet yet troubled scherzos. Most unusually, the dominant key, A major, is absent throughout, and modulations are either inconclusive or favour minor keys – F sharp minor, for example, at the end of the first section. However, the persistent opening motive is easy to follow and the scale motive concluding the outer sections and underpinning the flowing Minore recalls the celebratory peal of bells in the first movement and provides the movement with a sense of unity.

Presto   Variants of the scale motive appear in the finale as well, most notably in the transition and closing section – a triumphant descant, high above the first subject (ex. 10.19).

Ex. 10.19

There is the same uncertain tonality, with the tonic key only reached in the twenty-sixth bar after boisterous and discordant *sforzandi*. But in this brilliant *perpetuum mobile*, rich in *opera buffa* tunes and witty counterpoint, such unruly behaviour is surely meant to tease rather than to unsettle – as are the excitable three-note phrases (*z*) at the start of the movement, and the identical three-note farewells with which it quietly ends.

String Quartet no. 4 in C minor, op. 18 no. 4

Allegro ma non tanto
Scherzo: Andante scherzoso quasi Allegretto
Menuetto & Trio: Allegretto
Allegro – Prestissimo

Sketches for the C minor Quartet have not yet come to light and, partly
as a result, perhaps, it has become the most controversial of the six op. 18
quartets. Joseph Kerman, for example, has described it as 'exceptional by
its weakness in the entire corpus of Beethoven quartets',[14] while others
have argued that no sketches were necessary, as Beethoven must surely
have reworked the quartet from much earlier material composed in Bonn.
However, as Barry Cooper has shown, among more than 8,000 pages
that are known to have survived, there are almost no sketches either for
the Septet or First Symphony, composed at much the same time as the
C minor Quartet (1799–1800) so the 'obvious inference is that a single
sketchbook has been lost'; and as Beethoven always 'made sketches for the
simplest and most minor works ... it is inconceivable that he made none
for such large and complex works as these.'[15] When the second instalment of a further three op. 18 quartets was published in October 1801,
Beethoven decided to introduce the set with the C minor Quartet, so he
himself must have thought highly of it. Like the F major Quartet heading
the first instalment, the C minor certainly makes a powerful impression
in performance and, whatever its alleged weaknesses, remains a favourite
among chamber musicians and audiences alike.

Allegro ma non tanto   Though sharing the same key and something of
the same tensions, Beethoven's four C minor works to date – the Piano
Trio, op. 1 no. 3, the String Trio, op. 9 no. 3, the *Pathétique* Sonata and this
quartet – are very different in character. For a start, the opening movements of the first three, marked 'Allegro con brio' or 'Allegro con spirito',
are here replaced by a more spacious tempo, Allegro ma non tanto. What
is more, the first subject (ex. 10.20a) is one of Beethoven's longest and most
powerfully sculpted melodies – twelve bars of increasing tension, four
bars of *fortissimo* close combat and four of expressive intensity, leading to
the comparative security of the dominant key, G major. Unlike the youthful *angst* and passion of the three earlier C minor works, this authentically
original theme conveys feelings of supreme confidence in the face of adversity: 'Now I ask the reader just to cast a glance at the music', wrote Theodor Helm in 1875, 'and earnestly ask himself whether a quartet movement
by Haydn or Mozart can display such a broad and unified, forward-driving
melody? You will definitely have to answer "no".'[16] How right he was.

However, there are gentler emotions too; indeed at least half of the
movement is quiet. For example, the transitional *pas de deux* (bars

[14] Kerman, *The Beethoven Quartets*.
[15] Cooper, 'The Compositional Act', p. 36.
[16] Quoted in Kinderman, *The String Quartets of Beethoven*, p. 3.

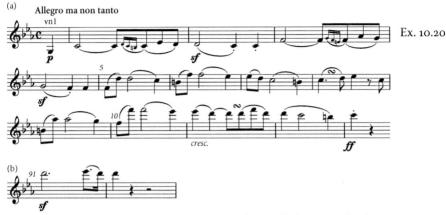

Ex. 10.20

26–33), shared by the two violins, seems carefree and the second subject is especially beguiling, not least because of its charming descant. Tensions mount again in the development section, reaching an impassioned climax in a *cri de cœur* from the first violin (ex. 10.20b), and the movement ends in uncompromising style.

Scherzo: Andante scherzoso quasi Allegretto 'The young composer whose rude manners could shock', wrote Robert Simpson, 'was also at this time very careful about his dress';[17] and although there is enough under-stated learning in the Scherzo to engage Beethoven's older listeners, there is more than enough charm to please the younger ones. It is one of his earliest lightweight 'slow' movements – among them the G major Violin Sonata, op. 30 no. 3, and the First and Eighth symphonies – and it is in sonata form, though of an unusual kind because both subjects begin con-trapuntally, the first, fugal (ex. 10.21a) and the second, a canon (ex. 10.21b).

Ex. 10.21

Apart from occasional outbursts, the general dynamic level is soft and secretive, and forward momentum is maintained not only by frequent hemiolas, but also by shortening the gap between each fugal entry from five bars to four, then to three, with canonic entries in the second sub-ject only one bar apart. Both subjects share a simple three-quaver figure

[17] Simpson, 'The Chamber Music for Strings', p. 246.

which plays an increasingly important part in the development section, creating yet another example of those moments of introspection (bars 114–21) noted in previous chapters. In the recapitulation, the second subject appears much as before, but the first is framed by delicate contrapuntal traceries, including a new tongue-in-cheek idea of a quietly subversive kind (*x* in ex. 10.21c) – brilliant!

Menuetto & Trio: Allegretto   The Minuet threatens violence with its searing chromaticisms, contrapuntal twists and turns, unexpected modulations and third-beat *sforzandi*, and Beethoven raises the emotional temperature still further in the recapitulation with the instruction: *La secunda volta si prende il tempo più Allegro.* In the Trio, however, the conversation between the second violin on the one hand and the viola and cello on the other could hardly be more civilized, or the conclusions reached by the first violin expressed more graciously.

Allegro – Prestissimo   The finale begins energetically, though without the violence of the first movement, and the formal layout is unusually clear – a rondo, with a principal theme and two episodes neatly hedged in, at least initially, by double bars, and each in two repeated sections: A–B–A–C–A–B–A+coda/prestissimo. The principal subject is in ternary form and, although varied in texture in its later appearances, it retains its dynamic contours (*piano–crescendo–forte*) throughout; a motive taken from it (*y* in ex. 10.22) is put to significant use in the final bars of the movement.

Ex. 10.22

The most serene music in the quartet is to be found in the expressive first episode (ex. 10.23).

Ex. 10.23
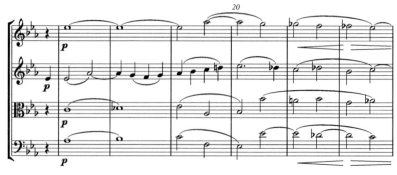

The second episode is rustic – a musette, firmly based on tonic and dominant drones. Violence returns in the coda, however, suggesting that the quartet may end tragically – the principal theme *sempre fortissimo*, and the first violin perilously high at times. The second violin and viola tentatively suggest C major with a variant of *y*, but the three unison flourishes with which the quartet ends are so inconclusive as to seem ambiguous.

String Quartet no. 5 in A major, op. 18 no. 5

Allegro
Menuetto & Trio
Andante cantabile
Allegro

Though eventually published in October 1801, as no. 5 in the second set of op. 18 quartets, preparatory sketches for the A major Quartet appeared two years earlier in the same sketchbook as nos. 1 and 2 (Grasnick 2, dated early 1799 – late August the same year). Much has rightly been made of parallels between this quartet and Mozart's Quartet in A major, K464, which Beethoven had recently studied, but the differences in character between them are far greater than their mostly structural similarities. Certainly, comments describing Beethoven as an 'aspiring student … learning here with such docility all his older brothers [Haydn and Mozart] can teach him',[18] as one critic wrote when discussing this quartet, are wide of the mark, because the writer fails to take into account the originality of this fine quartet and the other early masterpieces of Beethoven's 'first maturity', discussed in previous chapters.

Allegro   In contrast to the urbane elegance of Mozart's first movement, this carefree music breathes the fresh air and magic of the countryside, its mischievous themes flying, like the fairy in Shakespeare's *A Midsummer Night's Dream*, 'over hill, over dale … over park, over pale'. The first subject (ex. 10.24) establishes its pastoral credentials at once and, like the fairy, the three-note motive with which the Allegro begins, and so charmingly ends, finds its way into almost every corner of the movement, leaving its imprint wherever it can.

Ex. 10.24

The second subject is in two sections, the first appearing in mysterious unison in the dominant minor, modulating into the major with Schubertian grace in time for the second, a light-textured two-part canon. At the end of the development, an appropriately pastoral theme (ex. 10.25) emerges, recalling the aria 'He shall feed his flock' in Handel's *Messiah* – a canon this time (*y*), accompanied by a new *cantus firmus* on the viola (*z*) which will reappear prominently in the finale (ex. 10.26b).

---

[18] Mason, *The Quartets of Beethoven*, p. 56.

Ex. 10.25

Menuetto & Trio   At first, the Minuet seems as conventional as those Twelve Minuets, WoO 7, which Beethoven composed in 1795 for the annual ball of the Gesellschaft der bildenden Künstler. But it is not long before ambiguities which match his individual brand of humour interrupt the even flow of the music – a six-bar tantrum in C sharp minor, for example, brings the dance to a complete standstill, while a closely argued contrapuntal development of the opening theme raises the intellectual level of the movement higher perhaps than most dancers would wish. In the Trio the scene shifts from the elegance of a ballroom to the good cheer of a country inn, as the melody is pulled out of shape by bucolic *sforzandi* on the third beat of every bar.

Andante cantabile   Critics have sometimes commented on the thematic profligacy of Beethoven's earlier music, but few mention the simplicity of so many of his melodic ideas, a direct result, no doubt, of his improvisatory skills; it is, after all, more impressive to improvise brilliantly on a few notes from an upside-down cello part, as he did in his celebrated 'competition' with Steibelt described in Chapter 9, than on the loveliest of melodies. The theme for this set of five variations and coda, itself a variant of y in ex. 10.25 in the first movement, is a case in point. It is hard to imagine anything simpler than the theme itself, yet the variations that follow are extraordinarily rich and inventive. Beethoven had already composed more than twenty sets of variations, most of which broadly reflect the view of his contemporary, Christian Michaelis, in an article written in 1803, that 'Variation arouses admiration in so far as everything latent in the theme is gradually made manifest, and unfolds [into] the most attractive diversity.'[19] Traditionally, contrapuntal variations appeared late in a set, but the first variation is a fugato, so there is to be no gradual unfolding here. Elaine Sisman sees this as a 'manifesto, asserting [Beethoven's] control over the language of the classical variation, while challenging its decorum'.[20]

[19] Christian Michaelis in *The Cambridge Companion to Beethoven*, quoted in Sisman, 'Beethoven's Musical Inheritance', p. 60.

[20] Sisman, 'Beethoven's Musical Inheritance', p. 61

By introducing each of the four instruments in turn, as in a fugue, it is also perhaps a graceful acknowledgment that in this, Beethoven's first set of variations for string quartet, each instrument is to be fully involved and equally regarded. The first violin, for example, fulfills its traditional solo-istic role in the second variation but takes its turn as accompanist else-where. The viola and cello dominate the expressive third variation and all four instruments contribute to the exquisitely soft chromatic harmonies and strange modulations of the fourth, while the second violin and viola share the fifth variation above the hearty, tub-thumping cello. However, the finest music is to be found in the coda – an extended polyphonic dia-logue, which focuses on the first two bars of the theme (*y*), together with a countersubject based on its inversion shared by all four instruments in equal measure.

Allegro   The opening bars of the finale are also shared – a mischievous four-note motive (*u*), which dominates the first subject (ex. 10.26a), tran-sition, development and coda, and would surely be happy to return two or three decades later to star in one of Mendelssohn's magical scherzos. Only the introspective second subject (ex. 10.26b), a radiant version of the Handelian passage (*y* in ex. 10.25) in the first movement, escapes its attentions. Here, however, the roles are reversed: the *cantus firmus* (*z*) is now the principal theme and it is the canon's turn (*y*) to provide a flowing

Ex. 10.26

accompaniment. Both subjects are discussed in increasingly complex polyphony in the development, and one of Beethoven's subtlest and most entertaining early finales ends as it began – softly, though now with the four-note motive (*u*) contentedly legato.

String Quartet no. 6 in B flat major, op. 18 no. 6

Allegro con brio
Adagio ma non troppo
Scherzo & Trio: Allegro
La Malinconia: Adagio – Allegretto quasi Allegro

Allegro con brio   With striking symbolism, the last of Beethoven's op. 18 quartets – the only one to be composed entirely in the first year of the new century – combines elements of the classical past and the early romantic present with two remarkably prescient visions of the future. Sketches for the quartet appear in a sheaf of folios, dated May to August 1800, together with further revision of the first two op. 18 quartets and two particularly powerful sonatas – the Piano Sonata, op. 22, also in B flat major, and the Violin Sonata in A minor, op. 23, discussed in the next chapter.[21] The first subject (ex. 10.27a), with its characteristic turn (*x*) and jaunty conversation between the first violin and cello, above the plainest of accompaniments, is a cheerful, perhaps ironic, caricature of Beethoven's classical roots and those of his great teachers. However, the off-beat *sforzandi* and vigorous scales in the transition (ex. 10.27b) present a more balanced view of classical virtues, as does the development section with its clear focus on both themes, adventurous modulations and delicate polyphony.

Ex. 10.27

The prophetic second subject is another matter altogether. It starts crisply enough as a march in F major, but is quickly unsettled by oscillating major/minor modulations and sudden dynamic changes (ex. 10.28) to become a yearning, romantic theme of the bittersweet kind that Schubert would make so much his own in the future.

---

[21] Sketch sources in Cooper, *Beethoven and the Creative Process*, p. 88.

Ex. 10.28

A further theme (ex. 10.29), characterized by the extensive use of romantic thirds, appears at the end of the development; a second transition leading into a full recapitulation.

Ex. 10.29

Adagio ma non troppo   For all its decorative features, the Adagio is in simple, if unusually proportioned, ternary form. The opening theme is in two sections, one ornamental and tranquil (ex. 10.30a), the other searching (ex. 10.30b), and each concludes with similar ornamental refrains, which recall the characteristic turn (x) in the opening bar of the quartet. The second theme (ex. 10.30c), a mysterious, unsettled two-bar phrase, is first played in unison and then developed contrapuntally with some intensity in a series of eight mini-variations. Both themes are further embellished in the recapitulation, and an extended version of the turn (z) brings the movement to a gentle conclusion.

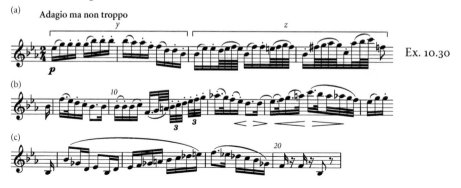

Ex. 10.30

Scherzo & Trio: Allegro   Beethoven frequently uses cross-rhythms, syncopations or *sforzandi* on weak beats, marked as often as not by unexpected dynamics, to induce a sense of metrical ambiguity, unease or conflict – sometimes charming, sometimes humorous and sometimes (as here) unnerving and complex. Indeed, there is no precedent for this extraordinary Scherzo (ex. 10.31), which looks more than a century ahead to the rhythmic complexities of Bartók's string quartets.

An uneasy compromise is eventually found in time for the sparkling Trio, but in the meantime, there are plenty of unexpected thrusts and parries in this rhythmic duel, and the violent mood returns later with unprecedented ferocity in the short transition which leads from the Trio back to the Scherzo.

Ex. 10.31

La Malinconia: Adagio – Allegretto quasi Allegro   Beethoven was generally sparing in his use of descriptive titles, but he seems to have realized that a few of his compositions – among them the *Pathétique* Sonata composed two years earlier than *La Malinconia*, and the *Eroica* Symphony, composed three years later – were so unprecedented, and yet so specific in intention, that a short title was necessary, even essential, if a movement or a work was to be fully understood. Beethoven had had typhus in 1796 and suffered from bouts of severe depression ('melancholy') from time to time thereafter, so he knew only too well what it is like to experience feelings of total despair. In *La Malinconia* (ex. 10.32) he expressed those feelings in awesome, almost clinical detail, anticipating the psychological and spiritual insights of his later years.

Ex. 10.32

Most intriguing of all is the second theme (*u*) at the heart of *La Malinconia* (ex. 10.33), a tragic motive which Beethoven had earlier explored in the G minor Cello Sonata and the C minor String Trio (*x* in ex. 8.15a) and to which he would return in several later works – the second subject in the finale of the String Quartet in C sharp minor, op. 131, for example – as a specific metaphor for depression.

Ex. 10.33

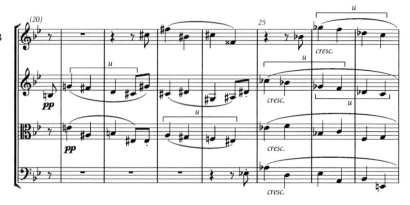

The opening bars of *La Malincolia* intervene twice more during the ensuing Allegretto quasi Allegro, unsettling the feelings of resignation, if not
contentment, that the gentle, wayward dance (ex. 10.34), with its characteristic second-beat accents, seems to evoke.

Ex. 10.34

But such raw and increasingly anxious emotions are hard to control for
any length of time, and the movement ends suddenly and violently in the
briefest of codas – *prestissimo* and *fortissimo.*

PART THREE ⅏ 1800–1803

*'I am not satisfied with what I have
composed up to now. From now on,
I intend to embark on a new path.'*

Beethoven in conversation with
Wenzel Krumpholz, 1802

Two Violin Sonatas, op. 23 & op. 24

During the early years of the new century, Beethoven became increasingly impatient with those who could not keep pace with his ideas, among them Haydn. 'His first works pleased me considerably', Haydn told Giuseppe Carpani, his first biographer; '[but] I must admit that I don't understand the later ones. It seems to me that he continually improvises.'[1] Partly as a result perhaps, Beethoven became less content with his earlier, more popular music like the Septet, as is shown in his celebrated conversation with Wenzel Krumpholz, quoted above.[2] However, the music he composed during the first three years of the new century – alternating periods of hope and all but total despair as his hearing gradually deteriorated – suggests not so much a single path as a number of new initiatives. Among them was an increased emphasis on such attributes as heroism and courage illustrated, for example, in the first movement of the *Kreutzer* Sonata (1802–3) or deeply felt emotions and spirituality, as in the slow movement of the *Spring* Sonata (1800–1801).

Beethoven composed his fourth and fifth violin sonatas during the summer and autumn of 1800 and they were first advertised on 28 October 1801 in the *Wiener Zeitung* as 'Deux Sonates pour le Pianoforte avec un Violon, op. 23', with a dedication to Count Moritz von Fries, one of the original subscribers to the op. 1 piano trios. When they were first published, however, they appeared with the separate opus numbers which they have today[3] – appropriately so, as they could hardly be more different from each other. The A minor Sonata, in its outer movements at least, is spare textured and impetuous; the *Spring* Sonata in F major is expansive and lyrical. They were enthusiastically reviewed in the *Allgemeine musikalische Zeitung* in May 1802, the critic praising 'their strict order, clarity and craftsmanship', a pleasant change for Beethoven after the hostile review his three op. 12 violin sonatas had received three years earlier in the same journal.

Count Moritz von Fries

A generous patron and a keen amateur musician, Count von Fries (1777–1826) had studied the violin with Giacomo Conti, leader of the orchestra at the Italian opera in Vienna. Haydn benefited from Fries' support

---

[1] Quoted in Landon, *Haydn: Chronicle and Works: The Years of the 'Creation'*, p. 503.

[2] Carl Czerny, quoted in Lockwood, *Beethoven: The Music and the Life*, p. 124.

[3] Nottebohm suggested that the 'reason for the separation was probably the fact that the separate violin parts had been engraved in different sizes, and that the publisher [Mollo] was unwilling to go to the expense of having one of the parts re-engraved.' Quoted in Brandenburg, *'Beethoven's Violin Sonatas, Cello Sonatas and Variations'*, p. 137.

and Schubert would later dedicate one of his finest early songs to him – *Gretchen am Spinnrade.* According to Beethoven's brother Carl, the Count commissioned the two violin sonatas under an agreement common at the time: 'He who wants a piece pays a fixed sum for its exclusive posses-sion for a half or a whole year, or longer, and binds himself not to give the manuscript to anybody; at the conclusion of the period the composer can do what he pleases with the work.'[4] Over the years Count von Fries contin-ued to help Beethoven in various practical ways and received two further important dedications from him – the String Quintet in C major, op. 29, discussed in the next chapter and the Seventh Symphony.

The House of Fries, a bank with property and other business interests, was involved on Beethoven's behalf in dealings with George Thomson of Edinburgh (arrangements of Scottish songs); with Coutts Bank in London (the Violin Sonata in G major, op. 96, and the *Archduke* Trio, op. 97); with Probst of Leipzig (Ninth Symphony) and Schott of Mainz (the *Missa Sol-emnis*). But like Prince Lobkowitz, another of Beethoven's patrons, Fries overreached himself in his enthusiasm for music and the arts, and in 1826 he was declared bankrupt. Although the firm was later rescued by the Count's son, Beethoven sensibly put his business affairs into other hands when he was told that there were serious problems at the bank.[5]

The cheerful atmosphere at Count von Fries' soirées when the Clarinet Trio, op. 11, was first performed, and Beethoven was unwillingly involved in a 'competition' with Daniel Steibelt, is described in Chapter 9. Ferdinand Ries also remembered another soirée at Count Johann Browne's home, which included an early performance of the A minor Violin Sonata; his description again brings to life the charm and informality of such musi-cal evenings. Much to Ries's alarm, Beethoven insisted that he should play the new sonata during the evening – perhaps with Schuppanzigh – even though he had not yet studied it:

> As usual, Beethoven turned pages for me. In a jump in the left hand, where one particular note must be brought out, I went com-pletely astray and Beethoven tapped me on the head with one fin-ger. Princess L[iechtenstein], who sat leaning on the piano facing me, watched this with amusement. When I had finished playing, Beet-hoven said: 'Very good. You did not need to study the Sonata with me first. The finger was just meant to prove my attentiveness.' Later Beethoven had to play, and chose the D minor Sonata [op. 31 no. 2], which had just appeared. The Princess, who was expecting that Beet-hoven would surely make a mistake somewhere, now placed herself behind him while I turned the pages. At bars 53 and 54, Beethoven missed the beginning and instead of going down two notes and then two more, struck with his whole hand all the crotchets ... The

[4] From a letter written by Beethoven's brother, Carl, to Breitkopf & Härtel: Thayer, *The Life of Beethoven*, p. 311.

[5] *Letters of Beethoven*, Letter 1485, 20 May 1826: Beethoven to Schotts of Mainz.

Princess gave him several not exactly gentle slaps on the head with the observation, 'If the pupil gets one finger for one wrong note, the Master must be punished with the whole hand for making bad mistakes.' Everyone laughed, and Beethoven first. He started again and played wonderfully, particularly the Adagio.[6]

Sonata no. 4 in A minor for violin and piano, op. 23

Presto
Andante scherzoso, più Allegretto
Allegro molto

The A minor Violin Sonata is a volatile and original work, still controversial enough to provoke strong and sometimes opposed reactions. Lewis Lockwood, for instance, describes it as 'bleak, odd, and distant, a neglected child in the family of Beethoven's violin sonatas, despite its original and experimental moments.'[7] Max Rostal, on the other hand, salutes its 'true dramatic power ... the breathlessness and tension of its outer movements', finding it 'incomprehensible that this work ... is not heard more often in concert halls.'[8] It can certainly make a dramatic impact, especially as the opening work in a recital, and deserves to be played much more often.

Presto Feelings of despair and hope jostle one another in the opening movement, reflecting, perhaps, Beethoven's anxieties as various remedies for his increasing deafness were tried. Textures are unusually spare, recalling similar textures in Mozart's late Violin Sonata in A major, K526. Contrasts in mood are illustrated by two very different versions of the same motive (*x*). The first version, curt and threatening, dominates the opening bars of the Presto (ex. 11.1a), while the second version, which appears late in the development, is miraculously purged of despair by the addition of a quaver at the start and another tucked in the middle, to create a carefree new theme (ex. 11.1b), played alternately by the violin and piano and then more darkly in canon.

Ex. 11.1

[6] Ferdinand Ries, quoted in Landon, *Beethoven: A Documentary Study*, p. 99.

[7] Lockwood, *Beethoven: The Music and the Life*, p. 142.

[8] Rostal, *Beethoven: The Sonatas for Piano and Violin*, pp. 67–8.

There are similar contrasts in the transition – angry unison passages alternating with crisp, though unsettled ones. The flowing, contrapuntal second subject, for example, is violently swept aside by pounding double octaves and *sforzandi* on every beat. With the focus on extensions and variants of the two-bar motive (*x*) in the development, no place can be found for the second subject, but even in this hostile environment, with its cruel, needling harmonic clashes (ex. 11.2), there are signs of hope – an aspiring violin descant, for example, apparently unaware of subversive threats (*x*) in the bass.

Ex. 11.2

After the development and recapitulation have been repeated in full, the second version (ex. 11.1b) returns, seemingly without a care in the world, suggesting that there may be a positive outcome after so much overt anger. But it is not to be; violence returns and the movement ends haltingly and in despair.

Andante scherzoso, più Allegretto   The Andante, an oasis of calm and quiet humour after so much tension, is also in sonata form, though so understated that it hardly sounds like it. Textures are fragile, silences as organic as sounds in the first theme, a reminder that Beethoven, the improviser, had yet more to say about a rising or falling semitone or tone, already explored in the first movement of the A major Violin Sonata, op. 12 no. 2. A business-like fugato (ex. 11.3) is more clearly defined and provides a bridge to two ideas in the second group.

Ex. 11.3

The first recalls Haydn's cooing doves in Gabriel's great aria, 'Auf starkem Fittige' ('On mighty wings uplifted high') at the start of Part 2 in *The Creation*; and the other is light-hearted. There are a few surprise interventions in the development (close imitation, *sforzandi* on weak beats), but the prevailing mood of calm returns in the recapitulation – a delicately ornamental mirror of the exposition.

Allegro molto   Textures in the finale are similar to those of the first movement and, although there are five times as many soft as loud bars, the prevailing mood is deeply troubled. There are four identical statements of the rondo theme (*z* in ex. 11.4) and its mirrored bass, and two further varied statements near the end of the movement – the first with the melody and bass interchanged and the second with the bass line picked out by the violin in a brilliant string-crossing passage (ex. 11.4).

Ex. 11.4

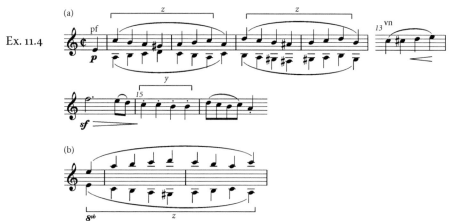

There are three episodes in the finale: the first, with mirrored diminished sevenths and menacing scales, is as unsettling as the darker moments in the first movement. The other two recall the gentle character of the Andante and two specific phrases in the rondo theme itself (*y, z*). The second episode is a quiet reflection on the most basic motive in the sonata (*y*), while the third episode in F major (ex. 11.5), accompanied simply, note for note, as in first-species counterpoint, shares much the same outline as the rondo theme (*z*), though it is more serene in character.

Ex. 11.5

All three episodes reappear later, though the gentler ones eventually fade away and an angry version of the principal theme leads inexorably to an impetuous and ultimately a bleak conclusion.

Sonata no. 5 in F major for violin and piano, op. 24 (*Spring*)

Allegro
Adagio molto espressivo
Scherzo & Trio: Allegro molto
Rondo: Allegro ma non troppo

The key provides a clue: from the Pifa in Handel's *Messiah* and from Adam and Eve's glorious duet of self-discovery in the Garden of Eden ('Der Sterne hellster') in Part 3 of Haydn's *Creation*, to Beethoven's own *Pastoral* Symphony, his Eighth Symphony and his last String Quartet, op. 135,

F major seems to have been the key in which to meditate on the joys, but also on the spiritual inspiration, of Nature. The *Spring* Sonata is no exception – an exquisite testament to Beethoven's profoundly religious feeling for the natural world. It also reflects his current interest in melody, seen in the slow movements of the F major Quartet, op. 18 no. 1 (ex. 10.4–5), for example, or the Piano Sonata in B flat major, op. 22 – a change of emphasis warmly welcomed by a Leipzig music critic in 1802: 'The original, fiery and bold spirit of this composer ... sometimes unfriendly, wild, sombre and impetuous, is now becoming increasingly serene, is steadily rejecting all excesses, and is being manifested in ever more agreeable forms, without losing its character.'[9]

Allegro   Unconventional in so many other ways, Beethoven remained attached, even in some of his more mature music, to eight-bar phrase-lengths generally favoured by classical composers; so the ten-bar first subject, introduced by the violin at the beginning of the sonata, and then extended by the piano for a further fifteen bars to reach the dominant, C major, proclaims from the start that this is to be an expansive movement, with each instrument sharing melodic and accompanying material in equal measure. The lyrical motive (x) in the first two bars inspires numerous twists and turns throughout the first movement – in the assertive transition, unexpectedly in D flat major, for example – and later extends its influence to include the whole work. The serene melody (ex. 11.6) dives and soars over a flowing accompaniment (y), which would not be out of place in the quiet upper reaches of the mill-stream in Schubert's song-cycle *Die schöne Müllerin*, composed twenty-three years later.

Ex. 11.6

Just such an accompaniment will return in the Adagio and, still more beguilingly, in the fluent Rondo. Finally, the unhurried harmonic steps taken in the bass (z) look ahead not only to the almost static harmony in much of the Adagio, but also to the plain harmonic foundations and the thematic repetitions characteristic of the *Pastoral* Symphony. There are some stormy moments, but they appear to be meteorological rather than psychological. Two motives in the second subject – a dialogue between rising thick-textured arpeggios (rare in the generally light piano textures

[9] Brandenburg, '*Beethoven's Violin Sonatas, Cello Sonatas and Variations*', p. 136.

Beethoven employs in his violin sonatas) and anxious triplets – provide most of the material in the dramatic development section. There are few surprises in the recapitulation, but the coda is enriched by some bars of chromatic counterpoint and the lyrical motive *x* provides material for yet further dialogue between violin and piano.

Adagio molto espressivo   The Adagio is as simple as the thoughts expressed in it are profound. The spellbinding melody (ex. 11.7) with its characteristic turn (*v*) and flowing accompaniment (*u*) inspired by the opening bars of the first movement (*x, y*), creates a reflective, even a mystical atmosphere – mood music as in the *Moonlight* Sonata, op. 27 no. 2, composed at much the same time.

The theme is followed by three unnumbered variations. After an extended transition – questions, answers, modest key changes, further variants of the lyrical motive – the opening melody (*v*) returns, introduced by the piano, now more ornamental and improvisatory in character. The second variation, expanded to sixteen introspective bars, is played by the violin in darker, minor keys and heard as from a distance. The third variation, which resembles the opening bars of the sonata most closely (*x* in ex. 11.6), is shared by both instruments, drawing together various strands from both movements, alternating with shimmering textures in the coda.

Scherzo & Trio: Allegro molto   The *Spring* is the first of Beethoven's violin sonatas to include four movements rather than three, and this one is undoubtedly the joker in the pack. In the scurrying Trio, played so quickly that it seems to be over before it begins, both instruments are united – or should be! But the mischievous Scherzo (ex. 11.8) is one of Beethoven's more subtle jokes, with the lord of misrule in the ascendant. Clearly, the intention is to embarrass the violinist who, for much of the time, lags a beat behind the piano (*w*). Schumann later based the 'Children's March' in *Kinderscenen* note-for-note on this Scherzo, although his children were required, no doubt, to play it in time.

Rondo: Allegro ma non troppo   It is not to be expected that anything as serious as thematic relationships should be involved after such comedy, but oddly enough they are. For surely the child, as portrayed in the first section (*w*) of the Scherzo, becomes an ardent young adult in the opening bars of the Rondo. Indeed, the principal theme has much in common with the youthful outlines of the Scherzo and, with such flowing, sensuous harmonies, the mood is unquestionably romantic (ex. 11.9).

Ex. 11.9

There are two episodes – the first alternately crestfallen in C minor or cheerful in C major, recalling the lyrical motive in the first movement (*x*). The magnificent second episode, with its manly strides and extended tessitura, played in turn by each instrument over lively accompanying triplets, dominates the middle of the movement. Radiance and humour in the finale can also be found in the various reappearances of the principal theme, presented here as a series of enchanting, kaleidoscopic vignettes – the same face, so to speak, but observed from different angles and in different moods. In its first reappearance, played by the pianist, the melody and accompaniment are unchanged, but the violinist contributes two unmannerly and bizarre *sforzandi* before snatching the principal theme, as yet unfinished, from the pianist and playing it in full. There are two further versions of the rondo theme after the dramatic central episode – the first in D major, with a serene violin descant; and the second back in the tonic, accompanied for the first time in Beethoven's violin sonatas by pizzicato chords. The two final appearances are a delight: the first decorated with dancing triplets on the piano; the second with spritely dotted rhythms on the violin. Then a complete surprise: a beautiful new melody (ex. 11.10a) played only twice – the first and shortest of Beethoven's many 'hymns of thanksgiving', which would later include the final bars of the *Pastoral* Symphony and the deeply spiritual *Heiliger Dankgesang* movement in the A minor String Quartet, op. 132.

Ex. 11.10

Fortunately this beautiful miniature was not forgotten as it reappears in a more rustic setting as the principal theme (ex. 11.10b) in the hilarious finale of the Violin Sonata in G major, op. 30 no. 3, discussed in Chapter 13.

String Quintet in C major, op. 29

The C major Quintet, composed in 1801, and like the op. 23 and op. 24 violin sonatas dedicated to Count von Fries, has remained something of an outsider in Beethoven's chamber music, considered 'important' by most writers, but not often played. Robert Simpson regards its neglect as 'shameful', claiming, perhaps provocatively, that it 'could be in some ways regarded as a crown to op. 18', praising in particular its 'breadth and economy of line', and adding that 'fine works for this medium are not so plentiful that chamber players can afford to ignore it as often as they do.'[1] Other writers suggest that its importance lies in reflecting Beethoven's current interest in melody, and pass on without much further comment. Although Beethoven's recent studies with Salieri had broadened his approach to lyricism, melody, however defined, had already played an important part in the music he was composing in the late 1790s, and would continue to do so throughout his life.

The Quintet got off to a shaky start. Beethoven sold it to Breitkopf & Härtel as soon as the agreed six-month period during which Count von Fries had sole rights to it had expired, only to discover that Artaria had somehow got hold of the parts and planned to publish it without permission. A furious correspondence ensued, and the matter was resolved only after a court hearing. Happily, Count von Fries carried on with his support of Beethoven in the years that followed – he later became the dedicatee of the Seventh Symphony – and both Breitkopf & Härtel and Artaria continued to publish his music.

Beethoven's other string quintets

Apart from op. 29, Beethoven seems not to have warmed to the string quintet as a genre, though he toyed with it from time to time during his later years; indeed, he was working on one at the time of his death. He wrote the eighty-three-bar Fugue in D major for string quintet, op. 137, in a few hours on 28 November 1817, as a personal gift to Tobias Haslinger, who was planning to publish a complete edition of his music. He was increasingly absorbed in polyphonic studies at the time, and op. 137 is a poised and spritely study in five-part counterpoint, though not, of course, a quintet in the classical sense.[2] Beethoven's other two quintets are arrangements.

---

[1] Simpson, 'The Chamber Music for Strings', p. 251.

[2] In addition, a few original, though unfinished, quintet sketches survive, including a fragment in D minor (Hess 40) also written in 1817, and the unfinished String Quintet in C (WoO 62), commissioned by Diabelli, on which Beethoven was working just before he died – an almost exact contemporary, incidentally, of the undisputed masterpiece in the genre, Schubert's String Quintet, D956, also in C major.

The first is a string version of his early Wind Octet written, at least in part, as a self-imposed exercise during his early years in Vienna. Mozart had rescored the Wind Serenade in C minor, K388, for string quintet, so he would do the same with his Octet. In doing so he made substantial changes to the music itself, and he was sufficiently pleased with the result to agree to its publication in 1796 as the String Quintet in E flat major, op. 4. It is an appealing work, though inevitably limited in its range of keys,[3] and strangely out of place when compared to the adventurous music, discussed in Part 2, which he was writing or planning at much the same time.

The second arrangement is modelled on one of Beethoven's early masterpieces, the Piano Trio in C minor, op. 1 no. 3, and is musically much stronger than op. 4. Herr Kaufmann, a composer not previously known to Beethoven, paid him a visit in 1817, and proudly showed him his own quintet arrangement of the trio. Beethoven was so appalled by what Herr Kaufmann had done, however, that he resolved at once to bring it, in his own words, 'to the light of day in five real voices, therebye elevating it from abject wretchedness to moderate respectability'.[4] In a letter to the publisher Sigmund Steiner, dated 14 August 1817, he emphasized that Kaufmann had only provided him 'with the occasion to undertake this complete revision',[5] and consequently the work was his own. Judging by the result, he must have enjoyed rescoring one of his favourite early works at a time when he was composing very little, though the first momentous sketches for the Ninth Symphony appeared the following month and he would soon be busy working on the *Hammerklavier* Sonata – exalted company indeed for an opus 1 arrangement.

The Quintet received its premiere on 10 December 1818, and it was published by Artaria the following year as op. 104. Although the general outlines of the trio remain unchanged, the piano part is so imaginatively revoiced and the string writing so beautifully conceived that it almost seems like a new work. To take one colourful and dramatic example: a bravura passage in the last movement, a single line played as an unaccompanied piano solo in the Trio, is vigorously shared by all five instruments in the quintet (ex. 12.1).

---

[3] As discussed in Chapter 8, contemporary clarinets were limited in their choice of keys.

[4] Quoted by Sabine Kurth in the introduction to Henle's urtext edition of Beethoven's quintets. See also Schwager, 'A Fresh Look at Beethoven's Arrangements'. Readers may have read Vikram Seth's fine novel, *An Equal Music*, which was inspired by the String Quintet in C minor, op. 104.

[5] *Letters of Beethoven*, Letter 801, 14 August 1817: Beethoven to the publisher Sigmund Steiner.

Ex. 12.1

Quintet in C major for two violins, two violas and cello, op. 29

Allegro moderato
Adagio molto espressivo
Scherzo & Trio: Allegro
Presto – Andante con moto e scherzoso

Allegro moderato Extended melodies in Beethoven's earlier first movements are less common than in his slow movements, but there are some precedents for the expressive first subject here, among them the *Spring* Sonata, op. 24, and the Piano Sonata in D major, op. 28 (*Pastoral*), both recently completed. Unlike them, however, there is at times a tantalizing lack of continuity and growth in parts of the movement, very rare if not unique in Beethoven's chamber music, with the first subject and the four short sections of the ensuing transition (triplet quavers) framed and set apart from each other like paintings in a picture gallery.

The opening melody (ex. 12.2a), introduced by the first violin and mirrored by the cello, is a more mature and considered version of the first subject in the earlier string quintet arrangement, op. 4 (ex. 12.2b), and shares something of its self-absorbed, sequential character. Noble and spacious, it anticipates in spirit and solemnity some of the great opening melodies of Beethoven's middle years, such as the first *Razumovsky* quartet, or the Cello Sonata in A major, op. 69. But Roger Fiske has a point when he writes that 'this promising mood is cut off in its prime and replaced by a trivial short-breathed triplet figure, effective enough combined with the 'noble' theme in the development, but sadly out of place here.'[6]

Ex. 12.2

[6] Fiske, 'String Quintets', p. 117.

Be that as it may, there can surely be no disagreement over the exquisite second subject (ex. 12.3) – as timeless as Renaissance polyphony and as pure as water from a mountain spring.

Ex. 12.3

Nonetheless the first subject dominates, even overwhelms, large swathes of the movement, flooding the closing and development sections, the recapitulation and coda with expressive, contrapuntal and thematic material; too much of a good thing, perhaps, for some, but for others mesmerising, among them Brahms, who was surely inspired by it when he wrote the opening theme and flowing accompaniment for his Sextet in B flat major.

Adagio molto espressivo If the first movement looks forward to the romantic future, the Adagio looks back, perhaps with some nostalgia, to the glories of Mozart's later operas. Fiordiligi would surely have enjoyed the long expressive melody (ex. 12.4), relished its coloratura and understood its idiom. There are no picture frames here, no cut-off points. One idea leads seamlessly to another, and subsidiary material – the cello pizzicatos in the opening bars, for example – is almost as beguiling as the melody itself.

Ex. 12.4

Two further themes take their lyrical cue from parts of the opening melody to create a satisfying blend of unity and diversity – the first an expressive dialogue and the second a clear reference to the slow movement in Mozart's String Quintet in G minor, K516.

Scherzo & Trio: Allegro At first sight the Scherzo looks conventional enough – a cheerful, cantering theme, which finds its way into every corner of the movement, supported by a series of musette-like drones. Proportions are extraordinary; the first section is eight bars long, the second ten times as many, and phrase-lengths are mischievously uneven, with four-bar phrases jostling with one, two, five and even seven-bar phrases. Thematically the Trio is more ambitious: a bold, sweeping melody, followed by a precarious roller-coaster ride, focused on a three-note motive, up, down and over increasingly challenging modulations. All but the second viola are united in octaves, held together by strong on-beat accents, and it is left to the second viola to assert its individuality with contrary off-beat accents and yet another musette-like drone; a curiously unbalanced division of labour, yet a remarkably effective one.

Presto – Andante con moto e scherzoso   The last movement is as full of musical metaphors as a crossword puzzle is of clues. For a start, it is among the earlier examples of Beethoven's use of tremolo, a technique he applied sparingly for specific, if not always for the same, reasons – to suggest fear and horror in the dungeon scene in Act 2 of *Fidelio*, for example, awe and mystery at the beginning of the Ninth Symphony, or extreme nervous tension in the recitative leading into the finale of the A minor Quartet, op. 132. Here, however, in the opening bars of almost continuous tremolo, the metaphor is surely meteorological, as in the first movement of the *Spring* Sonata – wind? thunder? driving rain? sometimes distant, sometimes explosive; indeed, the three-note cell (ex. 12.5b) is almost identical to the 'lightning motive' used by Beethoven to such dramatic effect during the storm in the *Pastoral* Symphony, composed seven years later. Two strongly contrasted dances invite further speculation. The first, in A flat major sliding dangerously to G major, is rustic in character and asymmetric in shape, and suggests a hurdy-gurdy rather than a string quintet. The second dance (Andante con moto e scherzoso) – one of Beethoven's many slow movement scherzos (ex. 12.5a) – is more elegant, though still tongue-in-cheek – the sort of *opera buffa* music that the ten-year-old Rossini would soon be writing so engagingly; note especially the formal bows and curtseys (*x*) and the smartly clicked heels (*y*).

Ex. 12.5

But the heart of this unashamedly melodramatic finale is to be found in the development section (ex. 12.6) – three distinct motives played simultaneously: a march (*w*) in simple duple time, with a syncopated descant (*u*), threatened by a raging storm in compound duple time (*v*), sometimes distant, sometimes near at hand – magnificent!

Ex. 12.6

Three Violin Sonatas, op. 30

Beethoven moved to the village of Heiligenstadt on doctor's orders in April 1802, hoping that a few months of peace and quiet might lead to an improvement in his hearing. He took with him sketches[1] for the three op. 30 violin sonatas which he had begun the previous month, and in an extraordinary outpouring of creative energy completed them in May – a remarkable achievement, not least because he had to compose a new finale for the first of the three, the Sonata in A major, when he realized that the original Presto had outgrown itself. He was certainly right to do so, as it is twice as long as the first movement, five times as long as the second and altogether too brilliant as the finale for such a gentle work.

The following year, a far more suitable home was found for it as the third and last movement of the *Kreutzer* Sonata, discussed in the next chapter. The three sonatas were published in 1803 with a dedication to the young Tsar of Russia, Alexander I, whose apparently enlightened views Beethoven admired. In spite of his many worries, Beethoven's creativity never slackened during that fateful year. After completing the violin sonatas, he went on to compose the three innovatory piano sonatas, op. 31, between June and September, and in October he completed two sets of piano variations, including the *Prometheus* Variations, op. 35, which would soon provide inspiration for the *Eroica* Symphony.

The year of the Heiligenstadt Testament

Early that month, however, hopes of an improvement in his hearing turned to despair, movingly recorded in a letter known as the Heiligenstadt Testament, which he wrote to his brothers, but never sent. Two incidents which he described in the letter affected him deeply: 'What a humiliation for me, when someone standing next to me heard a flute in the distance and I heard nothing, or someone heard a shepherd singing and again I heard nothing. Such incidents drove me almost to despair; a little more of that and I would have ended my life – it was only my art that held me back.'[2] It would be surprising if such feelings were not reflected in at least some of the music that Beethoven composed during those anxious months. The outer movements of the C minor Violin Sonata, for example, certainly reflect his 'fiery, active temperament' (also referred

---

[1] Sketches for the three op. 30 violin sonatas occupied 87 pages of the *Kessler* sketchbook. As Richard Kramer has shown (*'Sonate, que me veux-tu?'*, p. 48), 'they are exceptional in that they have survived perfectly intact within the single sketchbook that was not vandalized in the years following Beethoven's death.'

[2] All the quotations from the Heiligenstadt Testament are to be found in Solomon, *Beethoven*, p. 152. The Testament was among Beethoven's papers when he died.

to in the Testament) and seem to convey, or at least provide metaphors for, the anger, depression and frustration he must sometimes have felt. It is equally clear from the very different character of other music he composed in Heiligenstadt – the serenity and radiance of the A major Violin Sonata, op. 30 no. 1, for example, and the life-affirming humour of the G major Sonata, op. 30 no. 3 – that in adversity his art and his spiritual life were becoming more important to him than ever. 'I hope my determination will remain firm to endure ... Perhaps I shall get better, perhaps not ... Divine One, thou seest my inward soul; thou knowest that therein dwells the love of mankind and the desire to do good.'[3] In its quiet way, this sublime sonata shows that Beethoven's belief in a personal destiny, his strength of character and the deep spirituality revealed in those words from the Heiligenstadt Testament, could overcome his despair. Strangely, however, the first of the op. 30 Violin Sonatas is not often played, and remains a well-kept secret for those who understand it and share Max Rostal's 'special affection [for it] ... I regard its neglect as a real wrong ... [and] I feel the first two movements to be especially serious, profound and masterly.'[4]

Sonata no. 6 in A major for violin and piano, op. 30 no. 1

Allegro
Adagio molto espressivo
Allegretto con Variazioni

Allegro   The first movement begins (and touchingly ends) with a gentle eight-note motive (*x*) which, like the opening bars of the *Spring* Sonata, draws disparate elements in the movement together, reappearing in the transition, closing section, development, recapitulation and coda, as well as being structurally productive in its own right. The opening theme (ex. 13.1), a spacious, beautifully sculpted melody framed by the motive (*x*), is introduced by the piano, then shared and extended to twelve bars by the violin, its ethereal mood conveyed by suspended tonality and by the clarity of Beethoven's part-writing. The elusive character and the subtlety of the movement owes much also to its rhythmic diversity. The first subject (ex. 13.1), for example, is in triple time, although with its long, extended phrases, it seems almost timeless.

Ex. 13.1

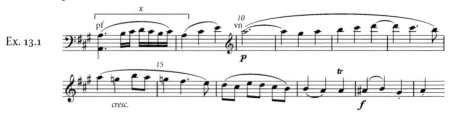

[3] Solomon, *Beethoven*, p. 152.

[4] Rostal, *Beethoven: The Sonatas for Piano and Violin*, p. 90.

The leap-frogging transition (ex. 13.2) is most assertively in duple time.

Ex. 13.2

The expressive second subject (*z* in ex. 13.2), perhaps remembered later by Schubert in his Impromptu in A flat major, suggests both triple and compound duple time. Underlying note values are significant too as the movement gradually gathers momentum: flowing crotchets lead to quavers and triplet quavers to joyful semiquavers. Although there are no significant changes in the recapitulation, each idea is discussed in varied form in the development – the second subject (*z*), for instance, is further extended and explored in canon (ex. 13.3).

Ex. 13.3

Adagio molto espressivo　The slow movement is a simple rondo, with three statements of the principal theme (ex. 13.4), two episodes, each of which appear only once, followed by a spellbinding coda. Playing or listening to this exquisite movement, it is hard to disagree with Max Rostal's wonderful tribute: 'It belongs for me among the most beautiful and moving things that have ever been expressed in music … the end of [the

Ex. 13.4

movement] equals late Beethoven in its rapture.'[5] With its gently rocking accompaniment and almost unbroken stream of melody, this sublime and intimate music, as tender as a cradle-song, could hardly be further from the violence and deep sadness expressed in the C minor Sonata that follows or the heroic, extrovert aspirations Beethoven was beginning to explore.

The short first episode, in the relative minor, is an extension of the theme itself; but the second episode (ex. 13.5a), an aching variant of the theme's second bar (*u*), is more troubled. Serenity returns in the coda, however (ex. 13.5b), with a meditation on the opening theme which offers comfort to the most despairing of minds.

Ex. 13.5

Allegretto con Variazioni The mystical spell cast over the first two movements extends also to much of the pastoral theme and variations which Beethoven composed in place of the original finale. The theme, in two eight-bar sections played alternately by each instrument (ex. 13.6), is as spontaneous as a folk-song; both its companionable countersubject (*v*), and the perky rhythmic figure with which it ends (*w*) will be structurally important later. The first four variations are contained within the sixteen-bar frame of the theme, but are very different in style and mood. The galloping first variation, for example, owes more to the countersubject (*v*) than to the theme itself while, in the second, the theme is traced expressively in long, sinuous phrases.

Ex. 13.6

The powerful third variation explores significant intervals from the theme in double counterpoint over a brilliant triplet bass, and the fourth

---

[5] Rostal, *Beethoven: The Sonatas for Piano and Violin*, pp. 90, 94.

is a highly original dialogue, in which the violin plays increasingly assertive unaccompanied chords; a foretaste, perhaps, of the introduction to the *Kreutzer* Sonata which Beethoven would compose early the following year – but fails to rouse the piano from its reverie. The fifth variation (ex. 13.7a), however, is much longer.

Ex. 13.7

Opening in bleak double counterpoint, the theme is joined by an equally prominent countersubject (*s*), which recalls almost note for note the slow movement in Beethoven's earlier A major Violin Sonata, op. 12 no. 2 (ex. 13.7b). The mood lightens as Beethoven improvises for a while on the cheerful rhythmic figure *w* and this provides a charming bridge to the sixth variation. With its slightly faster tempo (Allegro, ma non tanto), compound time and tonic pedal, the mood is contentedly pastoral – and that is how the sonata eventually ends: happy and carefree. But before it does so, Beethoven is carried away once again into a trance-like, improvisatory world of his own, the contrapuntal texture and suspended tonality recalling the elusive spirituality of the first two movements. A critic in the *Allgemeine musikalische Zeitung* singled out this beautiful digression for particular scorn: 'The reviewer is least satisfied with the play on minor and diminished sevenths and augmented sixths, unworthy of Herr Beethoven … In the reviewer's opinion Herr B. can have written this only as a result of working in great haste, or when improvising, when not in the right frame of mind.'[6] At least he was right about the improvising.

Sonata no. 7 in C minor for violin and piano, op. 30 no. 2

Allegro con brio
Adagio cantabile
Scherzo & Trio: Allegro
Finale: Allegro – Presto

Allegro con brio   There is no doubting the depth of Beethoven's feelings in this masterpiece, in which heroism, anger, tension and sorrow all play a part, foreshadowing the intensity, if not the scale, of the *Eroica* Symphony composed the following year. The forward thrust of the first movement

---

[6] Brandenburg, *'Beethoven's Violin Sonatas, Cello Sonatas and Variations'*, p. 139.

– all the more tense because so much of it is played softly – is underlined by the rare absence of a double bar dividing the exposition from the development; clearly, there must be be no turning back in this restless, turbulent music. The curt commands (*x*) in the first subject (ex. 13.8), accompanied by threatening semiquavers, suggest a military metaphor – not unlikely at a time when the Napoleonic Wars were tearing Europe apart – but also, perhaps, an emotional one.

Ex. 13.8

Further evidence for such an interpretation is provided by the second subject (ex. 13.9), a crisp march heard in the distance, as lean and fit in its two-part texture and call to arms (*y*) as an élite regiment of the Imperial Guard.

Ex. 13.9

It is not long before battle is joined in a violent, close combat version of the march (ex. 13.10).

Ex. 13.10

Both motives (*x*, *y*) underpin the formal structure of the movement. The sorrowful closing section, for example, with its melting enharmonic modulations, is repeatedly challenged by crisp dotted rhythms and commanding gestures. Fuller harmonies do appear from time to time, providing violent punctuation at the end of sections; but sometimes, as at the end of the development, they reflect a deep sadness.

Adagio cantabile   The form of this heart-felt elegy is simple in its ternary outlines, but complex in detail. The opening theme (ex. 13.11) is in two repeated eight-bar sections, with the melody and accompaniment played in turn by each instrument to create an unusually long span of thirty-two bars.

Ex. 13.11

The poignant central theme, first played by the violin in A flat minor and then partially repeated by the piano in B flat minor, is framed by delicate ascending traceries. But metaphors of war and emotional anguish cannot be easily forgotten and the gentle violin descant (ex. 13.12) erupts unexpectedly with a crisp reminder, both rhythmic and melodic, of the march (*y*) in the first movement; a wake-up call, perhaps, and also a comparatively rare example of Beethoven's simultaneous use of different dynamics for dramatic effect.

Ex. 13.12

The unusually long and introspective coda is interrupted unexpectedly by a bold sweep of interlinked C major scales, played *fortissimo*. In the language of keys, which Beethoven would endorse later in *Fidelio* (Chapter 15), C major is the key of Providence; so this dramatic intervention, repeated a second time to reveal in each case the opening two bars of the movement (ex. 13.11), high in register and in the pastoral key of F major, is surely benevolent – a vision of hope and strength, perhaps, but one which soon fades to make way for sad acceptance.

Scherzo & Trio: Allegro   According to Anton Schindler, his one-time secretary and general factotum, Beethoven considered reducing many of his four-movement sonatas to three when he was planning the definitive edition of his complete works in 1823: 'he definitely wished to delete the Scherzo allegro from the highly emotional Violin Sonata in C minor, op. 30, because of its incompatibility with the character of the work as a whole.'[7] Fortunately, the project failed to materialize. The Scherzo shares dotted rhythms, off-beat accents and explosive chords with the first movement. But there is an air of gallantry and élan in the canonic Trio, with its teasing hemiolas; reason enough surely to justify their 'compatibility' and inclusion.

Finale: Allegro – Presto   Beethoven is at his most uncompromising in the finale, a study of emotional extremes: anger and serenity, despair and hope, war and peace. The first group is in two sections which together dominate the movement. The first section (ex. 13.13a), implacably rooted in

---

[7] Schindler, *Beethoven as I Knew Him*, p. 403.

the same key for all seven of its appearances, is as gruff and incisive as a sergeant-major's parade-ground commands, and the short opening motive (*z*) hovers menacingly in the background, reappearing frequently and unexpectedly. The second section (ex. 13.13b) is gentler, its dynamic shape (*piano–crescendo–sforzando–decresc*) almost pleading, though it stands its ground later in the development section in a powerful fugato.

Ex. 13.13

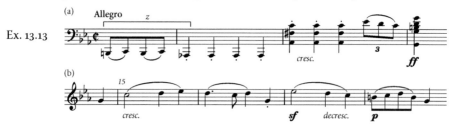

There is yet another march (ex. 13.14); quicker and rhythmically simpler than the one in the first movement, but no less swashbuckling with its fife-like descant (*u*) high on the piano.

Ex. 13.14

The coda, a dramatic Presto, is introduced by a variant of the opening motive (*z*) and concludes with a magnificent *coup de théatre* (ex. 13.15a) – an insistent variant of the two-bar motive (*x*) at the beginning of the first movement (ex. 13.15b). With two such powerful motives at the beginning and the end of the sonata united in this way, there is to be no happy release into C major, and the finale ends, to the accompaniment of insistent drumbeats (piano left hand), in a mood of unsurpassed ferocity.

Ex. 13.15

Sonata no. 8 in G major for violin and piano, op. 30 no. 3

Allegro assai
Tempo di Menuetto ma molto moderato e grazioso
Allegro vivace

By contrast, the G major Violin Sonata is one of Beethoven's most contented chamber works, its outer movements high-spirited, and the central movement beguiling. Tensions, such as they are, are musical ones resolved by musical means, and although such characteristics are generally associated with Beethoven's earlier classical style, there are new ideas here too, looking ahead to such later music as the Piano Trio in E flat major, op. 70 no. 2, and also, as Nigel Fortune suggests, to Schubert and Schumann: 'There is no Beethoven sonata remotely like it ... he seems at once to revitalize the past and to point to the future.'[8] The great violinist Joseph Szigeti was equally enthusiastic: 'With the Eighth Sonata we are in the realm of a kind of conflict-less perfection where the proportion and the sunny gaiety of the first movement, the stately beauty of the Tempo di Menuetto, and the good humoured bounce of the concluding Rondo combine to give us one of the most harmonious works of the set.'[9]

Allegro assai   The first movement may be short, but it is brimming with ideas. There are three in the first group alone (ex. 13.16): a spinning top of a motive (x) followed by a daring trajectory (y) which establishes the sonata's carefree mood; then a lyrical (z) and lastly an energetic melody (u), full of confidence and *joie de vivre*.

Ex. 13.16

The transition (ex. 13.17), on the other hand, is pensive, as questions are asked in sinuous counterpoint and searching tonality, foreshadowing a similar moment in Schubert's Quartettsatz in C minor, D703, composed eighteen years later.

[8] Fortune, 'The Chamber Music with Piano', p. 217.

[9] Joseph Szigeti, *The Beethoven Sonatas for Piano and Violin*, ed. Paul Roland, p. 28.

Ex. 13.17

The second group is more purposeful, though happy to be distracted by a rustic hurdy-gurdy above a dominant pedal. Tonality remains ambiguous in the eventful closing section with its misplaced accents and high cadential trills, and it is this material which dominates the early bars of the development, and does so with style. However, the main topic to be discussed is the engaging 'spinning-top' motive (*x*) first heard softly low on the piano, then high on the violin, sliding down a tone every four bars through a series of unnerving modulations – from C sharp minor to B minor, then A minor and finally G major, in time for a foreshortened recapitulation.

Tempo di Menuetto ma molto moderato e grazioso   The contrasting timbres and expressive qualities of the violin and piano are explored in long, trance-like melodies in the Tempo di Menuetto, and in colourful and imaginative accompanying figures. Repeats are written out in full so as to ensure that both instruments have an equal share of the material. The principal melody, an astonishing fifty-eight bars long, is itself in ternary form; the outer sections warm yet elegant, the short middle section in G minor, with its characteristic, yearning augmented second, still more expressive. There are two further, though much shorter, themes; the first (ex. 13.18) is as spontaneous as a Schubert song, with the characteristic second-beat *sforzandi* in the accompaniment as carefree as the melody itself, creating just the imaginative partnership between voice and piano that Schubert would later make his own – indeed Schubert provided a very similar accompaniment for his beautiful setting of Shakespeare's *Who is Sylvia? (Was ist Silvia?*, D891).

Ex. 13.18

The second theme, in E flat minor, is more distant in mood and makes only one appearance, providing a poised link back to a full recapitulation. The movement ends with a wistful, fragmentary restatement of the opening melody, shared alternately by each instrument, phrase by phrase.

Allegro vivace   The last movement would not be out of place at an international folk festival; it is eccentric, unbuttoned and hilarious. A distinctly earthy reincarnation of the heavenly coda at the end of the *Spring* Sonata, the rondo theme (ex. 13.19) occupies more than half of the movement's 221 bars. It is three-dimensional: a bucolic dance (*v*) in partnership with an energetic ostinato (*w*), each interchangeable and equally important, above an all-pervasive tonic/dominant hurdy-gurdy drone, which famously reminded Bartók of bagpipes.

Ex. 13.19

Structurally, the movement is tightly controlled: a series of variants of the peasant dance, for instance, provides rhythmic and melodic material for the two cheerful episodes (ex. 13.20a) and also for the coda (ex. 13.20b).

Ex. 13.20

Dynamics throughout the movement are subtly controlled too. There are plenty of hearty *fortissimo*s, of course, but for much of the time the bagpipes are kept at a safe distance – as is perhaps best for bagpipes. The headlong momentum of this cheerful *moto perpetuo* is maintained throughout, visiting a bewildering maze of keys, while savouring lively cross-rhythms and contrapuntal development on the way, only to be brought to a dramatic standstill by a pause on the dominant seventh of G major. Instead of the expected resolution, four *pianissimo* 'oom-pah' bars creep out of hiding in the unrelated key of E flat major, providing a precarious perch for the ostinato theme and fiddle tune. After some poised canonic imitation the movement ends with a cheerful coda, the accompanying hurdy-gurdy drone broken up into rustic off-beat *sforzandi* – the 'pah' in other words, without the 'oom'.

Violin Sonata in A major, op. 47 (*Kreutzer*)

Rodolphe Kreutzer

Beethoven first met Rodolphe Kreutzer (1766–1831) in 1798, when the violinist visited Vienna as a member of the French ambassador, General Bernadotte's, entourage. Though German by birth, Kreutzer had been brought up in Paris and became a leading exponent of the influential French Violin School, which Beethoven admired so much. During the visit, Kreutzer and Beethoven performed together on at least one occasion – a soirée at the Lobkowitz palace on 5 April 1798 – perhaps playing one or more of Beethoven's newly composed violin sonatas, op. 12. After Kreutzer returned to Paris they never met again, but Beethoven wrote friendly letters to him from time to time, including a letter of recommendation[1] written as late as 1825, in which he referred to himself as 'votre ancien ami'.

His admiration was not reciprocated, however. Kreutzer seems to have disliked German music in general and Beethoven's music in particular; he was even said to have walked out of a performance of the Second Symphony in Paris, blocking his ears as he did so. Moreover, it is unlikely that he ever performed the sonata which would later immortalize his name as, according to Berlioz, he regarded it as 'outrageously unintelligible'.[2] Not knowing what Kreutzer thought of his music, Beethoven instructed his Bonn friend, the music publisher, Nikolaus Simrock – who seems to have been dragging his feet – to include a dedication to the distinguished French violinist:

> I have waited and waited with longing for the sonata which I gave you, but in vain. Where is that dilatory devil who is to shove out my sonata? ... When you let me know the date you have fixed, I will send you at once a little note for Kreutzer and you will be so kind as to enclose it when you send him a copy ... This Kreutzer is a dear, kind fellow who, during his stay in Vienna, gave me a great deal of pleasure. I prefer his modesty and natural behaviour to all the exterior without the interior which is characteristic of most virtuosi. As the sonata was written for a competent violinist, the dedication to Kreutzer is all the more appropriate.[3]

---

[1] *Letters of Beethoven*, Testimonials and Letters of Introduction, no. 6, p. 1416.

[2] Berlioz, *Voyages en Allemagne et en Italie*.

[3] *Letters of Beethoven*, Letter 99, 4 October 1804: Beethoven to Nikolaus Simrock. The Sonata was eventually published in 1805 by Simrock in Bonn and Birchall in London.

George Bridgetower

An incomplete manuscript of op. 47, discovered in 1965 and now in Bonn, suggests, however, that Beethoven originally intended to dedicate the sonata to George Bridgetower (?1779–1860), who gave the first performance with him on 24 May 1803. By all accounts, Bridgetower was a magnificent violinist. He was brought up in Haydn's musical establishment at Eisenstadt, where his father, probably West Indian in origin, had been Prince Nikolaus Esterházy's personal page, and he made his debut in Paris in 1789 at the age of ten:

> A curious debut which aroused much interest was that of M. Bridge-Tower, a young [violinist] from the colonies, who played several concertos ... with a neatness, a facility, an execution and even a sensibility which are rarely met with at so tender an age. His talent, as genuine as it is precocious, provides one of the best answers that one can make to the philosophers who would deny to those of his nation and of his colour the faculty of distinguishing themselves in the arts.[4]

As revolution tightened its grip on France that fateful year, Bridgetower left Paris for London with his father where, under the patronage of the Prince of Wales, he continued his studies with the emigré French violinist Barthélemon; later, according to Samuel Wesley, he also 'practised much with the celebrated [violinist] Viotti, and imbibed largely of his bold and spirited style of execution'.[5] Bridgetower gave frequent concerts in London, including at least one conducted by Haydn, and after obtaining the Bachelor of Music degree at Cambridge University and his election to the newly formed Philharmonic Society in London, he became an admired member of the English musical establishment. Early in April, 1803, after visiting his mother in Dresden, Bridgetower arrived in Vienna determined to persuade Beethoven to take part in his benefit concert, booked for late May, and perhaps even to compose something for the occasion. Beethoven was busy at the time writing his oratorio *Christ on the Mount of Olives*, op. 85 – a spiritual response perhaps to the recent traumas expressed in the Heiligenstadt Testament – but he was also sketching the first movement of a ninth violin sonata to match the splendid finale in A major which he had originally composed for op. 30 no. 1, discussed in the previous chapter.[6] After hearing a recital by Bridgetower in Schuppanzigh's rooms, playing which he later described as 'that of a very able virtuoso and complete master of his instrument',[7] Beethoven readily agreed to complete the sonata in time for Bridgetower's benefit concert.

---

[4] Landon, *Beethoven: A Documentary Study*, pp. 149–50.

[5] Brown, 'Ferdinand David's Editions of Beethoven', p. 119.

[6] Cooper, *Beethoven and the Creative Process*, pp. 88, 89. Sketches for both op. 30, no. 1 and the *Kreutzer* appear in the *Kessler* sketchbook (late 1801 – June 1802).

[7] *Letters of Beethoven*, Letter 73, 18 May 1803: Beethoven to Baron von Plankenstern,

The excitement of those few weeks, during which Beethoven and Bridgetower were 'constant companions', may have reminded him of his visit to Berlin seven years earlier, when he composed the two op. 5 cello sonatas for another virtuoso, the cellist Jean-Louis Duport. Bridgetower seems to have played a similar role to Duport in stimulating and supporting Beethoven in his unprecedented decision to compose a sonata 'scritta in uno stilo molto concertante, quasi come d'un concerto', as he put it in the published score, with virtuoso parts of equal importance for each of them to play. Technical difficulties for the violinist in the finale, which Beethoven had composed the previous year, are no greater than those encountered in his other violin sonatas and less challenging than some, but the technique required to play the first two movements, mostly composed after Bridgetower's arrival in Vienna, is in a different league altogether. Clearly, however, this presented him with no problems, and it suggests that the individuality and brilliance of his playing was indeed a source of inspiration for Beethoven.

The first performance should have taken place at midday on 22 May 1803 at the Augarten, but because the sonata was still unfinished, it had to be postponed to 24 May. It was an extraordinary event; Beethoven had woken his long-suffering pupil Ferdinand Ries at 4.30 that morning, with instructions to copy out the first two movements in the violin part – the finale had been copied the previous year. Not surprisingly, Ries managed to complete only the first movement in time for the concert, so Bridgetower had to play the Andante from Beethoven's manuscript; moreover, the piano part was still incomplete, with some sections only sketched. Greatly to his credit, Bridgetower seems to have been unfazed by the postponement of what was, after all, his personal benefit concert at an awkward rescheduled time.[8] He even managed to surprise Beethoven at the premiere by repeating on the violin the short piano cadenza in bar 36 of the first movement, extending it to still greater heights. 'Beethoven leaped out of his seat', Bridgetower noted in his own copy of the sonata; he 'embraced me and said, "My dear boy! Once more!" Beethoven's expression in the Andante was so chaste, always a characteristic of the execution of his slow movements, that everyone unanimously insisted that the passage be repeated twice.'[9] After the performance Beethoven wrote an informal dedication to Bridgetower above the first line of the opening Adagio in the jokey, punning language he reserved for close friends: '*Sonata mulattica composta per il Mulatto Brischdauer, gran pazzo e compositore mulattico.*'[10] Many years later, in conversation with J. W. Thirlwell, the editor of

---

recommending the violinist, George Polgreen Bridgetower, to a wider circle of music lovers.

[8] Landon, *Beethoven: A Documentary Study*, p. 149. According to Joseph Rosenbaum, 'The Concert took place at 12 o'clock noon.' Ferdinand Ries, on the other hand, remembered that the premiere of the *Kreutzer* Sonata took place at 8 a.m. that day.

[9] Landon, *Beethoven: A Documentary Study*, p. 149.

[10] Landon, *Beethoven: A Documentary Study*, p. 148.

The Musical World, Bridgetower ruefully acknowledged that although they were 'constant companions' in the weeks leading up to the premiere, and Beethoven had inscribed a dedication to him on the first copy, 'we had some silly quarrel about a girl and in consequence Beethoven scratched out [my] name and inserted that of Kreutzer.'[11] As a result, he has never been given the credit he deserves for his role in the later stages of op. 47.

Reactions and legends

The spontaneity of that extraordinary premiere is the stuff of legend, whether the *Kreutzer* Sonata is regarded with some reserve as a work in which 'virtuosity has rather mastered him',[12] or loved and admired as among the greatest of all violin sonatas. Early reactions were mixed; one critic in the June edition of the *Allgemeine musikalische Zeitung* described Beethoven as 'brilliant' and the sonata as 'important'. This was followed four months later by a particularly virulent review in the same journal: 'The addition to the title "scritta in uno stile molto concertante, quasi come d'un concerto" appears eccentric, presumptuous and ostentatious … One would have to be in the grip of some kind of aesthetic and artistic terrorism … to fail to find in this work a new, obvious proof of the fact that for some time now this artist has been indulging in caprices [and] above all striving to be absolutely different from other people.'[13]

History has been much kinder. As a sonata in *concertante* style, the *Kreutzer* has even been included in orchestral and choral programmes. Mendelssohn, for example, thought so highly of it that he performed it with Ferdinand David as the centrepiece of a concert given for King Friedrich August II in 1840, placing it between Weber's *Oberon* Overture and his own *Lobgesang*. According to Clara Schumann, 'he played it the way he plays everything – masterfully, full of spirit, but in my opinion without sufficient grandiosity, on the whole too hastily … David truly had to fight in order to keep in step with the piano.'[14] The following year Berlioz, who considered the *Kreutzer* 'one of the most sublime of all violin sonatas', also included a performance by Liszt and Lambert Massart in an all-Beethoven programme at the Paris Conservatoire, placing it between the *Emperor* Concerto and the *Pastoral* Symphony. Wagner, who was present, was deeply moved and exclaimed: 'How willingly would we all give concerts for Beethoven!'[15]

A fine performance of the *Kreutzer* Sonata invariably arouses feelings

[11] Landon, *Beethoven: A Documentary Study,* p. 150.

[12] Truscott, 'The Piano Music', p. 119.

[13] Brandenburg, '*Beethoven's Violin Sonatas, Cello Sonatas and Variations*', pp. 140–1.

[14] Schumann, *The Marriage Diaries,* p. 44.

[15] Cairns, *Berlioz,* vol. 2, p. 238. The concert was one of many such fund-raising events given at the time in support of the Beethoven monument in Bonn. Wagner was in the audience and later wrote an article on the *Kreutzer* Sonata in the Dresden *Abendzeitung.*

of awe, as Leo Tolstoy found in 1888 when his son played it in the family home in Moscow with his friend, the violinist Yuli Lyasota. Tolstoy, who was himself an able pianist, already knew the sonata, but on that occasion the performance made a particularly strong impression on him and inspired him to write his novella *The Kreutzer Sonata*, a powerful study of jealousy, sexuality and love: 'On me, at any rate, that piece had the most shattering effect; I had the illusion that I was discovering entirely new emotions, new possibilities I'd known nothing of before ... What this new reality I'd discovered was, I really didn't know, but my awareness of this new state of consciousness filled me with joy.'[16]

Thirty-five years later, Leoš Janáček was inspired by Tolstoy's novel – and arguably by Beethoven's op. 47 as well – to compose his intensely passionate String Quartet no. 1 (1923), also called *The Kreutzer Sonata*. Many contemporary writers share Tolstoy's enthusiasm for the work. Far from objecting to the Sonata's *concertante* character, Lewis Lockwood, for example, sees in it a blending of 'elements of concerto and sonata in a new and brilliant synthesis';[17] and Charles Rosen describes the first movement as 'unequalled in formal clarity, grandeur and dramatic force by anything that Beethoven had yet written.'[18]

The finale as a source of inspiration

Two or three weeks after the first performance of the *Kreutzer* Sonata, Beethoven began work on the epoch-making *Eroica* Symphony, and when that was finished in October, he moved on to the *Waldstein* Sonata, completing it in December. So, together with the oratorio *Christ on the Mount of Olives*, the year 1803 was dominated by four of Beethoven's most powerful and individual works to date – remarkable evidence of his resilience and strength of character in the aftermath of the severe depression he had suffered a few months earlier in Heiligenstadt.

In both the *Kreutzer* and the *Eroica*, he found thematic inspiration in music he had already composed. In the case of the *Eroica*, the underlying seminal idea first appeared in his *Prometheus* ballet (1800–1801) followed by the op. 35 Variations (1802). In the *Kreutzer*, material from the finale, originally intended for op. 30 no. 1 and completed the previous year, provided inspiration for the other two movements as well. Indeed, all the principal themes can be traced to a two-note cell consisting of a rising or falling semitone or tone (*x*), which appears with emphatic *sforzandi* in the finale (ex. 14.1) while its second subject (*y*) suggests in outline the great heroic third theme (ex. 14.6) in the first movement.

---

[16] Tolstoy, *The Kreutzer Sonata*, pp. 13, 97–8. The passage quoted is spoken in the novel by the narrator but, according to Tolstoy's son, it precisely expressed his father's views on Beethoven's ninth Violin Sonata, op. 47.

[17] Lockwood, *Beethoven: The Music and the Life*, p. 144.

[18] Rosen, *The Classical Style*, p. 399.

Ex. 14.1

In addition, the striding dotted minims (*z*) which briefly stem the onward rush of triplet quavers in the finale (ex. 14.2) may be the inspiration for the imposing opening bars of the sonata (ex. 14.3). Consciously or not, such connections provide the listener with an overarching sense of unity, essential in a work composed on such a massive scale.

Ex. 14.2

Beethoven made only one change in the finale when he incorporated it into this sonata, and it was a significant one: a *fortissimo* eight-note chord of A major for the piano, marked with a pause and added, in Ferdinand Ries's writing, at the beginning of the movement. Superficially, the chord may seem unnecessary; the key-signature after all is clear enough. But at a deeper level, it provides an unequivocal link to the Adagio sostenuto with which the first movement begins.

Sonata no. 9 in A major for Violin and Piano, op. 47 (*Kreutzer*)

Adagio sostenuto – Presto
Andante con Variazioni
Finale: Presto

Adagio sostenuto   The violin's monumental introduction (ex. 14.3), played unaccompanied, also begins with a powerful (though ebbing) chord of A major, and its outline (*z*) recalls those striding dotted minims in the finale (ex. 14.2).

Ex. 14.3

In both cases what follows is *not* in the tonic key, and this highlights the tonal ambiguities which provide the outer movements of the *Kreutzer* Sonata with such tension and drama; indeed, in none of Beethoven's other chamber works is the tonic abandoned so quickly and so completely. After a mere four bars the piano responds no less powerfully with a series of beautifully sculpted modulations, as affirmation turns to doubt and A minor is finally established as the tonic key of the ensuing Presto. So Clara Schumann had a point when she referred in her *Marriage Diaries* to the *Kreutzer* as the 'A minor Sonata, op. 47'.[19]

Presto   There are three principal themes in the exposition, linked together by two independent, but equally turbulent, transitional passages. Although completely different in character, all share the same parentage: a rising or falling semitone or tone (*x*). The first theme, in A minor, is in two sections: one brusque, even petulant (ex. 14.4a), though full of bravado in the assertive C major cadenza with which it ends; while the other (ex. 14.4b), which appears after the piano cadenza that Bridgetower so successfully echoed, asks questions and receives emphatic answers.

Ex. 14.4

The second theme is also in two sections and recalls the major/minor confrontation in the opening bars of the introduction (ex. 14.3) – the violin's melody expressive and warm in E major (ex. 14.5), the piano's response poignant in E minor.

Ex. 14.5

The third theme, also in E minor (ex. 14.6), a reinvention of the second subject in the finale (see *y* in ex. 14.1) above – is one of Beethoven's most inspiring heroic melodies and is self-evidently the principal theme in the movement, dominating as it does the rest of the exposition and almost the entire development section, where, in a flurry of increasingly challenging flat keys, it fights off wave after wave of violent assault.

Ex. 14.6

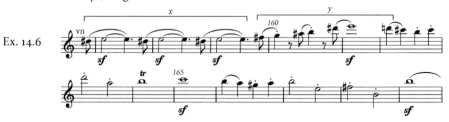

[19] Schumann, *The Marriage Diaries*, p. 44.

The recapitulation broadly mirrors the exposition after an attempted (though corrected) 'false' recapitulation (D minor to F major). The coda is quite simply magnificent, one of the great moments in chamber music, reached by both instruments in octaves up a rough-hewn chromatic path (ex. 14.7), like climbers triumphant as they finally conquer the summit.

Ex. 14.7

Andante con Variazioni   It is hardly surprising that the theme (ex. 14.8), which Beethoven played with such a 'chaste expression', was twice encored at the premiere, as it is one of his loveliest melodies, involving simple materials (*x*, *z*) borrowed yet again from the finale.

Ex. 14.8

There are four variations, all quiet and unassertive, though increasingly complex. The first is *pointilliste* in texture, as the piano picks out the melody with extreme delicacy; the second, with its unobtrusive accompaniment, is a flirtatious scherzo for the violin; while the third, shared by both instruments in F minor, is more serious with its expressive dynamics, rich harmonies and interweaving part-writing. In the fourth variation, repeats are written out in full as Beethoven creates an aerial sound-world of extraordinary originality and beauty with each instrument exploring ever higher regions, decorating both the theme and accompanying textures in a variety of ways, including unusually high violin pizzicatos. However, the most sublime music is kept for the end: an improvisatory coda (ex. 14.9), forty-five bars long, in which Beethoven reflects on the opening bars of the first movement (ex. 14.3), at times almost reinventing them.

Ex. 14.9

Finale: Presto   Schubert must surely have been familiar with this irrepressible and energetic finale when he composed the wild tarantella for his *Death and the Maiden* quartet a little over two decades later, though

the mood here in this joyful celebration of life could hardly be more different. A cheerful two-part duel (ex. 14.10a) follows the introductory chord of
A major. There is a suggestion of E major in the third bar, B minor in the
eighth and, after a glance at E minor and D major, the tonic key, A major,
is finally re-established in the twenty-eighth bar. This lively, if wayward,
preamble provides material for three interconnected themes each in turn
an extension of the one before: three rising steps (ex. 14.10a) in the first,
five in the second (ex. 14.10b) and a full octave in the third. The prevailing
mood is one of supreme confidence – so much so that Beethoven insists
that the principal theme in the finale (ex. 14.1), should be played softly in a
devil-may-care, insouciant way, not triumphantly, as the music appears to
suggest.

Ex. 14.10

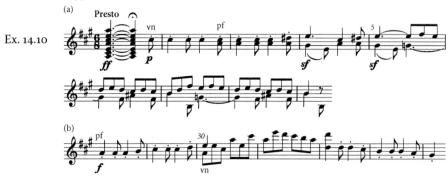

There is plenty of drama elsewhere, not least in the development section with its assertive F major pedal. There are some surprises too, among
them the abrupt change of key from E major down a tone to D major (bar
70) in the second subject, an idea which Beethoven would soon return
to in the first movement of the *Eroica* Symphony. Most surprising of all,
however, are the few moments set aside by Beethoven for quiet reflection
(ex. 14.11) in simple duple time on the two-note motive *x*, which, more
than anything else, provides this towering masterpiece with the firmest
foundations.

Ex. 14.11

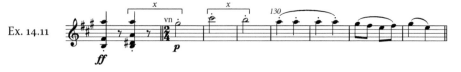

PART FOUR ✺ 1804–9

'A force and reality that makes music an intelligible language, possessing an illimitable power of pouring forth thought in sound.'

Thomas Love Peacock, from his review of
the London premiere of *Fidelio* in 1832

In the wake of *Fidelio*

After completing the *Kreutzer* Sonata and the *Eroica* Symphony in 1803, Beethoven devoted most of the next two and a half years to *Fidelio*, his only complete opera. During those years he composed the Triple Concerto, op. 56, and three important piano sonatas – op. 53 (*Waldstein*), op. 54, and op. 57 (*Appassionata*) – but, for the time being, he wrote no chamber music. The opera was not well received, and Beethoven set it aside after revision and a second round of performances early in 1806. However, after yet further revision, it was revived to great acclaim during the Congress of Vienna in 1814.

In the meantime, Beethoven had returned to his instrumental roots and, from 1806 to 1816 a flood of distinctive compositions followed one after another: five more string quartets, three cello sonatas, three piano trios and the last of his violin sonatas, all these in addition to five new symphonies (nos. 4–8), three concertos, and the piano sonatas, songs and choral music he was also writing during the same years. Composed in the wake of *Fidelio*, these masterpieces could hardly have been unaffected by one of the greatest of all operas, just as they were enriched, and in many cases empowered, by the *Eroica* Symphony during what has traditionally, if somewhat misleadingly, come to be known as Beethoven's 'Heroic Decade'.

Fidelio is indeed about heroism, but it is also concerned with other human attributes: love, faithfulness, tenderness, pity, hope – anger, vengeance and despair too. Many of Beethoven's loveliest compositions written during that decade are neither heroic nor 'externalized', but reflective and spiritual: the Violin Concerto, the Fourth Piano Concerto and the *Pastoral* Symphony, for example or, in his chamber music, the first three movements of the Piano Trio in E flat major, op. 70 no. 2, the Violin Sonata in G major, op. 96, and the slow movements in all three of the *Razumovsky* quartets, op. 59.

The primacy of song in opera and the need to focus on real characters, their situations and their emotions, rather than on abstractions, may well have contributed to the still greater emphasis on melody, the directness and lucidity of form, and the emotional intensity of Beethoven's post-*Fidelio* instrumental music. Moreover, at a technical level, the use of such dramatic effects as tremolo in Pizarro's aria 'Ha! Welch'ein Augenblick!' (no. 7) in Act 1 of *Fidelio*, or in the terrifying orchestral Introduction to Act 2 (no. 11) – as earlier in the finale of the String Quintet in C major, op. 29 – inspired similar dramatic effects in Beethoven's later instrumental music: the Storm in the *Pastoral* Symphony, for example, or the Largo in the *Ghost* Trio, the opening bars of the Ninth Symphony and the recitative leading into the last movement of the A minor Quartet, op. 132.

There are several examples of thematic links, whether conscious or not, between *Fidelio* and Beethoven's later instrumental music, notably in the Violin Concerto, which was composed in 1806 at much the same time as the first revision of the opera. The first tenors' entry, for example, in the Prisoners' Chorus (ex. 15.1a) closely resembles the opening theme of the Violin Concerto (ex. 15.1b).

Ex. 15.1

In addition, a four-note phrase (*x*) in the Terzetto (no. 13), signals the first stirrings of hope when Florestan becomes aware of the 'assistant gaoler' (Leonore's) unexpected kindness (ex. 15.2a). In the Violin Concerto a similar phrase heralds the solo violin's first entry (ex. 15.2b), while Florestan's solo in the Terzetto (*y*) is close in shape and mood to the reflective second theme (ex. 15.2c) in the slow movement.

Ex. 15.2

Such thematic links suggest that the instrumental music Beethoven composed in the wake of *Fidelio* may also have been touched by the opera in other, equally profound ways. Lewis Lockwood,[1] for example, sees the four-note phrase *x* as 'an unforgettable expression of tenderness and love. And it is exactly this quality that Beethoven brings to his Violin Concerto, often noted for the ideal tranquility of its first two movements, the vivid spirit of its finale, and the sense of emotional cogency and connectedness which binds the work together.'

---

[1] Lockwood, *Beethoven: The Music and the Life*, p. 245.

The 'Farewell' motive

There are other thematic links between *Fidelio* and Beethoven's later instrumental music. For example, the opening phrase (*z*) of Florestan's aria (ex. 15.3a) at the beginning of Act 2, as he bids farewell to joy and perhaps to life itself, chained and helpless in his dungeon, reappears as a 'Farewell' motive on two occasions in 1809 and on two further occasions later.

Ex. 15.3

The first is specific, with three syllables – *Le-be-wohl* ('Farewell') – written by Beethoven beneath the first three crotchets (ex. 15.3b) of the *Lebe-wohl* Piano Sonata, op. 81a, composed for his young pupil, Archduke Rudolph, when he left Vienna with other members of the royal family for the security of Hungary as Napoleon's troops approached the city. Later that year, Beethoven created the Haydn-like theme for the finale of the *Harp* Quartet, op. 74, from the same primary motive (ex. 19.4a); it appears fifteen times in the theme alone, almost certainly as his personal tribute to Haydn, who had died in May that year. The motive appears for the fourth time in the slow movement of the G major Violin Sonata, op. 96 (ex. 22.3, 22.4a) arguably as Beethoven's farewell to his 'Immortal Beloved', Antonie Brentano, who finally left Vienna for Frankfurt in 1812. It reappears finally in the Cavatina – the slow movement of the Quartet in B flat major, op. 130 (ex. 27.7) – which Beethoven composed in 1825 'with tears in the writing'.

Symbolism, key structure and the sublime in *Fidelio*[2]

The emotions and aspirations which Beethoven portrays in his later instrumental music precisely mirror the concerns he expresses in the opera. What is more, after the anguish which he had experienced in Heiligenstadt in 1802 and the great religious themes he had addressed in the *Gellert Lieder*, op. 48 (1801–2) and the oratorio *Christ on the Mount of Olives* (1803–4), he must have been conscious from the outset not only of the libretto's enlightened ideals but also its powerful Christian symbolism. Beethoven had been brought up a Catholic and as a young man in Bonn he had played the organ regularly at Mass, both in the Court Chapel and at a

---

[2] Aspects of Christian symbolism in *Fidelio* were discussed by Bishop David Connor, Dean of Windsor, when Senior Chaplain at Winchester College and the author, then the Master of Music at the College, in preparation for performances of *Fidelio* staged in celebration of the College's sixth centenary in 1982.

neighbouring monastery. That he was fully aware of the symbolism of the Mass was powerfully demonstrated later in the Mass in C and in the *Missa Solemnis*.

Some of the symbolism in *Fidelio* is metaphorical; imprisonment, for example, is the Christian symbol for Mankind's bondage after the Fall, so Florestan and his fellow prisoners may be seen as symbols of Mankind. Other symbols are clear enough and play an active part in the story. Rebirth, resurrection, freedom can only be achieved by self-sacrifice, and the Christ-like heroine, Leonore, is prepared to suffer every humiliation and death itself to protect so helpless a prisoner, even before she knows for certain that he is her husband, Florestan. Woven into the fabric of these symbols is Beethoven's careful choice of keys at moments of special significance, and it is possible that by using the implicit 'language' of keys rather than referring to the libretto's Christian imagery, he was able to evade the strict theatrical censorship imposed by the authorities in Vienna at the time. As it is, performances of the first revised version of *Fidelio* were banned by the censor on 30 September 1805 and the ban was only lifted five weeks later after a successful appeal by Beethoven's librettist, Joseph Sonnleithner.

Throughout the opera C major, sometimes approached from unexpected angles, is the divine key, the key of Providence, as it is in Haydn's *Creation*. All three *Leonore* overtures are in C major, and in the finale (no. 16) Don Fernando tells Florestan and his incredulous fellow-prisoners (in C major) that in his Master's kingdom 'his subjects are his brothers'. Rocco presents Florestan to Don Fernando with the words: 'God Almighty has raised him from the dead', and as the opera reaches its triumphant conclusion in C major, the chorus sings of love, self-sacrifice and fidelity.

By contrast, E major is the heroic key and also the key of hope. The *Fidelio* Overture, for example, composed by Beethoven for the triumphant performances staged during the Congress of Vienna in 1814, begins in E major, but after only twenty-two bars modulates into C major with horns, clarinets and oboes giving notice that this is to be a story of divine deliverance as well as of heroism. The turning point is Leonore's great recitative (no. 9). Opening in a mood of complete despair in G minor (a dark key for Mozart too), the vision of divine love and grace in C major – 'I see a rainbow shining brightly against the storm-clouds' – stills her fears and gives her hope, confidence and strength, expressed in the magnificent aria in E major that follows, buoyed up by three obbligato horns in full cry: 'Komm Hoffnung' ('Come Hope!').

During the grave-digging duet (no. 12), there is a similar modulation – this time from D minor to C major – when Leonore, still unsure of the prisoner's identity, swears that 'Whoever he is, I will save him; I will not let him die.' And in the next movement – the Terzetto (no. 13) in A major – there is a further act of symbolism, central to Christian belief and practice. Florestan begs for water, and the kindly gaoler gives him wine. Soon afterwards, there is yet again a sudden modulation into C major when Rocco allows the persistent Leonore to give Florestan some bread as well – 'Da nimm das Brot du armer Mann' ('Oh take and eat this bread, unhappy man') (ex. 15.4) – a spontaneous Eucharist, expressed in some of Beethoven's loveliest music.

Ex. 15.4

So   sei es   ja,   so sei's   du kannst es   wa-gen

Da nimm, da nimm das Brot,   du ar-mer, du ar - mer Mann,

Beethoven knew all too well from personal experience how much courage was needed in the face of adversity – faith and heroism too: 'Every day brings me nearer to the goal I feel but cannot describe. And it is only in that condition that your Beethoven can live. There must be no rest', he told his old friend Franz Wegeler in 1801, as various remedies failed to cure his increasing deafness. 'I will seize Fate by the throat; it shall certainly not bend and crush me completely.'[3] As *Fidelio* reflected his own predicament so closely, he brought to it more focused intensity and even raw emotions at times, as in Leonore and Florestan's ecstatic duet, 'O namenlose Freude!' (no. 15).

The spiritual legacy of *Fidelio* includes the rarest of all qualities, the *sublime*[4] – a word that is hard to define but easy to recognize. The word comes to mind increasingly in Beethoven's later instrumental music, not least after the triumphant revival of *Fidelio* in its final version in 1814 – in the late piano sonatas, the *Missa Solemnis*, the Ninth Symphony and the late string quartets. In 1818, for example, Beethoven remembered the hymn sung by the prisoners' spokesman (ex. 15.5a) – 'Our songs of praise be given to God enthroned in Heaven' – when finding a sublime response to the brutal opening bars of the *Hammerklavier* Piano Sonata, op. 106 (ex. 15.5b).

Ex. 15.5

(a)

Wir   wol-len mit   Ver-trau-en auf Got-tes   Hil-fe, auf Got-tes Hil-fe bau-en

(b)

Thomas Love Peacock's magnificent article, written soon after the London premiere of *Fidelio* and published in *The Examiner* on 27 May 1832, applies no less to the instrumental masterpieces that Beethoven composed

[3] *Letters of Beethoven*, Letter 54, 16 November 1801: Beethoven to Franz Wegeler in Bonn.

[4] The 'sublime' was a post-Enlightenment concept, providing a significant link between classicism and romanticism. See Edmund Burke's *Treatise on the Sublime*.

in the wake of the opera: 'It carries to a pitch scarcely conceivable the true musical expression of the strongest passions and the gentlest emotions, in all their shades and contrasts ... with a force and reality that makes music an intelligible language, possessing an illimitable power of pouring forth thought in sound.'[5]

---

[5] Quoted in Coldicott, 'Arrangements of His Own Music', p. 251.

Three String Quartets, op. 59 (*Razumovsky*)

'Oh, they are not for you, but for a later age!'[1] Beethoven told the Italian violinist Felix Radicati, who, at his request, had just added some fingering to the violin parts of his three new string quartets. Radicati had found them incomprehensible – not surprisingly perhaps, as the op. 59 quartets are about as far removed from the op. 18 set, completed six years earlier, as is the *Eroica* from the Second Symphony. Nonetheless, Beethoven himself was pleased with his 'new violin quartets', as he called them in a letter to Breitkopf & Härtel, dated 5 July 1806: 'Indeed I am thinking of devoting myself entirely to this type of composition.'[2]

His confidence proved to be justified and, in Vienna at least, the 'later age' dawned sooner, perhaps, than he had expected. His circle of friends, among them the loyal Schuppanzigh and members of his quartet, had learnt from experience that all his new compositions were challenging to start with; whatever their initial reactions, it was their job to catch up with him. They set to work, at first with many misgivings and even some boisterous laughter, suspecting that Beethoven was springing one of his practical jokes on them, and gave the premiere of all three quartets in February 1807. The concert was respectfully reviewed soon afterwards by the Vienna correspondent of the *Allgemeine musikalische Zeitung*, who found them 'very long and difficult ... deep in thought and well worked out, but not generally comprehensible, except perhaps the third, whose originality, melody and harmonic power will surely win over every educated music lover.'[3] Three months later, the same journal noted that 'in Vienna, Beethoven's most recent, difficult but fine quartets have become more and more popular.'[4]

Count (later Prince) Andreas Razumovsky

Count Andreas Razumovsky (1752–1836) commissioned the quartets late in 1805 and they were probably composed between May and November 1806.[5] Under the usual arrangement by which a patron commissioning a work had possession of it for six months or a year before it could be released for publication, those two concerts (and many others, no doubt) would have been given with the Count's active support and perhaps

---

[1] Thayer, *The Life of Beethoven*, 409.

[2] *Letters of Beethoven*, Letter 132, 5 July 1806: Beethoven to Breitkopf & Härtel.

[3] Abraham, *Beethoven's Second-Period Quartets*, p. 10.

[4] Solomon, *Beethoven*, p. 261.

[5] In a fair copy of the first quartet Beethoven wrote: 'work began on 26 May 1806.' It is not clear whether this refers to the autograph or to Beethoven's original work on the quartet.

occasional participation. Sometimes Beethoven composed quickly – unbelievably so in 1806 when, in an almost nonchalant display of inspiration, confidence and energy, he revised *Fidelio*, completed the Fourth Piano Concerto, and composed the Fourth Symphony, the Violin Concerto and *Leonore* Overture no. 3, as well as the three op. 59 string quartets. However, he always liked to have plenty of time to try out his compositions and revise them if necessary before they were published, and in Count Razumovsky he found the ideal patron to ensure that this was possible.[6]

The Count was among Beethoven's more interesting and cultured patrons. His father, Kyril Razum, born of humble parents in a small Ukrainian village in 1728, was a singer in the Russian Imperial Choir in St Petersburg. He became one of Catherine the Great's favourite lovers and was generously rewarded by her – first ennobled, then married off to a suitably aristocratic lady, Catherina Ivanovna, given a huge estate and finally, for good measure, appointed a Field Marshal. For a time, their son Count Andreas was an officer in the Imperial Navy (his training included six months on a British warship); later he became a diplomat, serving as Russian Ambassador in Copenhagen, Stockholm and Naples, where he is said to have charmed the Queen. Finally, in 1792, he was appointed Ambassador to the Austrian Court and, apart from a two-year gap at the turn of the century, he remained in Vienna for the rest of his life.

Count Andreas Razumovsky inherited from his father not only a vast fortune, but also his talents as a musician; and as his first wife was Prince Lichnowsky's sister-in-law, he was naturally drawn into the Lichnowsky's lively musical circle when he arrived in Vienna, meeting Haydn and later Beethoven there. The splendid palace he built for himself outshone every other embassy – so much so that, on one occasion, the Emperor described him, ironically no doubt, as 'the King of one of my suburbs'. Baroness du Montet viewed him with mixed feelings as 'one who commands respect and is generally most amiable, [but] his presence and appearance are imperious [and] sometimes he is downright haughty.'[7] In musical matters, however, he knew his limitations, and unlike the Emperor, who insisted on leading his own string quartet, Razumovsky always played second violin in the quartet he employed for a number of years. When his palace was accidentally destroyed by fire in 1814 he was forced to disband the quartet, but thoughtfully awarded a pension to each member – Schuppanzigh, Sina, Weiss and Linke. Least of all was he 'haughty' with Beethoven, who was 'cock of the walk' in his establishment, insistent that any performance should be 'just as he wanted it and not otherwise.'[8]

[6] The op. 59 Quartets were first published by the Bureau des Arts et d'Industrie in Vienna in 1808. Three complete autographs survive.

[7] Baroness Du Montet, quoted in Landon, *Beethoven: A Documentary Study*, p. 206.

[8] Ignaz Seyfried, quoted in Thayer, *The Life of Beethoven*, p. 444.

The Count commissioned the three quartets at about the time of the Battle of Austerlitz on 2 December 1805 when the Austrian and Russian armies suffered catastrophic defeat at the hands of Napoleon; for months afterwards hospitals, schools and convents in Vienna were filled with wounded soldiers. It is inconceivable that Beethoven would remain unaffected by such a catastrophe and, whether or not as a direct result, he agreed to the Count's suggestion that each quartet should include a Russian song. He found two that he could use in a collection published by Ivan Prach in 1790[9] – one for the finale of the first quartet and one for the Allegretto in the second; for the third quartet he decided to compose a folksong, or rather a mysterious and magical folk-tale of his own. Less specifically, the depth of feeling expressed in much of the music he composed in 1806 – the Adagio in the F major Quartet, op. 59 no. 1, for example – must surely owe something to those tragic events at Austerlitz, described so movingly many years later in Tolstoy's novel *War and Peace*.

It was not only the length of the op. 59 quartets that was to cause some initial bewilderment. After all, in addition to the massive *Eroica* Symphony, Beethoven had already composed several long movements – the Allegro molto (509 bars) of the G minor Cello Sonata, op. 5 no. 2, for example, or the outer movements of the *Kreutzer* Sonata, op. 47 (599 and 539 bars respectively). Perhaps it was more the boldness, the sweep, the originality, not to mention the technical difficulties of the three quartets, each so different from the other, that first mystified, but later impressed, Beethoven's contemporaries.

A few years earlier Schuppanzigh had instituted the first public chamber music concerts in Vienna, and one suggestion, commonly made, is that in the *Razumovsky* quartets Beethoven changed the nature of chamber music, making it more 'symphonic' in response to changing times. With the increasing influence of the middle classes throughout Europe in the early nineteenth century, the expectations of audiences were changing. The rapturous reception given to the Seventh Symphony, for example, at its premiere on 8 December 1813, or later to the Ninth Symphony on 27 May 1824, showed that Beethoven's symphonic works were beginning to inspire and challenge mass audiences, as they have continued to do ever since. However, as Beethoven's letter to Breitkopf & Härtel suggests, chamber music was of the greatest importance to him, a spiritual arena in which he could explore his innermost nature and in which only the most dedicated audiences could participate fully. 'Actually, there was not a large assembly there', wrote Johann Reichardt of a concert sponsored by Count Razumovsky and given by the Schuppanzigh Quartet in 1808, 'but one consisting of very zealous and attentive music-lovers. And that is the proper public for this finest and most intimate of all musical associations.'[10] It still is.

---

[9] Cooper, *Beethoven* [Master Musicians], p. 158.
[10] Johann Reichardt, quoted in Landon, *Beethoven: A Documentary Study*, p. 96.

String Quartet no. 7 in F major, op. 59 no. 1

Allegro
Allegretto vivace e sempre scherzando
Adagio molto e mesto
Thème Russe: Allegro

Allegro   The opening bars of the F major Quartet seem simple enough – the reason, perhaps, for Schuppanzigh and his colleagues' initial reactions – but prove to be highly complex as the movement unfolds. It is easy to admire such an appealing melody for the cello (ex. 16.1a), and at the same time to be surprised by the apparent naïvety of the accompaniment of repeated quavers and very basic harmonies. However, as Philip Radcliffe has noted, 'The combination of slow harmonic motion and rhythmic energy is very characteristic of Beethoven.'[11] He had already introduced a similarly basic accompaniment in the second movement of the first Cello Sonata, op. 5 no. 1, also in F major, and more recently in the opening bars of the *Eroica* Symphony. It might take longer to appreciate the tensions and the strong sense of forward momentum created by the suspended tonality of the accompaniment – tonic/second inversion alternating with dominant harmonies – which remains unresolved until the nineteenth bar; longer still, perhaps, to realize that the opening melody contains two motives in particular (*x* and *y*) which will shape and inspire several later themes and motives, providing this spacious movement with a remarkable degree of cohesion. There are, for instance, two interlinked and closely related themes in the first group (ex. 16.1), parts of which inspire the closing section as well.

Ex. 16.1

The second group is similar to the first in expressive line and mood; not so much a new initiative as a gentle response. Both groups are framed by a variety of transitional motives, one crisply rhythmic, providing contrast and ensuring that momentum is maintained; the other a sequence of seemingly unrelated chords, mystical and strangely aloof. The central double bar and repeated exposition are omitted, as in the first movement of the C minor Violin Sonata. An apparent repeat is briefly suggested, only to veer away after only four bars into the dramatic development section, where a four-note cell (*z*), which has already appeared earlier in the movement

[11] Radcliffe, *Beethoven's String Quartets*, p. 51.

(ex. 16.2), provides a lively, though secretive, companion for a new fugal motive (*u*).

Ex. 16.2

The climax of the movement occurs at the start of the coda – the opening theme (ex. 16.1a) played *fortissimo*, challenged by off-beat *sforzandi* over massive chords (root position this time); simple enough, but magnificent.

Allegretto vivace e sempre scherzando   Rhythmic patterns play an important part in Beethoven's music – sometimes assertive as in the Fifth Symphony, sometimes expressive as in the opening bars of the Violin Concerto, where the timpani's four-crotchet introduction casts a magical spell over the entire first movement. Both play an integral, if contrasting part in this cheerful dialogue, full of secrets and confidences (*pianissimo*), uninhibited laughter (*fortissimo*), and hints of romance – a rare, if not unique example of a scherzo in sonata form.

The childlike rhythmic figure in the introduction, which so enraged the cellist Bernhard Romberg, that he 'trampled under foot as a contemptible mystification the part which he was to play',[12] links and defines the melodic material that follows. There are two themes in the first subject: the first pieced together from a variety of related fragments, teased apart and then triumphantly reunited *fortissimo*; the second, lyrical and expressive. There is only one theme in the second subject (ex. 16.3a), a sweeping, romantic melody shared by each member of the quartet in elegant counterpoint. But there are other ideas too in the development section, including an enchanted, if fragile waltz (ex. 16.3b).

Ex. 16.3

Adagio molto e mesto   In one of his sketches for this movement, Beethoven left a possible clue to the meaning of the opening theme: 'A weeping willow or acacia over the grave of my brother' – a tribute, perhaps, to the memory of his brother Georg,[13] who had died at the age of two in 1783, or

[12] Wilhelm von Lenz, quoted in Thayer, *The Life of Beethoven*, p. 409.

[13] There were seven children in the Beethoven family; two daughters and two sons died as infants.

more generally to those Austrian and Russian soldiers killed or wounded at
Austerlitz. However, no clue is really needed, for the mood of deep sorrow
(*mesto*) is clear from the start: the unfolding of a desolate one-note introduction on the dominant, followed by a bleak open fifth (*v*), introduces
the profound elegy (ex. 16.4) that follows, a melody which explores in particular the extreme emotional tensions in F minor between the sorrowful
flattened seventh (E♭) and the comforting leading note (E♮). Played softly
by the first violin above weaving, contrapuntal lines, the melody is later
repeated with increased intensity by the cello, high in its register.

Ex. 16.4

In structure, this movement, like the previous one, is in sonata form,
but in meaning it is without question a personal meditation on despair and
tragedy 'unmatched', as Lewis Lockwood suggests, 'outside the world of
Florestan's dungeon',[14] not a public expression of grief as in the slow movement of the *Eroica* Symphony. All the melodic ideas, including the transition, the short, sequential second subject, and a closely related new theme
in the development are similarly expressive, though accompanied in different ways – among them the unusual use of harp-like pizzicatos played in
turn by all four instruments, a texture to which Beethoven would return
three years later in the *Harp* Quartet.

Further emotional depths are explored in a new tearful motive, but
the mood of deep sorrow and pity is finally purged in a spectacular and
wholly unexpected way: a violin cadenza, soaring high and diving low as it
sweeps F minor aside and basks in divine C major, a spiritual metaphor to
which Beethoven would return many years later in the violin obbligato (G
major – C major – G major), which weaves its radiant way throughout the
'Benedictus' in the *Missa Solemnis* (ex. 24.3b). Sorrow makes way for joy,
and then laughter so infectious that everyone joins in (mirrored staccato
scales), leading companionably and without a break to the carefree finale.

Thème Russe: Allegro It is in the nature of folk music to evolve and
change, and it could be argued that Beethoven's treatment of the two
Russian songs, though in Philip Radcliffe's amused comment 'decidedly

---

[14] Lockwood, *Beethoven: The Music and the Life*, p. 321.

high-handed', was in line with that tradition. When Beethoven noted them in his sketchbook, he marked them respectively 'Molto Andante' and 'Andante', but 'eventually introduced them at a far brisker pace, regardless of the fact that one tells of a soldier prematurely aged by the rigours of military life, and the other is a hymn of praise to God.'[15] As in the first movement, it is some time before the tonic, F major, is finally established, postponed by sustained trills on the dominant which link the cadenza to the theme. The jaunty folk-song (ex. 16.5) is played by each instrument in turn, appearing below, above and in the middle of accompanying textures, reappearing in the busy transition and also providing a link to the closing section.

Ex. 16.5

There are two further motives in the second subject: the first full of charm, though playing little part in the movement as a whole. The second (ex. 16.6), which may have been in Dvořák's mind when he composed the second subject in the opening movement of his String Serenade, op. 22, is a neatly controlled and understated march, enlivened by teasing rhythms that recall parts of the second movement.

Ex. 16.6

The cadenza appears twice more, played *fortissimo* in unison and in paired thirds by all four players in the closing and development sections. But Beethoven's most charming gesture is his 'amende honorable' to that exhausted soldier: the Thème Russe played slowly just before the final Presto, as intended in the original song.

String Quartet no. 8 in E minor, op. 59 no. 2

Allegro
Molto Adagio
Allegretto [Minore] – Maggiore
Finale: Presto

During the summer of 1806, Beethoven spent several months with the Lichnowskys at their castle in Grätz. He took with him the unfinished E minor Quartet and the *Appassionata* Sonata, but set them aside after a neighbourly visit to Count Oppersdorff, who commissioned him to compose a new symphony. The Count was passionately fond of music – it was

[15] Radcliffe, *Beethoven's String Quartets*, p. 49.

said that every member of his household was expected to play an instrument – and his private orchestra was good enough to perform the Second Symphony in Beethoven's honour. The new symphony, the Fourth, was written quickly, and by September Beethoven was again at work on the quartet and the sonata, only to be interrupted once more the following month – not this time by another commission, but by his famously explosive quarrel with Prince Lichnowsky. According to Alexander Thayer, he had been 'so pestered by the guests ... who wished to hear him play, that he grew angry ... A threat of arrest, made surely in jest, was taken seriously by him.'[16] Beethoven at once left Grätz for Vienna during a violent thunderstorm worthy of the storm in Act 3 of Shakespeare's *King Lear*, the rain so heavy that water seeped into his trunk, damaging, though fortunately not destroying, the completed manuscript of the the first two movements of this quartet and of the *Appassionata* – an appropriate metaphor perhaps for his long, though unsettled, friendship with the Prince.

Allegro Beethoven fully understood the emotional and dramatic importance of silence, most recently explored in *Fidelio* and in the slow movement of the G major Piano Concerto, and he returned to it here. There are no fewer than twelve silent bars, all associated with the first subject; far from impeding momentum, however, they play a vibrant part in this elusive movement by creating feelings of suspense and tension – tension further increased by tonal ambiguity, extreme contrasts in dynamics and by quietly placing weak beats (y) higher than strong beats. The quartet opens with two brusque chords (x in ex. 16.7), followed by a series of challenging questions, each in outline a variant of the chords: the first in the tonic, E minor; the second up a semitone to F major – a destabilizing Neapolitan relationship,[17] which Beethoven was exploring at much the same time in the opening bars of the *Appassionata* and would return to later, among other compositions, in his F minor Quartet, op. 95.

Ex. 16.7

The questions (y) become increasingly insistent (ex. 16.8) and the answers (z) increasingly emotional, with each motive contributing to the discussion both melodically and contrapuntally. The argument comes to a head in the heated transition with its unsettled rhythmic patterns – groups of four semiquavers (u) at cross purposes with groups of six.

---

[16] Thayer, *The Life of Beethoven*, p. 403.

[17] The 'Neapolitan sixth' – an expressive and emotional tool usually defined as 'the first inversion of the triad on the lowered supertonic', i.e. F–A♭–D♭ in C major. See Apel, *Harvard Dictionary of Music*, p. 685.

Ex. 16.8

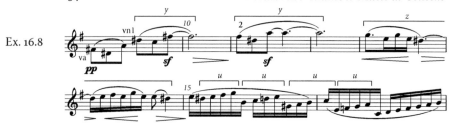

Peace is restored in the second group (ex. 16.9), a radiant preview of Beethoven's late-period style: a soaring melody inspired by a variant of (*z*) with 'something in it of divinity more than the ear discovers':[18]

Ex. 16.9

A rhythmic variant of the same figure (*z*), now assertively *marcato*, shares the second motive in the group with another expressive phrase, marked *dolce* and full of pathos, played first by the viola and repeated, high in register, by the first violin. A mysterious transition follows – shifting harmonies, strange syncopations, misplacement of the first beat in every bar – growing in intensity to reach the explosive closing section. There is no place for radiance in the concise development, but other motives are explored to the full in this highly charged drama, especially variants of semiquaver motives (*z*, *u*), played in thirds, sixths or octaves and colouring the opening bars of the recapitulation to brilliant effect. The coda is full of mystery, ending bleakly with those earlier questions still unresolved.

Molto Adagio   The mood of this beautiful chorale-like movement, which 'must be played with great feeling' ('Si tratta questo pezzo con molto di sentimento'), is one of awe. According to both Czerny and Holz, Beethoven was inspired to write it after gazing 'up at the stars, contemplating the harmony of the spheres', while perhaps at the same time recalling a quotation from Kant, which he had underlined in his copy of Bode's *Guide to a Knowledge of the Starry Heavens* – 'The moral law within us, and the starry sky above us.'[19] The inspiration Beethoven drew from 'the harmony of the spheres' that summer in Grätz also inspired the introduction to the Fourth Symphony, which shares with this quartet the same slow-moving minims and the same feelings of awe and wonder.

In contrast to the first movement with its many silences, there are no pauses or breaks in this serene Adagio but, in John Donne's immortal

---

[18] Abraham, *Beethoven's Second-Period Quartets*, p. 33. 'It is such music as the author of *Religio Medici* conceived to be an hierographical and shadowed lesson of the whole world.'

[19] Mason, *The Quartets of Beethoven*, pp. 110–11.

words, 'one equal music', as each exquisite phrase merges imperceptibly into the next – the chorale (ex. 16.10a), for example, merging into the slow moving transition, illuminated, starlike, by descants created from delicate staccato patterns. The chorale is played five times during the movement and harmonized differently on each occasion – most impressively in its glorious final appearance at the start of the coda. The second group of themes, as awe-struck as the first, includes a mystic fanfare (ex. 16.10b) followed by a seamless and reflective episode.

Ex. 16.10

Allegretto [Minore] – Maggiore   Feet scarcely touch the ground in the mazurka-like Allegretto with its second-beat stresses, airy texture, secretive *pianissimos*, assertive *fortissimos* and effervescent quavers, passed in turn from melody to accompaniment and back again (ex. 16.11). The Neapolitan relationship between E minor and F major in the first movement is again explored, with E minor delicate and F major boldly assertive.

Ex. 16.11

Maggiore – Thème Russe   Beethoven's treatment of the 'Thème Russe' (in E major) may not be as dignified as Mussorgsky's later version of the same theme in *Boris Godunov*, but it is colourfully presented in a series of vignettes, the theme ever-present and played in turn by each member of the quartet: first, a fugato with a fluent triplet countersubject and the lightest of textures; then a more incisive variant in thirds and sixths accompanied by sparkling quavers, to reach a forceful climax in a canon 'as rough as some of Beethoven's puns', as Robert Simpson puts it;[20] then finally played softly in richly chromatic polyphony, the resulting harmonies as creamy as the smooth interweaving lines.

Finale: Presto   Schoenberg relished this sparkling sonata-rondo as a prime example of tonal ambiguity: 'We can say that in the development of art it must always be as it is in the Spring! One does what the situation demands, unconcerned about the approval or disapproval of others',[21]

---

[20] Simpson, 'The Chamber Music for Strings', p. 257.

[21] Schoenberg, 'Problems of Harmony', in *Style and Idea*, pp. 268–9.

quoting a verse from Wagner's *Meistersinger* in support: 'Your closing key is not the same. / This gives the masters pain; / But Hans Sachs draws a rule from this: / In Spring it must be so, 'tis plain.' Why Beethoven composed a finale (ex. 16.12a) almost entirely in C major for a quartet in E minor is one of the intriguing mysteries of music.

Ex. 16.12

Gerald Abraham's theory that he may have felt that 'he had overdone E major and minor as the tonic in the previous movements'[22] is persuasive as far as it goes, but there may be more to it than that. Beethoven was passionate about the appropriateness of keys for different moods and situations, and he must have decided that the character of the principal theme demanded the greatest tonal resonance from open strings that a string quartet can provide, so only C major would do. If that meant visiting E minor briefly from time to time and finishing the movement in E minor as fast as possible (Più Presto) with a generous sprinkling of *sforzandi*, that would only add to the mystification – and the fun. As so often, Beethoven's dynamics are subtle and unexpected. The principal theme seems boisterous in character, but is firmly marked *piano*, not *forte*, with intermittent, short-lived *crescendo*s, suggesting that Beethoven meant it to sound poised and insouciant, in contrast to the expansive and lyrical nature of the second theme (ex. 16.12b). The transition, based on elements of the principal theme, is certainly boisterous, as is the ninth and final appearance of the theme in C major, played *fortissimo* just before the coda. But the dramatic heart of the movement is to be found later in contrapuntal development (ex. 16.13), with motives from each subject pitting their wits against the giant strides of an imposing *cantus firmus* (*w*).

Ex. 16.13

---

[22] Abraham, *Beethoven's Second-Period Quartets*, p. 39.

String Quartet no. 9 in C major, op. 59 no. 3

Introduzione: Andante con moto – Allegro vivace
Andante con moto quasi Allegretto
Menuetto & Trio: Grazioso
Allegro molto

Introduzione: Andante con moto   Several of Beethoven's earlier chamber works begin with a slow introduction, but this is the first of a distinguished line to appear in his later string quartets. Unresolved diminished and secondary sevenths, slow-moving contrapuntal lines played *pianissimo*, one groping its way upwards, another downwards through a series of uneven steps on the cello, an elusive melodic fragment, a mysterious trill and moments of silence – all combine to create feelings of extreme suspense. Generations of quartet players have shared Rebecca Clarke's experience when playing these opening bars: 'One hardly dares breathe, and can almost see the internal counting of one's companions floating like an astral shape above them. It is such a trying thing to play – wonderful as it is – that the entry into the Allegro vivace feels exactly like a sigh of relief at gaining solid ground again.'[23]

Critics have been less united as to the meaning or purpose of the introduction – mood music, solely concerned with creating an atmosphere? An echo of the visionary introduction to the Fourth Symphony composed a few months earlier? Most intriguing of all is Lewis Lockwood's observation that it draws on 'some of the same harmonic resources we find in the F minor introduction to Florestan's dungeon scene written in 1805–6 just before his main work on these quartets.'[24] Add to this the comment which Beethoven wrote on a sketch for the last movement: 'May your deafness be no more a secret, even in art'[25] – and it is not unreasonable to speculate that, far from being a mere sequence of mysterious chords, the introduction is an expression of deeply personal feelings.

Allegro vivace   If that is so, the outcome in the ensuing Allegro is surprisingly positive. Tentatively at first, with its two reversed cadences (*x*), unsettled tonality and delicate violin solos, the mood is increasingly one of elation as the divine tonic key, C major, is finally reached in the forty-third bar. Confinement gives way to freedom and introspection to celebration in some of the sunniest pages in Beethoven's chamber music. There is no time for melody in all the excitement; room only for a series of motives, played companionably in thirds or octaves or sometimes competitively as solos. Two short cells provide the basis for development, acting as signposts to guide both listeners and performers through the complexities that follow. The first – a two-note cell

[23] Clarke, 'Beethoven's Quartets as a Player Sees Them'; also quoted in Mason, *The Quartets of Beethoven*, p. 117.

[24] Lockwood, *Beethoven: The Music and the Life*, p. 325.

[25] Cooper, *Beethoven* [Master Musicians], p. 162.

(*x*) – crops up everywhere, though in many different guises. It introduces the two opening motives in the first subject (ex. 16.14a), inspires gentle dialogue leading to the transition (ex. 16.14b), provides the rhythmic basis for two rounds of a hard-fought sporting duel – the first in the development section, the second in the recapitulation – and reaches deep into the finale as well, where like a benign spirit it hovers serenely above the coda.

Ex. 16.14

The second cell (*y*) shapes and characterizes the second theme (ex. 16.15) and transition with supreme confidence.

Ex. 16.15

There are two delightful surprises later: the violin cadenza, which signals the start of the recapitulation, and the hilarious stringendo with which the movement ends.

Andante con moto quasi Allegretto   Long candle-lit evenings during the harsh Russian winter are perhaps evoked in trance-like repetitions and poignant phrases, as memories are stirred and stories retold. There are three themes in the exposition, shared mostly between the two violins and viola in expressive polyphony to form an almost continuous stream of melody. The role of the cello is more varied, occasionally joining the upper strings, but more often taking up the narrative in melodic pizzicato solos or marking the passing of time as majestically as a grandfather clock. The story unfolds mysteriously, as all good stories should, in one of Beethoven's most touching melodies (ex. 16.16) and haunting cadences are repeated tenderly as each paragraph comes to an end.

Ex. 16.16

The second melody, introduced by the viola above the cello's resonant pizzicato C, is more emotional, even at times anguished, while the third is delicate and child-like, though later called upon to create an unexpected fugato. However, as the development comes to an end, Beethoven delays the return of the opening theme and a full recapitulation with one of his many sublime moments of introspection and stillness (ex. 16.17), as the cello measures the passing of time in distant pizzicato quavers.

Ex. 16.17

Menuetto & Trio: Grazioso Beethoven retained an unexpectedly soft spot for the old-fashioned minuet. There are minuets in eight of his earlier chamber works, including the Septet and two of the op. 18 quartets (nos. 4 and 5). But this is the only one to appear in the chamber music of his post-*Eroica/Fidelio* years and it is perhaps 'the fairest of them all', with its mirrored phrases, cross-rhythms and flowing traceries (ex. 16.18a). By contrast, the Trio is a wake-up call, a fanfare which anticipates the frenetic activity to come – though not before a repeat of the Minuet and a thoughtful, self-explanatory coda which, in inverted form (*z*), links it seamlessly to the fugue subject (ex. 16.18b) which dominates the finale.

Ex. 16.18

Allegro molto Disparate elements are drawn together into a unified whole in this thrilling movement, a *moto perpetuo* like the finales of the G major String Trio or the *Kreutzer* Sonata, but one in which the contrapuntal possibilities of fugue are explored within the overall context of sonata form. The fugue subject/first subject, an extended version of the opening bars of the Menuetto, is exceptionally long, as the viola, second violin and cello in turn play the ten-bar theme in full. The first violin extends the subject still further, accompanied by a vigorous, striding *cantus firmus*, to reach the triumphant transition and its *fortissimo* fanfares. The exhilarating development section includes a highly competitive tournament – initiated by the first violin, and then followed by each instrument in turn

– centred on a motive (*u*) borrowed from the last two bars of the fugue subject. But even as the excitement intensifies, gentler voices are heard and,
before the final dénouement, the last word is awarded to the *second* violin
– a lyrical descant (ex. 16.19) which rises high above the busy quavers below
and includes the same two-note cell (E–F), significantly accented, which
launched the Allegro in the first movement (ex. 16.14a) – an inspired example of architectural design and also, perhaps, a graceful tribute to a Princely
second violinist.

Ex. 16.19

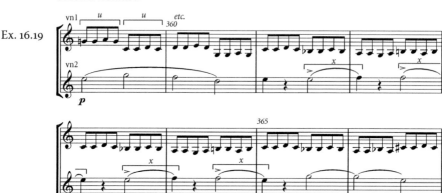

Cello Sonata in A major, op. 69

Ignaz von Gleichenstein

An attractive feature of Beethoven's post-*Fidelio* years was his decision to dedicate at least some of his compositions to close friends, rather than to grandees; friends like Ignaz von Gleichenstein (1778–1828), a keen amateur cellist and, in the opinion of another member of Beethoven's circle, the historian Julius Schneller, 'a man of the greatest probity and ... the kindest [of] men'.[1] Gleichenstein was a state counsellor working in the War Department and his official duties included at least one intelligence mission to assess Napoleon's troop movements, after war broke out yet again between France and Austria. He helped Beethoven in a number of practical ways. For example, it was Gleichenstein, at the instigation of Countess Erdödy, who negotiated the all-important contract agreed by Archduke Rudolph, Prince Lobkowitz and Prince Kinsky in February 1809 (see Chapter 19) designed to keep Beethoven in Vienna when he was considering a lucrative offer from the King of Westphalia.

The numerous letters Beethoven wrote to Gleichenstein suggest that, for some years at least, their friendship was especially warm. Beethoven even asked him for help with his marriage plans: 'Now you can help me look for a wife ... who would perhaps now and then grant a sigh to my harmonies.'[2] A month later, he begged Gleichenstein to undertake a particularly sensitive mission: to give as much support as he could to Stephan von Breuning, whose wife Julie, with whom Beethoven often played duets, had died after only a year of marriage. Her death upset Beethoven deeply, all the more because he felt that his attempts to comfort von Breuning had been a complete failure: 'You would hardly believe in what an excited condition I found him ... Hence, my dear Gleichenstein, I am entrusting to your care one of my best and staunchest friends.'[3] Apart from two periods of estrangement, Beethoven's friendship with von Breuning, who had recently revised the libretto for the 1806 revival of *Fidelio*, lasted from their years as children together in Bonn until Beethoven's death. Their friendship had been cemented earlier by his dedication of the Violin Concerto to Stephan and the piano version of the concerto to Julie.

---

[1] Clive, *Beethoven and his World*, p. 132. The friendship between Beethoven and Gleichenstein cooled after the latter's marriage to Anna Malfatti, the younger sister of Therese Malfatti, whom Beethoven had hoped to marry. He and his wife left Vienna in 1811 to manage the family estate near Freiburg. They returned to Vienna from time to time and it is known that Gleichenstein visited Beethoven during his final illness in 1827.

[2] *Letters of Beethoven*, Letter 202, 14 March 1809: Beethoven to Ignaz von Gleichenstein.

[3] *Letters of Beethoven*, Letter 216, April 1809.

Beethoven had originally intended to dedicate the Fourth Piano Concerto to Gleichenstein, but unfortunately Archduke Rudolph, his new royal pupil and one of the three signatories to the contract, particularly liked it. An embarrassed letter of explanation became necessary: 'My dear Gleichenstein! I have not yet had time to express to you my delight at your arrival or to see you – nor to enlighten you about something which presumably will greatly surprise you – but which cannot do you any harm because another work is appearing in which you will be given what is due to you – [and] to our friendship.'[4] The 'other work' was the Cello Sonata in A major, op. 69, a masterpiece not only in its own right, but also as the benchmark by which duo sonatas for cello and piano have come to be judged ever since, from Mendelssohn and Brahms to Debussy, Shostakovich and beyond.

Beethoven had become increasingly interested in advanced cello techniques, writing a particularly showy part for the solo cellist in the Triple Concerto (1804–5), a work which, like the *Kreutzer* Sonata, must have contributed significantly to virtuoso and other elements in op. 69. Ideas for the sonata, musically and melodically among the richest of Beethoven's fifteen duo sonatas for strings and piano, appeared in a sketchbook dated September 1807 to early 1808, together with preliminary ideas for the Fifth Symphony and *Leonore* Overture no. 1.[5] Judging by the innumerable alterations and experiments revealed in the sketchbook, he took even more trouble than usual over this important addition to the new genre which he himself had created – an impression confirmed by yet further alterations in the surviving autograph of the first movement, all the more surprising considering the sonata's apparent spontaneity and lyrical flow.

Nikolaus Kraft, hailed by Bernard Romberg for his lack of affectation, his clear, rich tone and technical mastery,[6] gave the first public performance on 26 July 1809, with Beethoven's pupil, Baroness Dorothea von Ertmann. The sonata was published the same year by Breitkopf & Härtel and later performances included one in 1816 by Carl Czerny and Joseph Linke, the cellist in Prince Razumovsky's quartet, whom Beethoven was known to consult on matters of cello technique. Czerny's involvement is particularly interesting, as he carefully noted the metronome marks for each movement in all five of the cello sonatas, presumably approved by Beethoven, and recommended the subtle use of *rubato* when playing them: 'Although each piece should be played 'from beginning to end … in the time prescribed by the author [there] occur in almost every line some notes or passages, where a small and almost imperceptible relaxation or acceleration of the movement is necessary to embellish the expression and increase the interest.'[7]

---

[4] *Letters of Beethoven*, Letter 172, Summer 1808.

[5] Cooper, *Beethoven and the Creative Process*, p. 89.

[6] Clive, *Beethoven and his World*, p. 194.

[7] Watkin, 'Beethoven's Sonatas for Cello and Piano', pp. 112–13.

Sonata no. 3 in A major for cello and piano, op. 69

Allegro, ma non tanto
Scherzo: Allegro molto
Adagio cantabile – Allegro vivace

In this sonata, one of his greatest celebrations of melody, Beethoven explored the character of the cello, its musical and technical possibilities, more deeply than either of his great Classical predecessors had done. Melodic material is scrupulously shared between the piano and the three voices of the cello – bass, tenor and alto – matching all but the highest octaves of the piano's range. As in the *Kreutzer* Sonata, short cadenzas and virtuoso passages for each instrument add zest and brilliance, and subsidiary material is as varied for the cello as it is for the piano.

Allegro ma non tanto Beethoven composed a number of noble melodies in his post-*Eroica/Fidelio* years, and the opening theme of this sonata is among the noblest of them all (ex. 17.1a). It is a shared melody: the first extended phrase played by the cello alone, low in register and with unassertive simplicity; the second by the piano, high above a flowing left hand accompaniment and the cello's sustained dominant pedal. After a short piano cadenza, positions are reversed, with the first phrase played more assertively by the piano in octaves, the second phrase and cadenza taken this time by the cello. As in so many of his mature masterpieces, this spacious melody provides much of the movement's structural material too, as Beethoven builds 'not on short incisive figures', Philip Radcliffe suggests, 'but on flowing and continuous melodies that are capable of being divided at a later stage [*x, y, z*] into smaller, separable units'.[8] The movement continues with just such a 'separable unit' (ex. 17.1b) – a much bolder version of the opening phrase (*x*), with its strong sense of purpose, minor key (A minor) and off-beat *sforzandi*.

Ex. 17.1

There are three further motives in the second group of themes – the first two played simultaneously (ex. 17.2), one thoughtful and contrapuntal (*u*), the other gently flowing (*v*).

---

[8] Radcliffe, *Beethoven's String Quartets*, p. 50.

Ex. 17.2

The third, again introduced by the cello, is heroic in character (ex. 17.3) and experimental in texture, with the melody played, as in Beethoven's first Cello Sonata, op. 5 no. 1, well below the piano accompaniment.

Ex. 17.3

The closing section and short development are based throughout on phrases from the first subject, particularly (*y*) and (*z*). One variant of (*y*) is of special interest (ex. 17.4a), as it is almost identical to the opening bars of the viola da gamba solo (ex. 17.4b) which introduces and weaves its way through the Alto aria, 'Es is voll-bracht' ('All is fulfilled') in Bach's St John Passion. Whether or not the reference is intentional, it is certainly intriguing to know that Beethoven wrote 'Inter lacrimas et luctus' ('Amid tears and grief') on Gleichenstein's copy of the sonata, words which precisely echo the mood of the aria sung shortly before the death of Christ, and suggest that the theme must have been of deeply emotional and spiritual significance for Beethoven – *in memoriam* Julie von Breuning, perhaps?

Ex. 17.4

Another reflective passage occurs just before the recapitulation, and reappears before the final flourishes at the end of the movement – not the expected grand climax, but a few moments of stillness and introspection – the simplest, most basic reduction of the opening phrase in the movement (*x*), beautifully moulded.

Scherzo: Allegro molto   The formal layout is clear enough: a scherzo in A minor played three times, alternating with a contrasting section in A major played twice. With its insistent syncopations and violent contrasts, the Scherzo (ex. 17.5) is deeply troubled.

Ex. 17.5

Interpreting the syncopations on a modern piano, however, is anything but simple. Czerny suggested a solution which, on the pianos of his day, might well have matched the cello's syncopated tied notes – 'the first note (with the fourth finger) very tenuto, and the other (with the third finger) smartly detached and less marked … the fourth finger must therefore glide aside and make way for the third.' The A major section, played expressively by the cello in sixths and thirds and marked *dolce*, might be thought to offer warmth and comfort, if it were not for the taunting two-note cell *w*, played low in the piano's bass register and repeated obsessively. Tonal and rhythmic ambiguities in this part of the movement anticipate similar ambiguities, melodic shapes and cadences that an eleven-year-old choirboy, Franz Schubert – awarded a scholarship at the Imperial and Royal City College in Vienna in the year that op. 69 was composed – would respond to and make so much his own a few years later. The opening phrase, for example, in the slow movement of Schubert's Piano Trio in B flat major, D898, is similar in shape and mood to the cellist's melody here.

Adagio cantabile   There is ambiguity of another kind in the Adagio. It promises to be one of Beethoven's most peaceful slow movements – a tranquil eight-bar melody, played first on the piano partnered by a gentle cello descant, then repeated with the roles reversed; and that is all, apart from an *ad libitum* bar linking the Adagio to the finale. Is it an introduction or a very short slow movement? Perhaps a bit of both, as the tensions in the Scherzo are gently replaced by this serene two-verse song.

Allegro vivace   Whatever Beethoven's intentions, those eighteen lovely bars are followed without a break by one of his sunniest melodies (ex. 17.6a) and, in the second subject, by one of his friendliest, if secretive, conversations (ex. 17.6b).

Ex. 17.6

Both give rise to brilliant cascades of semiquavers and breathless, off-beat rhythmic patterns, especially in the closing section. The development is more serious, however, focusing initially on the first two bars of the movement, and then on the first bar only (*s*) in a sinister chromatic sequence for the cello, climbing slowly to the accompaniment of insistent drum beats on the piano; then repeated with the roles reversed.

Accompanying textures are livelier than ever in the recapitulation. But the crowning glory of this consummate movement is the coda, introduced by a heroic new descant high on the piano – so high that in its splendid isolation it appears to be wholly unaware of the harmonic mayhem it is causing the cello far below (*t*). Differences are set aside in the last few bars, however, with the opening phrase first played in canon, then in friendly unison accompanied by lively semiquavers – and finally celebrated by more of those triumphant drum-beats.

Two Piano Trios, op. 70

Beethoven began work on the first of his two op. 70 piano trios early in 1808 and both were completed later that remarkable year, during which he also composed the A major Cello Sonata, the Fifth and Sixth symphonies, the Mass in C major and the Choral Fantasia. The trios were published in 1809, and appeared separately, the first in June and the second in August. In a letter to Breitkopf & Härtel, Beethoven remarked that his reason for writing them was that 'such trios are now rather scarce',[1] but he seems to have made a conscious decision in those rich post-*Eroica* and *Fidelio* years to revisit the principal genres of his earlier chamber music – violin sonatas, cello sonatas, piano trios and string quartets, though not string trios or wind chamber music.

The D major Piano Trio, op. 70 no. 1, familiarly known as the *Ghost*, is a foray, rare for Beethoven, into a violent and at times supernatural world. By contrast, the Piano Trio in E flat major, op. 70 no. 2, is a celebration of the wholesome, natural world which he loved so much. It may or may not be significant, but it is certainly intriguing to know that the sketchbook dated February to September 1808, which was used by Beethoven when working on the two trios, reflects these contrasts: on the one hand, it contains preliminary ideas for a chorus of witches for the opening scene of a projected opera based on Shakespeare's *Macbeth*, and on the other, extensive sketches for the *Pastoral* Symphony.

Anna Maria, Countess Erdödy

Beethoven dedicated the two trios to Anna Maria, Countess Erdödy (1778–1827), who had become one of his keenest supporters and dearest friends. He wrote detailed fingerings for her in the piano part of each trio and insisted that they should be included when the trios were published. The first performance of the *Ghost* Trio, given by Schuppanzigh, Linke and Beethoven himself, took place on 5 December 1808, and both trios were played six days later to an invited audience in the Countess's apartment, where Beethoven had rooms at the time. Among her guests was the composer and diarist Johann Reichardt, who was enthralled by the new trios and by the 'great bravura and resolution' of Beethoven's playing, in spite of his increasing deafness. The susceptible Reichardt confessed to being no less enchanted by the Countess's response to the music as it unfolded.

> The charming, sickly, yet so touchingly serene Countess and one of her friends, a young Hungarian lady, showed such enthusiastic enjoyment of every beautiful, bold passage and every fine, effective

---

[1] *Letters of Beethoven*, Letter 169, July 1808: Beethoven to Breitkopf & Härtel.

new idea in the music that the sight of them was as agreeable to me as was Beethoven's masterly work and execution. Fortunate the artist who can be certain of having such listeners![2]

Apparently the Countess was very pretty and, in spite of chronic ill-health, had

given birth to three healthy and charming children who are as close to her as burrs. The only pleasure left for her is music and she plays even Beethoven's music quite well, hobbling from one fortepiano to the other on her still very swollen feet. Withal she is so cheerful, so friendly and kind.[3]

For some years she had lived apart from her husband, bringing up her three children, two daughters and a son, in a large apartment in the Lichnowsky's palace in Vienna. She was a hospitable promoter of Beethoven's music at frequent soirées and it was she, together with Baron Gleichenstein, who initiated the successful plan referred to in the previous chapter to dissuade him from leaving Vienna for the Westphalian court. Her friendship with Beethoven appears to have been platonic, and it was strong enough to withstand periods of estrangement, one of which almost robbed her of the op. 70 dedication.

The longest breakdown in their relationship was caused by one of the strangest of many misunderstandings involving Beethoven and his closest friends. When he discovered in 1809 that the Countess was paying his steward a bonus to prevent him from leaving his difficult employer, he stormed out of her apartment, his pride hurt, suspecting, however implausibly, some kind of 'affair' between her and the steward. He wrote at once to Breitkopf & Härtel cancelling the op. 70 dedication but, fortunately for the Countess, his letter arrived too late. When he realized that she had only been trying to help him, he sent her an abject letter of apology: 'My dear Countess, I have acted wrongly, it is true. Forgive me … Only since yesterday evening have I really understood how things are; and I am very sorry that I acted as I did … do write just one word to say that you are fond of me again.'[4]

Though cool for a time, their friendship survived and over the years became even closer. Beethoven's later letters confirm his respect and deep affection for the Countess, symbolized in 1815 by his dedication to her of the two cello sonatas, op. 102. A shared interest in ill-health is a favourite topic in the letters and most include humorous, as well as thoughtful,

---

[2] Klugmann, 'Piano Trios and Piano Quartets', p. 122.

[3] Landon, *Beethoven: A Documentary Study*, pp. 221–2. The composer and writer Johann Reichardt stayed in Vienna from November 1809 to the spring of 1810, and later published a travel journal with enthusiastic comments on Beethoven and his circle.

[4] *Letters of Beethoven*, Letter 207, March 1809: Beethoven to Countess Anna Maria Erdödy.

philosophical comments. A letter addressed to the Countess, who was spending some months in Schloss Paukowitz, her family home in Croatia, is typical: references to medical problems and jokes at the expense of her son's tutor, Joseph Brauchle, and the cellist Joseph Linke are followed by profound reflections on the human condition: 'We finite beings, who are the embodiment of an infinite spirit, are born to suffer both pain and joy; one might almost say that the best of us obtain joy through suffering.' Finally he shows his affectionate concern for her and for her family: 'Your children must be a great joy to you. Their sincere affection and their endeavour to secure in every way the welfare of their dear mother must surely be an ample reward for her sufferings.'[5]

E. T. A. Hoffmann

The op. 70 trios soon attracted the attention of one of the most influential music critics of the early nineteenth century, E. T. A. Hoffmann (1776–1822), whose writings inspired many later composers and compositions, among them Schumann's *Kreisleriana*, Offenbach's *Tales of Hoffmann* and Busoni's *Die Brautwahl*. In a remarkable essay published in December 1813, based on two earlier reviews which he had written for the *Allgemeine musikalische Zeitung*, Hoffmann first defined the different romantic qualities to be found in each of the great triumvirate – Haydn, Mozart and Beethoven – and, after a powerful account of the 'indescribably profound, magnificent [Fifth] Symphony in C minor', wrote most perceptively about the op. 70 trios:

> With what joy I received [the] seventieth work, the two glorious trios. How well the master understood the specific character of [each] instrument and fostered it in the way best suited to it! A simple but fruitful theme, songlike, susceptible to the most varied contrapuntal treatments, curtailments and so forth, forms the basis of each movement; all remaining themes and figures are intimately related to the main idea in such a way that the details all interweave, arranging themselves among the instruments in the highest unity. Despite the good nature that prevails, Beethoven's genius is in the last analysis serious ... It is as though the master thought that, in speaking of deep, mysterious things – even when the spirit feels itself joyously and gladly uplifted – one may not use an ordinary language; only a sublime and glorious one.[6]

It was some time before Beethoven became aware of Hoffmann's article: 'You are often spoken of in the *Phantasie-Stücke* by Hoffmann', Friedrich Starke wrote in the current conversation book, dated March 1820. 'Hoffmann was musical director in Bamberg; he is now a government

[5] *Letters of Beethoven*, Letter 563, 19 October 1815.

[6] Strunk, *Source Readings in Music History*, pp. 778–80.

councillor.' Understandably, Beethoven was delighted with the article; more significantly, however, he clearly approved of Hoffmann's analysis of his music, its structures and meaning, because he wrote a warm letter to him soon afterwards and asked another friend, Herr Neberich, his wine merchant, to deliver it to Hoffmann personally: 'Herr Starke showed me in his album some lines of yours about me. So I am bound to think that you take some interest in me. Allow me to tell you that this interest on the part of a man like you, who is endowed with such excellent qualities, is very gratifying to me.'[7]

Trio in D major for piano, violin and cello, op. 70 no. 1 (*Ghost*)

Allegro vivace e con brio
Largo assai ed espressivo
Presto

Carl Czerny may or may not have known that Beethoven was considering Shakespeare's *Macbeth* as the subject for an opera, or that a few preliminary ideas for it had appeared in the same sketchbook as the op. 70 trios. But many years later he recalled that the central movement of the D major Trio had always reminded him of the appearance of Banquo's Ghost, and the work has been known as the *Ghost* ever since. Whether the evidence justifies such a specific 'programme' – and some writers remain sceptical[8] – Beethoven's extensive use of tremolo in the Largo, as in Pizarro's vengeful aria, 'Ha! Welch'ein Augenblick', in Act 1 of *Fidelio* or in the Introduction to Act 2, in which Florestan's feelings of horror, fear and despair are so graphically portrayed, suggests that he had some kind of surreal drama in mind when he composed this deeply unsettling work.

Allegro vivace con brio The Trio opens violently, and violence of one kind or another erupts repeatedly throughout the first movement with its lean, though productive, material and discordant counterpoint alternating, in Nigel Fortune's words, with 'aching, tender melodies'.[9] The exposition is short, and extreme contrasts in mood, dynamics and texture are evident from the start. The opening group (ex. 18.1) consists of two very different ideas. The first (*x*) is so ferocious that even its time-signature and key seem confused – it sounds as if it is in duple (*x'*), but is actually in triple time – and the cello's F natural in the fifth bar is both challenging and ambiguous. The second idea, the 'aching, tender melody' marked *dolce*, is created from

---

[7] Thayer, *The Life of Beethoven*, p. 759. For a time Friedrich Starke gave piano lessons to Beethoven's nephew Karl.

[8] Nicholas Marston, for example, finds the 'supposed connection' unconvincing. 'The sole basis for this is the presence of a short sketch in D minor, headed "Macbett", "Ende" at the top of a page of sketches for the Trio movement ... The connection cannot be proved or disproved on such flimsy evidence.' Cooper, *The Beethoven Compendium*, p. 230.

[9] Fortune, 'The Chamber Music with Piano', p. 222.

two further motives (*y, z*), both of which are productive later, particularly in the transition and in the impassioned development.

Ex. 18.1

All three motives in the first group exchange roles from time to time. The first (*x*), for instance, is sometimes delicate, sometimes overbearing (ex. 18.2).

Ex. 18.2

The second and third (*y, z*), however, are alternately passionate and cautious as they venture through a series of mysterious modulations and, in E. T. A. Hoffmann's words, arrange themselves 'among the instruments in the highest unity'. As a result, there is some challengingly discordant harmony and polyphony in places. Though no less impassioned, the spacious second subject, accompanied by an extended version of the opening bars (*x* in ex. 18.1) is increasingly fragmentary, and the recapitulation is extended by remote, wayward piano improvisations and further dark modulations. Issues remain unresolved in the reflective coda, and the movement ends as ferociously as it began.

Largo assai ed espressivo   Apart from the early Piano Trio in E flat major, published posthumously as WoO 38 and the Clarinet Trio, op. 11, the *Ghost* is the only one of Beethoven's piano trios with three rather than four movements, and because the Largo is so awe-inspiring, the outer movements not only frame it, but seem also to fall under its spell. Structurally, it consists of a simple theme in two sections, followed by four increasingly unnerving variations. The first section is a dialogue, with questions and answers only a bar apart; the second an anguished melody shared contrapuntally by all three instruments with the cello at times in a higher register than the violin. It is a movement of extraordinary, brooding presence, among the slowest ever written, with spine-chilling tremolandos, bleak, whispered conversations, weird chromatic passages and outbreaks of extreme violence. Czerny certainly had a point.

Presto   By contrast, the first subject in the finale is both expansive and lyrical (ex. 18.3), offering for a time at least some degree of emotional stability after so much tension – although two pauses are needed in the first eight bars for thoughts to be collected and nerves steadied before the movement gets fully under way.

Ex. 18.3

It soon becomes clear, however, that not all the demons conjured up in the Largo have vanished. The confident, striding transitional passage and the *dolce* second subject, for example, are challenged and even knocked off course at times, as in the combative development section. There are strange reminders too of incidents in the Largo: the piano's weird, needling improvisation (ex. 18.4) and the skeletal pizzicatos alternating with off-beat piano chords near the end which recall the final desolate bars of the slow movement.

Ex. 18.4

But gentle, pastoral voices are also heard from time to time – a flowing triplet version of the main theme, for instance, played in turn high on the cello, low on the violin and in octaves on the piano over a prolongued dominant pedal. So the Trio ends amicably with segments of the first subject shared alternately by the violin and cello in a friendly game of 'pass the parcel', followed by a long dominant pedal and finally by a triumphant chromatic flourish.

Trio in E flat major for piano, violin and cello, op. 70 no. 2

Poco sostenuto – Allegro ma non troppo
Allegretto
Allegretto ma non troppo
Finale: Allegro

Carl Czerny, who frequently played Beethoven's music in his presence, believed that he composed the E flat Piano Trio in honour of Countess Erdödy: 'In the Allegretto … he echoed Croation folk-melodies, which he had heard when staying [with her] in Hungary. The same is true of the middle section of the Finale in the same Trio.'[10] Apart from an occasional passing cloud, the music is warm, radiant and spiritually at peace with itself, so it is certainly possible that the Trio, at least in part, is an expression of his deep affection for the Countess. Reichardt considered the third movement 'the loveliest, most graceful thing I have ever heard – my spirit seems to soar and glow whenever I think of it';[11] and Lewis Lockwood describes the second movement most aptly as 'full of humour and kindness'.[12]

Poco sostenuto   Like Beethoven's letters to the Countess, the first movement is a mixture of serious thought, affection, charm and robust humour. The introductory Poco sostenuto (ex. 18.5), with its timeless polyphony and uncertain tonality, is tranquil, even mystical, as each instrument enters in turn a bar apart, the cello proposing C minor, the violin F minor, the piano B flat major and finally all three agreeing on E flat major.

Ex. 18.5

Further modulations lead to a piano cadenza above a dominant pedal (B flat major) and a complete change of mood in the ensuing Allegro.

Allegro ma non troppo   The first group consists of two contrasting themes: one wide-ranging and gallant (ex. 18.6a), all the richer for its mirrored counterpoint and varied dynamics; the other (ex. 18.6b), loud and energetic, built on the sturdiest of foundations.

---

[10] Carl Czerny, quoted in Klugmann, 'Piano Trios and Piano Quartets', p. 122.
[11] Friedrich Reichardt, quoted in Klugmann, 'Piano Trios and Piano Quartets', p. 122.
[12] Lockwood, *Beethoven: The Music and the Life*, p. 306.

Ex. 18.6

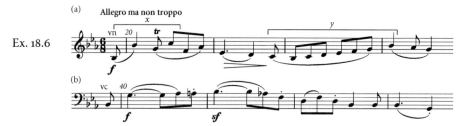

Ex. 18.7

The transition is a complete surprise: the return of the introduction (ex. 18.5), now in compound time and in the remote key of G flat major, leading to the fluent and emotional second group of themes, the cello at times venturing high above the violin in all the excitement (ex. 18.7).

The opening phrase in the second group (*z* in ex. 18.7) is also the central focus of the short development section, framed by the four-note cell (*x*) at the start of the Allegro. Further development takes place in the recapitulation, with the third bar of the opening theme (*y*) played in turn by the violin and cello in fervent conversation. The Poco sostenuto (ex. 18.5) returns twice more – the first time during the recapitulation and the second as an introduction to the coda.

Allegretto This enchanting Hungarian/Croatian dance is an example, quite rare in Beethoven, though not uncommon in Haydn, of a double theme with variations. The two-note rhythmic figure (*u*), with which the movement opens, known in Britain as the 'Scottish snap', is also characteristic of Hungarian music and familiar to audiences today in the music of Béla Bartók. It is catchy and easy to remember, provides a charming link between sections and adds spice to the coda. The first dance, in C major (ex. 18.8a), is poised, graceful and suitable for the politest society, while the second, in C minor (ex. 18.8b), is totally different, its clomping gait and heavily accented off-beats distinctly rustic.

Ex. 18.8

Variations on each dance appear alternately and differ in length and mood; delicately ornamental in the first dance, with the cello's pizzicatos high above the violin's accompanying demisemiquavers; then engagingly assertive in the two C minor variations of the rustic dance. Eventually the dancers disappear into the shadows and the movement ends in C minor, after tentative, perhaps rather sleepy, farewells (two indecisive *ritardandi*) (*u*) as the guests depart and doors are firmly shut.

Allegretto ma non troppo   It is not unusual for Beethoven to do without a slow movement, but to have two Allegrettos side by side in the middle of a four-movement work is very rare, if not unique; rare also to choose three different keys in a four-movement work as he does in this trio: E flat major, C major/minor, A flat major, E flat major. However, the second Allegretto is different in every way from the first – not a dance, but an ardent, romantic song, its spontaneity, expressive lines and flowing accompaniment anticipating the lieder which the twelve-year old Schubert would soon be composing. Each phrase is introduced by variants of the same three-note motive. The central part of the movement is in two contrasting sections: one, an antiphonal conversation between three-part unaccompanied strings and piano; the other, a yearning melody which, with its descanting triplets, rich harmonies and enharmonic modulations, again anticipates Schubert, though this time the impromptus rather than the songs.

Finale: Allegro   According to Carl Czerny, Beethoven 'got many of his ideas from chance occurrences and impressions'[13] and was inspired to write this magnificent finale, a movement of extraordinary energy, after watching a galloping horse. There was to be no let-up in tempo: 'If there is anywhere a ritardando', Beethoven wrote in a letter to Breitkopf & Härtel, 'then remove this too – there should be no ritardando in that whole movement.'[14] The finale is rich in melodic ideas with several themes and motives jostling for attention. The first group accounts for two of them: an arresting and brilliant introduction and a carefree melody (ex. 18.9) – the sort of open-air music which it is tempting to whistle.

Ex. 18.9

Like the first Presto in the *Kreutzer* Sonata, it is in true *concertante* style with brilliant passagework and short cadenzas for each instrument, a *moto perpetuo* development section and a strong sense of forward momentum – qualities which compelled Donald Tovey to resort to unprofessorial superlatives, when he described the recapitulation as 'stupendous'.[15] The brilliant introduction also launches the three cadenzas and adds glamour

[13] Carl Czerny, quoted in Cooper, *Beethoven and the Creative Process*, p. 43.
[14] *Letters of Beethoven*, Letter 218, Vienna; 26 May 1809: Beethoven to Breitkopf & Härtel.
[15] Tovey, *Beethoven*, p. 108.

to the development, recapitulation and coda. There are some moments of reflection too, but for the most part each succeeding idea seems more dramatic than the one before. The first of two magnificent themes in the second group, for example (ex. 18.10a), accompanied by pounding chords inspired perhaps by those galloping horses, is comparable in brilliance to the heroic third theme in the first movement of the *Kreutzer* (ex. 14.6), while the climax of the finale – and indeed of the whole Trio – is reached in the monumental second theme (ex. 18.10b), its supreme, magisterial authority underlined by several later appearances, not least in that 'stupendous' recapitulation.

Ex. 18.10

String Quartet in E flat major, op. 74 (*Harp*)

The year 1809 began well for Beethoven. The legal contract designed to provide him with an annual income for life, which had been initiated by Baron Gleichenstein and Countess Erdödy, was agreed on 26 February and signed by three of Beethoven's young patrons, Archduke Rudolph, Prince Kinsky and Prince Lobkowitz:

> The daily proofs which Herr Ludwig van Beethoven is giving of his extraordinary talents as a musician and composer awaken the desire that he surpass the great expectations which are justified by his past achievements. But as it has been demonstrated that only one who is as free from care as possible can ... create works of magnitude which are exalted and which ennoble art, the undersigned have decided to place Herr Ludwig van Beethoven in a position where the necessaries of life shall not cause him embarrassment or clog his powerful genius.[1]

Enemy occupation and the death of Haydn

Six weeks later, on 9 April 1809, Austria declared war on France for the third time, only to be defeated yet again after a series of disastrous battles. The imperial family, including Archduke Rudolph, left Austria on 4 May for the safety of Hungary, inspiring Beethoven to compose the affectionate first movement of the Piano Sonata in E flat major, op. 81a, *Das Lebewohl* (*Farewell*), which he completed after the Archduke returned the following year. The French were quick to lay siege to Vienna; the bombardment of the city was at times so severe that 'rich and poor, high and low, young and old ... found themselves crowded indiscriminately in cellars and fireproof vaults.'[2] Beethoven 'spent the greater part of the time in a cellar in the house of his brother, Carl, where he covered his head with pillows so as not to hear the cannons',[3] and also, no doubt, to protect his hearing.

In another part of the city a cannon-ball landed in the courtyard of Haydn's house, and throughout the day there was shooting from a fortress close by. Although 'our good Papa composed himself a bit', wrote Johann Essler, Haydn's faithful servant and copyist, 'his nerves were hit too hard ... his whole body sank.'[4] Vienna surrendered on 12 May, and its citizens were subjected to the usual humiliations and restrictions of enemy occupation. There was no doubt in anyone's mind that Haydn's death on 31 May

---

[1] Thayer, *The Life of Beethoven*, p. 457.

[2] Thayer, *The Life of Beethoven*, p. 465.

[3] Ferdinand Ries, *Notizen*, quoted in Thayer, *The Life of Beethoven*, p. 465.

[4] Johann Essler, Haydn's devoted servant and copyist, quoted in Landon, *Haydn: Chronicle and Works: The Late Years*, p. 386.

was hastened by what he himself described, with tears in his eyes, as 'this unhappy war [which] pushes me right to the floor'.[5] Inflation was rampant: 'We have been suffering misery in a most concentrated form', Beethoven wrote in a letter to Breitkopf & Härtel on 26 July 1809. 'Since 4 May I have produced very little work, at most a fragment here and there. The whole course of events has in my case affected both body and soul.'[6]

Not surprisingly, full implementation of the new contract was delayed by all this turmoil, and although the Archduke's contribution was paid regularly for the rest of Beethoven's life, the two other contributors were less dependable. For several years a series of delays and uncertainties caused Beethoven great distress – all the more so because he had kept his unwritten side of the bargain in a series of new dedications to all three of his patrons, among them the *Harp* Quartet to Prince Lobkowitz.[7] Prince Kinsky left Vienna for Bohemia soon after the contract was signed to raise a regiment from workers on his estates, and his first payment was delayed until June 1810. He was killed in a riding accident two years later and payments were again withheld until his widow, Princess Karolina, whom Beethoven described as 'one of the prettiest and plumpest women in Vienna',[8] agreed a new settlement, including arrears caused by the delay. Prince Lobkowitz was declared bankrupt in 1813 and his financial affairs were put in the hands of his brother-in-law, Prince Joseph Schwarzenburg. His contributions to the contract were also withheld for some time and only restored, again including arrears, after a court settlement in 1815.

To add to his woes during the occupation that summer, Beethoven was unable to take his annual holiday in the country. When he was too distracted to compose, he copied exercises and other extracts from various theoretical treatises – including those written by his admired teacher, Albrechtsberger, who had also died that year – in preparation for the composition lessons he planned to give the Archduke when he returned to Vienna, studies which must have contributed to his increasing interest in stricter forms of polyphony. In addition he asked Breitkopf & Härtel to send him 'all the scores you have … Haydn, Mozart, Johann Sebastian Bach, Emmanuel Bach and so forth',[9] partly for 'a little singing party' which he

---

[5] Haydn, in conversation with Georg von Griesinger, quoted in Landon, *Haydn: Chronicle and Works: The Late Years*, p. 385.

[6] *Letters of Beethoven*, Letter 220, 26 July 1809: Beethoven to Breitkopf & Härtel.

[7] Beethoven's dedications to the three signatories of the legal contract include: the Fourth and Fifth Piano Concertos and the *Lebewohl* Sonata to Archduke Rudolph (further dedications to the Archduke would follow later); the Mass in C to Prince Kinsky and several songs to Princess Kinsky; the Fifth and Sixth Symphonies to Prince Lobkowitz (jointly with Prince Razumovsky) in addition to several other important dedications: the op. 18 Quartets in 1801, the *Eroica* in 1806, the Triple Concerto in 1807 and the *Harp* Quartet, op. 74. One further work, the song cycle *An die ferne Geliebte*, op. 98, would be dedicated to Prince Lobkowitz in 1816 as a peace offering after a court settlement.

[8] Clive, *Beethoven and his World*; see Princess Karolina Maria Kinsky, p. 184.

[9] *Letters of Beethoven*, Letter 220, 26 July 1809: Beethoven to Breitkopf & Härtel.

had held every week in his rooms before 'this accursed war' started, and which he hoped to revive after it was over.

In spite of the horrors of the siege and the inevitable restrictions of the occupation, the list of works that Beethoven completed in 1809 is an impressive one, signalling in particular his re-engagement with the piano after some years of partial neglect. As it happens, four of the eight works listed that year – the Fifth Piano Concerto, the *Lebewohl* Piano Sonata, op. 81a, the Arietta buffa, *L'Amante impaziente*, op. 82 no. 3, and the *Harp* Quartet, op. 74, together with the Piano Trio, op. 70 no. 2, composed the previous year – are in E flat major; generally a resilient key, but a complex and ambiguous one in the *Harp* Quartet.

Beethoven's tribute to Haydn?

Beethoven composed his tenth string quartet in the months following Haydn's death on 31 May 1809, seemingly as an expression of his deep affection for Haydn and also of his thoughts, in Nicholas Marston's words, on the passing of 'the entire musical tradition that he had come to embody'.[10] The evidence is compelling – most obviously in frequent references in each movement to variants of a three-note motive (z in ex. 15.3) in Act 2 of Fidelio, where the starving, imprisoned Florestan bids farewell to joy and perhaps to life itself. Beethoven returned to the same phrase in the opening two bars of the *Lebewohl* Sonata, composed at much the same time as the *Harp* Quartet, and spelt out precisely what he meant by placing the three syllables of the word, *Le-be-wohl*, beneath the first three notes of the sonata (ex. 15.4). See 'The "Farewell" motive' in Chapter 15.

String Quartet no. 10 in E flat major, op. 74 (*Harp*)

Poco Adagio – Allegro
Adagio ma non troppo
Presto – Più presto quasi Prestissimo
Allegretto con Variazioni

Poco Adagio The depth of Beethoven's feelings is reflected in the restrained beauty of the introduction, its mystic polyphony, its silences, and above all its tonal uncertainties. The key of E flat major is certainly an appropriate choice for a tribute to Haydn, the most resilient of all composers, but from the first bar onwards the key is repeatedly challenged and dragged down by recurring D flats, variously harmonized – a compelling metaphor for sorrow and loss. Two phrases in particular, the first *sotto voce* (x in ex. 19.1a), the second, an expressive variant of the 'Farewell' motive (y in ex. 19.1b), provide inspiration for subsequent movements, most conspicuously the theme and variations with which the quartet ends (ex. 19.7).

---

[10] Marston, 'Haydns Geist aus Beethovens Handen', p. 125.

Ex. 19.1

Allegro   However, Beethoven's preoccupations were more visionary and complex than the extensive use of a leitmotif, important though that is, and are best summarized in the opening lines of T. S. Eliot's *Four Quartets* – 'Time present and time past / Are both perhaps present in time future / And time future contained in time past.'[11] The classical past is remembered and cherished in the Allegretto con Variazioni, and mystic visions of the future are explored in the introductory Poco Adagio, which no doubt prompted Adolph Bernhard Marx to describe op. 74 as the first of Beethoven's 'last quartets'.[12] Profound sorrow is expressed in the intro-

---

[11] T. S. Eliot, *Burnt Norton*, from *Four Quartets*, in *Collected Poems*, p. 189.

[12] Adolph Bernhard Marx, quoted in Marston, 'Haydns Geist aus Beethovens Handen', p. 110.

duction and in the slow movement, and extreme distress in the Presto. Experimental tone colours, notably the extensive use of pizzicato in the first movement, new kinds of structure as well as old, fantasy, variation, virtuosity, tonality – these surprise and delight, but also challenge performers and listeners alike.

Like many a novel or play, there is a plot and a sub-plot in the ensuing Allegro – a narrative in which two very different aspects of genius are explored and to some extent shared. One is complex, the other childlike in its simplicity – attributes which many of the greatest composers possess to some degree, Beethoven among them, but which Haydn possessed in full measure. There are three productive motives in the complex principal theme (x, y, z in ex. 19.2), the first (z) common to both narratives. The other two are explored contrapuntally at various points in the movement, and a variant of y stages a powerful and tragic drama in the development section.

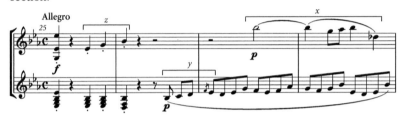

Ex. 19.2

However, as every actor knows, children will always steal the show, and the childlike pizzicato episodes somehow define the movement and remain in the memory when other, more complex and ambitious ideas, are forgotten. Beethoven had already begun to explore the use of thematic pizzicato for cello in the slow movement of the third *Razumovsky* quartet, and would do so again at some length for both violin and cello in the first movement of the *Archduke* Trio two years later.

But in this movement each pizzicato episode is based exclusively on simple arpeggio patterns, not on melodic lines. Some critics deplore the quartet's traditional nickname as trivializing the work, but a harp, universally associated in art and literature with 'flights of angels', such as those which Horatio so touchingly prayed for after the death of the Prince in Shakespeare's *Hamlet*, might well have been the instrument which Beethoven intended to evoke in Haydn's memory, not least because, with one exception – the first violin's extraordinarily violent cadenza – the pizzicato episodes are consistently played *pianissimo* or *piano* above or below a sustained and mystical background, as if heard from a great distance (ex. 19.3).

Ex. 19.3

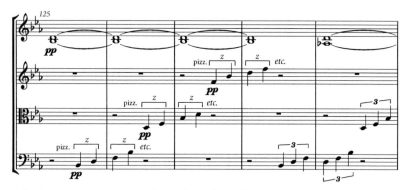

Adagio ma non troppo   In outline, the Adagio is a simple rondo (A–B–A–C–A+coda) but in practice it is an exquisite and almost unbroken song, characterized, Gerald Abraham suggests, by 'that masculine tenderness which is almost peculiar to Beethoven in the whole range of music'.[13] The opening melody (ex. 19.4a), an extended fantasy based on the 'Farewell' motive (y), is marked *cantabile* and accompanied warmly and lovingly, though soon darkened, as in the introduction, by grief-stricken flattened sevenths (y). Although the first episode (ex. 19.4b), with its recurrent weeping motive (v), is inconsolable, the second episode in D flat major (ex. 19.4c) offers comfort and encouragement for a time.

Ex. 19.4

In its two later appearances the rondo theme is more improvisatory and its accompaniment more florid – magically so in its final appearance, when joined by renewed pizzicato textures on the viola and by the second violin's fluttering demisemiquavers. The weeping motive introduces the coda as well, together with fragments of the rondo theme, and the movement ends with soft, expressive chords alternating with heart-broken, off-beat silences.

Presto   The Presto bursts into life in the same key and with the same all-pervasive rhythmic figure (w in ex. 19.5) as in the opening bars of the C

[13] Abraham, *Beethoven's Second-Period Quartets*, p. 60. Earlier examples of Beethoven's 'masculine tenderness' include the Adagio in the A major Violin Sonata, op. 30 no. 1, and later examples, the Arietta in the C minor Piano Sonata, op. 111, and the Cavatina in op. 130.

minor Symphony, which Beethoven had completed the previous year. Initially forceful, the dynamics become unsettled, with later bars increasingly distant, suggesting that the movement is not so much a protest against 'this accursed war' or a fist shaking at fate, as an expression of the emotional turmoil Beethoven must have experienced during those months after Haydn's death.

Ex. 19.5

At a later performance given by Schuppanzigh's quartet in December 1824, Schubert and his friend Joseph Lanz were particularly intrigued by rhythmic ambiguities in this movement 'where, within a 3/4 metre, the rhythm seemed to resemble 6/8 time. It was so well accentuated in performance that both of us could only detect the real beat with difficulty. This gave us a lot of fun.'[14]

Più presto quasi Prestissimo   The wild Più presto (ex. 19.6), played *sempre fortissimo* or *sempre forte* throughout, is even more of an emotional roller-coaster, as two diametrically opposed ideas face up to each other. The first (*s*), introduced by the viola, is an assertive and strangely archaic *cantus firmus*, with staccatos placed above each note suggesting the steady tolling of bells – a further metaphor for death. The second theme, introduced by the cello, is a ferocious version of the 'Farewell' motive (*y*).

Ex. 19.6

The Presto (ex. 19.5) is played three times, the Prestissimo (ex. 19.6) twice, both without alteration (A–B–A–B–A+coda). But tensions are gradually dissolved and eventually forgotten in the quiet forty-five-bar coda which leads without a break into the finale.

Allegretto con Variazioni   After so much emotional turmoil, the elegance and classic formality of the last movement comes as a complete surprise – a musical parterre in which the theme (ex. 19.7), mostly created from the 'Farewell' motive (*y*), and each succeeding variation is contained within the same precise dimensions, like flower beds encompassed by geometrically shaped and neatly clipped box hedges in a formal seventeenth-century garden.

[14] Steblin and Stocken, 'Reminiscences about Schubert by his Forgotten Friend', p. 232: *Studying with Sechter: Newly Recovered Reminisciences about Schubert by his Forgotten Friend, the Composer, Joseph Lanz.*

Ex. 19.7

Even the dynamics are arranged formally, with the first, third and fifth variation loud and the second, fourth and sixth soft, as Beethoven travels back in time, bypassing his own more adventurous sets of variations to embrace once more the classical certainties of his youth. Although earlier movements are not forgotten – the intrusive D flats in the opening bars of the quartet, for example, reappear as a throbbing triplet pedal in the second half of Variation 6 (ex. 19.8) – this was clearly a time for introspection, for remembering the good moments in Beethoven's long and complex relationship with Haydn, but also perhaps those less happy moments which should have been handled better.

Ex. 19.8

The beauty of this touching movement, one which Haydn himself would surely have enjoyed, is further enhanced by the ethereal nature of the theme itself and many of its variations, achieved by laying the stress on the weak second beat of each bar rather than on the first. There are some assertive moments in the odd-numbered variations and the coda. But after a final, distraught *cri de cœur*, played *fortissimo* with *sforzandi* on the second beat of each bar, the quartet ends quietly and reverently with the simplest of cadences.

PART FIVE ※ 1810–15

'Interpreters must be able to dream, to enthuse;
the flower must blossom in their souls.'

Carl Flesch

String Quartet in F minor, op. 95
(*Quartetto serioso*)

Beethoven completed fewer compositions in 1810 than in previous years, partly as a result, perhaps, of his despair when Therese Malfatti turned down his proposal of marriage: 'Your news has plunged me from the heights of the most sublime ecstasy down into the depths', he told his friend Ignaz von Gleichenstein, who had been given the unenviable task by the Malfatti family of telling Beethoven that he was no longer welcome at their home, except on musical evenings. 'For your poor B, no happiness can come from outside. You must create everything for yourself in your own heart; and only in the world of ideals can you find friends.'[1] As a parting gift he presented *Für Elise* to Therese Malfatti on 27 April, no doubt with a lump in his throat. Finding friends in 'the world of ideals' was not a figment of his imagination, however. 'Quartets every week', he noted cheerfully in one of his sketchbooks referring, no doubt, to the many musical gatherings held, among other venues, in Nikolaus Zmeskall's apartment in the Bürgerspital in central Vienna, and attended by members of his inner circle of friends.

Baron Nikolaus Zmeskall von Domanovecz

Nikolaus Zmeskall (1759–1833), a lawyer in the Hungarian court chancellery in Vienna, was a gifted and enthusiastic amateur cellist who devoted every spare moment to playing, discussing, promoting and listening to music. His admiration for Beethoven, whom he helped in numerous, often very mundane, ways never faltered. He was one of the original subscribers to the op. 1 piano trios and a founder member of the Gesellschaft der Musikfreunde, bequeathing to the Society his music library, which included such valuable manuscripts as Mozart's Quintet for Piano and Wind, K452, discussed in Chapter 8, and over 130 notes and letters written to him by Beethoven.

Zmeskall, a confirmed bachelor, and Beethoven, a most unwilling and frustrated one, often lunched together at the Zum weissen Schwan. Relations between them were generally warm and affectionate in spite of Beethoven's frequent teasing and jokiness. It may have been the essential seriousness of Zmeskall's character, as well as his key position as host at many of those chamber music soirées, which earned him the dedication,

---

[1] *Letters of Beethoven*, Letter 254, Spring, 1810: Beethoven to Gleichenstein. Therese Malfatti kept the autograph of the Bagatelle WoO 59, throughout her life. There was some confusion, however, when it was eventually published in 1867 and mistakenly given its present title, *Für Elise* (not *Für Therese*.)

inscribed by the composer himself on the original autograph: '*Quartetto serioso*, 1810, dedicated to Herr von Zmeskall, and written in the month of October by his friend LvBthvn.'[2]

Beethoven certainly valued the interest and support of his most loyal friends, especially when early versions of his more experimental compositions were first tried out. Initially, he wanted to restrict performances of the F minor Quartet to 'a small circle of connoisseurs'. In a letter to the conductor Sir George Smart, his most influential advocate in England, he even went so far as to insist that it was 'never to be performed in public', adding that, if he wanted 'some quartets for public performance, [he] would compose them for this purpose occasionally.'[3] No doubt, there were several private performances of the F minor Quartet at gatherings of 'connoisseurs' in Nikolaus Zmeskall's apartment and elsewhere, and some further revision as well, but Beethoven postponed its public premiere until May 1814, and it was not published until December 1816.

Goethe, *Egmont* and the String Quartet in F minor

Before embarking on the F minor Quartet, Beethoven celebrated Archduke Rudolph's safe return to Vienna in January 1810, by completing the last movement ('Das Wiedersehn') of the *Lebewohl* Sonata, and then spent some months composing extensive incidental music for a production in June of Goethe's play *Egmont*. The magnificent Overture is familiar to every concert-goer, but the other nine movements do not fit easily into a concert programme, and are rarely heard. Beethoven shared the play's ideals, and was moved by the historic events on which it was based, all the more perhaps because Count Egmont was Flemish and the Beethoven family on his father's side was of Flemish descent. Like *Fidelio*, *Egmont* is a story of love and heroism on the one hand and of oppression on the other. Unlike *Fidelio*, however, the play ends tragically: a Flemish nobleman, Count Egmont, challenges the oppressive regime of the Duke of Alba during the Spanish occupation of the Netherlands in the sixteenth century, but is captured and imprisoned. His beloved Clärchen tries to rescue him, but takes her own life when she fails to save him from execution.

Johann Wolfgang von Goethe (1749–1832) had mixed feelings about musical settings of his work, but he was uncharacteristically complimentary when he attended a later production of the play, commending in particular Beethoven's setting of the Melodrama: 'He entered into my intentions with an admirable stroke of genius',[4] he wrote, referring to the scene where the spirit of Liberty, in the form of Count Egmont's beloved, appears to him in a dream the night before his execution. She places a wreath on

---

[2] Stitch, 'String Quartets', p. 97.

[3] *Letters of Beethoven*, Letter 664, 11 October 1816: Beethoven to Sir George Smart in London.

[4] Daschner, 'Music for the Stage', p. 220.

his head and tells him that his fellow-countrymen, inspired by his example, will rise up and regain their freedom and independence.

When they eventually met at Teplitz in July 1812, Goethe was also impressed by Beethoven himself, telling his wife that he had never seen a 'more intensely focused, dynamic or fervent artist'.[5] For his part, Beethoven had always revered Goethe: 'I have done [so] since my childhood',[6] he had told him in an earlier letter. Like most young people, he would surely have been impressed by Goethe's celebrated novella *The Sorrows of Young Werther*, one of the earliest intimations of the new romanticism, and also by his confession that, in writing the book, he had decided 'to surrender to his inner self',[7] a decision that Goethe himself later rejected, but which Beethoven certainly understood and increasingly embraced. *Egmont* was still on his mind six months later: 'that glorious *Egmont*, on which I have again reflected through you', he told Goethe in the same letter, 'and which I have … reproduced in music as I felt when I read it.'[8] Both the Quartet and the Overture to *Egmont* share the dark, dramatic key of F minor with the dungeon scene in *Fidelio*, and both end in F major. In both, the submediant, D major, provides a foil to the tonic, a rare juxtaposition of keys perhaps defining, as Seow-Chin Ong has suggested, 'two different planes of activity, one spiritual and the other more earthly'.[9] There are thematic links as well; for instance, the opening motive in the quartet (*x* in ex. 20.2) is clearly a variant of sketches for the fifth movement in *Egmont* (*Zwischenakt III*) (ex. 20.1).

Ex. 20.1

After completing the F minor Quartet, Beethoven went on to compose three intensely romantic settings of poems by Goethe, published in 1811 as op. 83, and dedicated to Princess Kinsky. With lines like 'Do not dry, tears of unhappy love' or such titles as 'Longing', it is clear that Beethoven had yet to recover from the emotional turmoil at least partly caused by Therese Malfatti's rejection. Moreover, the raw intensity of the *Quartetto serioso* and those songs suggests that, like Goethe before him, Beethoven had indeed 'surrendered to his inner self' as never before when composing them, expressing his emotions in an unusually personal way – one of the reasons, perhaps, for his initial decision to restrict performances of the

---

[5] Clive, *Beethoven and his World*, p. 134. Goethe, in a letter to his wife.

[6] *Letters of Beethoven*, Letter 303, 12 April 1811: Beethoven to Goethe.

[7] Quoted in Davies, *Europe: A History*, p. 613.

[8] *Letters of Beethoven*, Letter 303, 12 April 1811: Beethoven to Goethe.

[9] Seow-Chin Ong, 'Aspects of the Genesis of Beethoven's String Quartet in F minor, op. 95', p. 133.

quartet to his circle of friends and supporters. He must also have realized that, with its remote modulations, extreme chromaticism and economy of texture and form, he had ventured into uncharted territory, and needed time to take stock before venturing further; certainly much of the quartet sounds, even looks on the page, like a late period work.

String Quartet no. 11 in F minor, op. 95 (*Quartetto serioso*)

Allegro con brio
Allegretto ma non troppo – Allegro assai vivace ma serioso
Larghetto espressivo – Allegretto agitato – Allegro

Allegro con brio As in *Egmont*, the first movement is about confrontation: power and oppression on the one hand; inner strength and heroism on the other. With the first act of the drama completed after a mere twenty-three bars, there is no room in this concise example of sonata form for repeats, introductions or lengthy transitions. The intimidating opening motive in F minor (*x* in ex. 20.2) and the harsh commands that follow (*y*) are to be played, in Daniel Mason's telling phrase, with 'tremendous force, as of a coiled spring released'.[10]

Ex. 20.2

They are met, however, with sustained, though by no means passive, resistance; the cello's thrusting arpeggios see to that. The challenge is repeated and again it is serenely confronted, leading to the spacious and ethereal second group (ex. 20.3). The first violin reaches for the heavens in a mood of spiritual ecstasy (*z*), while the other three instruments share

Ex. 20.3

[10] Mason, *The Quartets of Beethoven*, p. 146.

in turn a flowing, lyrical theme (*u*) and, in response to further goading (*x*), present a united front in an eloquent, though emphatic, unison scale of A major.

A chromatic melody follows (ex. 20.4), 'almost Franckian in its ripe romanticism', Gerald Abraham suggests,[11] and yet another triumphant unison scale, this time in affirmative D major emerging, as Seow-Chin Ong puts it, 'suddenly out of D flat major without any forewarning and, as a result … spotlighted with unusual clarity, even luminosity'.[12] Consciously or not, variants of a chromatic phrase (*v*) in the melody reappear at significant moments in each movement – a fine example of cyclic form, which occurs in several of Beethoven's mature compositions, including his recent Fifth Symphony.

Ex. 20.4

The turbulent twenty-two bar development is dominated by the first two motives (*x*, *y*) and, after a foreshortened recapitulation, the movement ends *pianissimo*, inconclusively on a unison F.

Allegretto ma non troppo   The second movement seems simple enough at first: a gentle, descending scale on the cello by way of introduction, followed by a restrained and poignant melody (ex. 20.5a) above a flowing accompaniment. It soon becomes clear, however, that emotionally the movement is anything but simple. For a start, the key is called into question almost at once with a hint of A major in the third bar of the introduction, while the tension between G minor and D major in the sorrowful opening melody (ex. 20.5a) suggests darker thoughts. Feelings of loss are expressed in the wandering fugato that follows (ex. 20.5b), recalling the chromatic inflections (*v* in ex. 20.4) of the previous movement. Though fugal entries are unevenly spaced, polyphonic lines flow naturally, and the emotional emptiness of the underlying drama is never compromised by contrapuntal necessity.

Ex. 20.5

The fugato, now joined by a decorative, though angular, countersubject, dominates the central section of the movement, and reappears later in

[11] Abraham, *Beethoven's Second-Period Quartets*, p. 68.

[12] Seow-Chin Ong, 'Aspects of the Genesis of Beethoven's String Quartet in F minor, op. 95', p. 133.

an extended recapitulation. As Daniel Mason has shown, there is one particularly intriguing mystery in the movement.[13] The opening melody (ex. 20.5a) is the perfect companion and countersubject for the fugal theme (ex. 20.5b), but they never appear simultaneously. It is inconceivable that Beethoven would have failed to notice the connection between them, so a symbolic explanation may be found in his *Egmont* music: Clärchen and Count Egmont separated in life, but mystically united in death, perhaps? Or there may be a raw, more personal explanation: the lives of Therese Malfatti and Beethoven destined to be for ever divided?

Allegro assai vivace ma serioso   The chromatic motive (*v*) is poignantly remembered as the Allegretto draws to a close, but the Allegro assai erupts with extreme violence (ex. 20.6), signalling a return to the confrontations of the first movement. Questions are left in the air, the rests as overbearing as the questions themselves, and momentum is maintained by the obsessive dotted rhythmic figures to which Beethoven would later return in such powerful movements as the Vivace alla Marcia in the A major Piano Sonata, op. 101, and the *Grosse Fuge*, op. 133. With its two alternating and contrasted sections, the broad outlines of the movement are similar to many of Beethoven's earlier scherzos (A–B–A–B–A+coda). But his unprecedented use of the word 'serioso' in the title of this movement, as well as in the quartet as a whole, underlines the importance he attached to the issues involved: sound and fury in the first section (ex. 20.6a), restraint and beauty in the second, with its gentle, aspiring melody (ex. 20.6b) – a further, more open version of the chromatic motive (*v*).

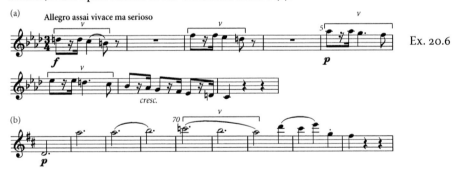

Ex. 20.6

Attempts to evoke a peaceful response are roughly thrust aside, however, and the movement ends with yet more violence, *più allegro* and *fortissimo*.

Larghetto espressivo – Allegretto agitato – Allegro   The finale opens with a short introduction, the dotted rhythms of the previous movement now more restrained. However, the recitative-like contours are angular, wide-ranging and emotional as they merge imperceptibly into the compact sonata-rondo that follows. The familiar chromatic motive (*v*) from previous movements is never far below the surface, and two further motives

[13] Mason, *The Quartets of Beethoven*, pp. 148–9.

(*w*, *s*) are vital components in one of Beethoven's most unsettled, nerve-end movements – a study of mental distress almost to the point of breakdown, with scarcely any let-up in tension or momentum. The rondo theme (ex. 20.7) provides most of the melodic and accompanying material, but it is persistently thrown off course before it can be completed.

Ex. 20.7

By contrast, the first episode, though short, is robust, with assertive *sforzandi* on every beat, and a degree of stability is eventually achieved in the first of two codas, in which two motives (*w*, *s*) play a significant part. F minor makes way for F major and the movement ends with an unexpected second coda: an excited, brilliant *tour de force*, part *opera buffa*, part fugato (ex. 20.8), and yet another version of the fugal motive (*v*), though now inverso and reverso – a further reminder of Beethoven's current studies in strict counterpoint.

Ex. 20.8

Predictably, this cheerful conclusion to an otherwise intensely concentrated and serious work has raised critical hackles over the years, most famously in Vincent d'Indy's comment that 'one might imagine [that] some light Rossinian finale had strayed into this atmosphere of sustained beauty, and we think that no interpretation could palliate this error of a genius.'[14]

However if, as the evidence discussed earlier seems to suggest, the F minor Quartet reflects the underlying spiritual tensions and emotional conflicts in Goethe's *Egmont*, and at the same time provides Beethoven with a metaphor for his own feelings during a truly disastrous year, everything in this powerful if enigmatic work falls into place. The brilliant coda with which the quartet ends may then be regarded as a joyful expression of spiritual renewal, whether for *Clärchen* as she rejoins her beloved in paradise or, as Robert Simpson suggests, for *Count Egmont* 'a fleeting sense of justification and release at the moment of death',[15] or for Beethoven as a victory over his many emotional troubles, 'as he surrendered to his [own] inner self' or for all three combined. So it may not be altogether surprising that Beethoven chose to dedicate such an intensely personal work to one of his closest friends and that, for some years at least, he allowed only an inner circle of connoisseurs to play it or listen to it.

---

[14] Vincent d'Indy, quoted in *Cobbett's Cyclopedic Survey of Chamber Music*, vol. 1, p. 97.

[15] Simpson, 'The Chamber Music for Strings', p. 262.

Piano Trio in B flat major, op. 97 (*Archduke*)

The Piano Trio in B flat major, op. 97, Beethoven's last complete piano trio,[1] could hardly be more different from the F minor String Quartet, even though sketches for the two works appear in consecutive sketchbooks.[2] In contrast to the personal traumas and tensions expressed in the *Quartetto serioso*, the *Archduke* Trio is unhurried, spacious and noble; an Olympian work unconcerned with the day-to-day cares of ordinary mortals. It has its enigmatic moments, especially in the last two movements, but there are plenty of enigmas, no doubt, on Mount Olympus too.

An early autograph dated 3 March – 20 March 1811[3] suggests that Beethoven may have composed the *Archduke* in a little over three weeks, though modern scholars disagree over the dates of the manuscript. It was played informally for the first time at Baron Neuworth's house two days after Beethoven finished it, but he then set it aside, as he often did with new compositions. The first public performance of the Trio, perhaps in revised form, was given by Schuppanzigh, Linke and Beethoven himself at a charity concert on 11 April 1814, in the hall of the Hotel Zum Römischen Kaiser, and it was repeated a few days later. Both were bittersweet occasions, because it was clear to all who were present in the hall, including the composer Louis Spohr and the pianist Ignaz Moscheles,[4] that although Beethoven was demonstrably at the height of his powers as a composer, his hearing was now so seriously impaired that he would have to give up performing in public.

The poignancy of the occasion was all the greater because Beethoven

---

[1] Beethoven wrote the tender, child-like Allegretto in B flat major for Piano Trio, WoO 39, in 1812, for Maximiliane Brentano, the ten-year-old daughter of Antonie Brentano, now generally accepted as his 'Immortal Beloved' (see Chapter 22 below) 'to encourage her in her piano playing.' Clearly, her piano playing was most successfully encouraged, because in 1821 Beethoven dedicated a much greater prize to her, the sublime Piano Sonata in E major, op. 109.

[2] Landsberg 11 (January–September 1810) and a dispersed sketchbook (late 1810 – Summer 1811).

[3] Nicholas Marston (Cooper, *The Beethoven Compendium*, p. 230) suggests that the 'dates, even if reliable, probably refer only to the writing of the autograph rather than to the total period of composition; moreover, the fact that the *Archduke* was probably revised in 1814–15 means that the composition of the work as we know it can no longer be confined solely to the years 1810–11.' Seow-Chin Ong ('The Autograph of Beethoven's "Archduke" Trio, op. 97'), on the other hand, believes that there was no later revision of the *Archduke* Trio, and Beethoven's dates are to be taken seriously.

[4] Ignaz Moscheles (1794–1870) was a fervent admirer of Beethoven. In spite of his growing reputation as an international concert pianist, he found time in 1814 to arrange a piano version of *Fidelio* – a project approved by Beethoven. As the project progressed, Beethoven treated him 'with the kindest indulgence' during their frequent meetings together.

had created in the last of his piano trios a new world of sound, almost symphonic in weight and texture, pointing forward to the rich tone colours of
nineteenth-century Romanticism, sounds which by then he himself could
imagine, but hear only partially. 'The densely sonorous textures are perhaps the most remarkable feature' writes Nigel Fortune. 'Beethoven uses
the developing resources of the most up-to-date pianos of his day – indeed,
causes the makers to keep up with him – and increases the sound of the
stringed instruments in order to match the piano; one feels the developments in instrument manufacture, instrumental technique and Beethoven's art to be indivisible.'[5] The Trio was eventually published in Vienna
by Sigmund Steiner in 1816 and at the same time by Robert Birchall in London, and dedicated to Beethoven's royal pupil, Archduke Rudolph.

Archduke Rudolph

As a member of the imperial family and later as Cardinal Archbishop of
Olmütz, Archduke Rudolph (1788–1831) was undoubtedly the grandest of
Beethoven's pupils. He was the youngest of Emperor Leopold II's twelve
children and he was only four when his oldest brother, Franz I, succeeded
to the throne on the death of their father in 1792. As a young man in Bonn,
Beethoven had admired Rudolph's grandfather, Joseph II, for his enlightened, reforming views, and in 1790 he composed the *Cantata on the Death
of Emperor Joseph II* in response to his death. Moreover, during his later
years in Bonn, he received encouragement and support from Rudolph's
uncle, Maximilian, the Elector of Cologne; so he was probably gratified to
be invited to teach such a talented member of the imperial family, who had
inherited the celebrated Habsburg musical gifts in full measure.

Like most music students at some stage of their development, the young
Rudolph realized that he had learnt what he could from his current teacher,
the court composer Anton Tayber, and that it was time for a change. It
is not known when his lessons with Beethoven began – possibly as early
as 1804, but certainly before 1808, when Beethoven dedicated the Fourth
Piano Concerto to him, the first in a series of masterpieces he would dedicate to the Archduke in future years.[6] Lessons in composition were added
later and were so successful that, on Beethoven's recommendation, Steiner
published in 1819 the Archduke's *Forty Variations on a theme by Beethoven*.
Composition lessons continued irregularly, often by correspondence, at
least until 1824, five years after the Archduke's election at the age of thirty-
one as Cardinal Archbishop of Olmütz. Although Beethoven sometimes

---

[5] Fortune, 'The Chamber Music with Piano', pp. 229–30.

[6] Beethoven's dedications to Archduke Rudolph included the Fourth and Fifth Piano
Concertos; the Piano Sonata in E flat major, op. 81a (*Das Lebewohl*); the piano
arrangement (by Moscheles) of the final version of *Fidelio*; the *Archduke* Piano Trio,
op. 97; the Violin Sonata in G, op. 96; the *Hammerklavier* Piano Sonata, op. 106; the
Piano Sonata in C minor, op. 111; the string quartet and piano duo versions of the
Grosse Fuge, op. 134; the *Missa Solemnis*, op. 123.

found the lessons irksome, he valued the Archduke's unvarying support – even his protection on occasion – and, of course, the regular contributions to his income, which had been agreed in the celebrated contract discussed in Chapter 19.

Famously quarrelsome, even with some of his dearest, most loyal friends, Beethoven never seems to have quarrelled with the Archduke. He was, after all, a member of the royal family and even for Beethoven that must have counted for something. Rudolph understood and admired the genius in Beethoven, and seems to have treated him and his many foibles with unfailing patience and respect: 'You would certainly not be made to feel his high rank',[7] Beethoven told his friend Gleichenstein, whom he planned to introduce to the Archduke at a rehearsal.

In later years Beethoven seems to have regarded the Cardinal Archbishop as a friend; indeed, it was his own idea to compose the monumental *Missa Solemnis*, op. 123, as a personal, if much delayed, tribute to him on his enthronement: 'Even though I am no courtier', he wrote in 1820, 'yet I think that Y[our] I[mperial] H[ighness] has got to know this about me, that it is no mere frigid influence that attaches me to you, but a true and deep affection which has always bound me to Your Highness and has ever inspired me.'[8] The many letters which Beethoven wrote to the Archduke were carefully preserved in his magnificent library and later bequeathed, like Nikolaus Zmeskall's library, to the Gesellschaft der Musikfreunde. Some letters are practical – lesson times, rehearsal arrangements or manuscripts to be copied by one of the royal copyists or requests to borrow scores of his own mislaid music. Others are serious, even political – 'In the world of art, as in the whole of creation', Beethoven wrote in a letter to the Archduke in 1819, 'freedom and progress are the main objectives.'[9]

Annus mirabilis

Whatever Beethoven's frustrations as a pianist after the first two public performances of the *Archduke* Trio, his mood was buoyant – and with good reason. After the triumphant premiere a few months earlier of the *Battle* Symphony (*Wellingtons Sieg*, op. 91) celebrating the Duke of Wellington's victory over Napoleon at Vittoria, everyone wanted to hear his music – not only further performances of the *Battle* Symphony at crowded fund-raising concerts for the war-wounded, but also premieres of the Seventh Symphony on 8 December 1813, and the Eighth on 27 February 1814. Both were performed by a large orchestra of sixty-nine amateur and professional string players, with wind, brass and percussion to match, and were followed a few weeks later by the premiere of the *Archduke* Trio.

---

[7] *Letters of Beethoven*, Letter 248, February 1810: Beethoven to Baron Ignaz von Gleichenstein.

[8] *Letters of Beethoven*, Letter 1016, 3 April 1820: Beethoven to Archduke Rudolph.

[9] *Letters of Beethoven*, Letter 955, 29 July 1819: Beethoven to Archduke Rudolph.

To cap this *annus mirabilis* the directors of the opera house decided to stage a revival of *Fidelio*, and, after yet further revision, the final version of Beethoven's opera was performed on 23 May 1814, with such success that twenty more performances followed, including one attended by several foreign heads of state who were in Vienna for the Congress.[10] Archduke Rudolph and Prince Razumovsky presented Beethoven to some of the 'assembled monarchs, and they acknowledged their regard for him in the most flattering terms'.[11] Before he was introduced to the Tsarina he had taken the precaution of composing the Polonaise, op. 89, as a tactful reminder that her husband, Alexander I, Tsar of Russia, had never acknowledged his dedication of the op. 30 violin sonatas, and he received from her 100 ducats for the three sonatas and 50 for the Polonaise. There is little doubt that Beethoven enjoyed being a celebrity among celebrities, but more significantly the occasion illustrated the increasingly fashionable shift in attitude at the time towards the Romantic view that great musicians, artists, poets, writers and thinkers deserved the respect of even the highest in the land.

Trio no. 7 in B flat major for piano, violin and cello, op. 97 (*Archduke*)

Allegro moderato
Scherzo & Trio: Allegro
Andante cantabile
Allegro moderato – Presto

Allegro moderato   Mantra-like repetitions, explored two or three years earlier by Beethoven in the first movement of the *Pastoral* Symphony, characterize this spacious and noble movement. Dynamics are restrained, the formal structure is unusually clear and the tempo is leisurely, so there is plenty of time to savour hemiolas, off-beat stresses, textural nuances and other matters of detail. Short, though eloquent, string recitatives divide two statements of the opening theme, the first introduced by the piano

[10] The Congress of Vienna, which lasted from September 1814 to June 1815, was a gathering of the allied crowned heads of Europe and their advisers after the initial defeat of Napoleon. Its purpose was to draft a peace treaty, redefine national borders and reassert the primacy of monarchical government in Europe. Although the *Battle* Symphony was perhaps Beethoven's least significant large-scale work, it did more for his popular and international reputation than any of the masterpieces he had already composed. However, the Seventh Symphony was also well received and piano arrangements of the symphony for two or four hands were quickly made and dedicated to the Tsarina of Russia. While the Congress was in full session in February 1815, Napoleon escaped from Elba, returned in triumph to Paris and created a new revolutionary army. The Congress was suspended, but Napoleon was finally defeated by the allied armies under the Duke of Wellington at the Battle of Waterloo on 18 June 1815. Napoleon's 'Hundred Days' were over and the *Battle* Symphony would, no doubt, have received many more performances.

[11] Schindler, *Beethoven as I Knew Him*, p. 205.

and the second played by the violin above an expressive countersubject on the cello (ex. 21.1). Four closely related phrases in this finely sculpted melody are the source of extensive development later. The first phrase (*x*) reappears in the transition, closing section, development and recapitulation; the second (*y*) inspires a lengthy pizzicato conversation between the cello and violin enlivened later by ornamental variants of *z* on the piano. In addition, the same phrase (*z*) generates momentum in the coda (bar 273) and an extension of *u* inspires the principal theme of the Scherzo.

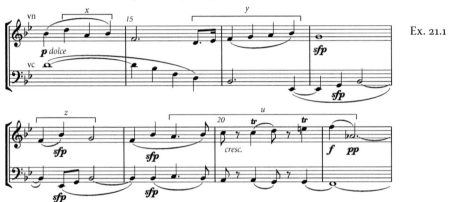

Ex. 21.1

In general, the piano is more independent than in Beethoven's previous piano trios, and the strings are more closely allied to each other, joining forces to create experimental tone-colours, such as the extended pizzicato duet or the swaying four-part chordal string textures in ex. 21.2.

Ex. 21.2

The three themes in the second group, all in the submediant, G major, rather than the more usual dominant, play no part in the development, but the first gives rise to some delicate polyphony, the second remoulds and extends the last two bars of the opening melody (*u*) and the third concludes the group with yet another richly expressive version of *u*. The recapitulation reflects the exposition in broad outline, but the opening melody (ex. 21.1) is triumphantly proclaimed *fortissimo* at the start of the coda, underlining the movement's 'symphonic' credentials.

Scherzo & Trio: Allegro The Scherzo starts innocently enough: a duo for unaccompanied cello and violin consisting of two statements of a cheerful theme – an extension of (*y, u*) in the first movement (ex. 21.1) – while the second section (eight times longer) is a series of variations on the theme and its inversion, by turns expressive, assertive and light-hearted.

There is something of the night, however, about the opening bars of the

Trio – a dark, chromatic fugato in B flat minor (ex. 21.3a), introduced by
the cello, then extended or sub-divided, amoeba-like, with each new entry;
in its search for daylight, it recalls the sinister, 'Gothic' atmosphere of the
Ghost Trio. By contrast, the second theme (ex. 21.3b) is an exuberant waltz
in D flat major.

Ex. 21.3

Variants of this enigmatic and seemingly incompatible pairing are
repeated twice more before fresh air returns in the Scherzo. But the tension between darkness and light is renewed in the coda, and sanity is only
restored in the final bars.

Andante cantabile   The sublime melody (ex. 21.4), played in turn by
piano and strings, unfolds gradually in a series of gentle, though profound,
sequences and ends with all three instruments united in expressing feelings of exaltation. Rich harmonic textures accompanying the theme suggest, and often receive, a full-toned performance, but Beethoven's dynamic
marks – *piano semplice* in the piano score and *piano dolce* for the strings
– indicate something more contemplative.

Ex. 21.4

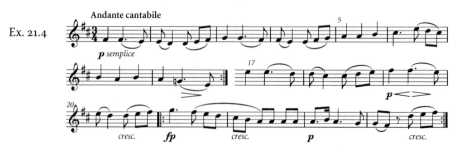

The first four variations share the theme's twenty-eight bar structure and, for the most part, its contemplative mood. Each variation flows
naturally from one to the other, with a gradual quickening of note-values
– triplet quavers in the first variation, semiquavers in the second, triplet
semiquavers for the third and demisemiquavers in the fourth, a variation especially rich and complex. In the exquisite final variation, each
instrument in turn reflects quietly on the theme – at times overcome,
even speechless, with emotion. A cadential phrase in the final bars (*v* in

ex. 21.5a) is the source of further dialogue and meditation in the introspective coda.

Ex. 21.5

Allegro molto – Presto   The same phrase (*v*) is also the unexpected
source of the rondo theme (ex. 21.6) in the finale, which follows without
a break. The first episode, with its canonic syncopation and chromatic
inflections seems to parody the chromatic fugato in the Trio (ex. 21.3a)
while, by contrast, the central episode is much stronger, even heroic in
outline. The movement ends with a substantial coda, based on the rondo
theme (*v* in ex. 21.5b) and marked 'Presto', followed by 'Più presto' – at 156
bars, well over a third of the finale in length. Opened by the strings in the
unlikely key of A major, it is a magnificent *perpetuum mobile* (ex. 21.6),
dominated latterly by the piano and accompanied admiringly (and perhaps
a little enviously) by sustained strings.

Ex. 21.6

If, as is sometimes suggested, the first movement of the *Archduke* Trio
is symphonic, the last movement is more like a piano concerto – a brilliant
tour de force, which Archduke Rudolph would, no doubt, have relished.
Almost uniquely, there is less involvement for string players here than in
any of Beethoven's earlier or later chamber music; the violin part, in particular, is mostly restricted to its lowest register. As usual, Beethoven's
dynamic markings are unexpected and suggest a much subtler interpretation of the principal rondo theme than its fragmentary shape and carefree
'oom-pah' accompaniment seem to suggest.

However, according to Schubert's friend, the organist and conductor
Franz Lachner,[12] the finale as a whole should not be played too gently:

> Suddenly Beethoven, on whose household affairs Frau Streicher had
> considerable influence, entered the room just as we had reached
> the beginning of the last movement. He listened for a few moments,

---

[12] Franz Lachner, organist and conductor, and a close friend of Schubert, later arranged
the *Missa Solemnis* for piano 'in a spirit of true devotion.' Quoted in Clive, *Beethoven
and his World*, p. 201.

using the ear trumpet he always carried with him, but soon showed that he was not in agreement with the too gentle interpretation of the principal motive of the finale. He leaned over Frau Streicher and played it for her, after which he left straightaway.[13]

---

[13] Quoted in Landon, *Beethoven: A Documentary Study*, p. 304.

Violin Sonata in G major, op. 96

Pierre Rode

'Only Kreutzer can be compared to him, but Rode only to himself', Ernst Ludwig Gerber declared in the *Tonkünstler-Lexicon*,[1] so expectations were high when Pierre Rode (1774–1830) visited Vienna on his way back to Paris from St Petersburg in December 1812. He booked the Redouten-saal for his celebrity concert in mid-January 1813, and the composer Louis Spohr, who had been overwhelmed by Rode's virtuosity in Brunswick ten years earlier, went to hear him in a state of 'almost feverish excitement'. He was quickly disillusioned, however: 'I now found his playing cold and mannered, missed his former audacity in overcoming great difficulties, and felt particularly dissatisfied with his cantabile playing.'[2] Others were critical too, including one reviewer who commented on the 'cutting edge of his tone'.[3]

Like other visiting celebrities, Rode would have received invitations to play at various soirées during his stay in Vienna. Among them was a particularly grand one: to give the first performance of Beethoven's G major Violin Sonata with a member of the imperial family, Archduke Rudolph, at Prince Lobkowitz's palace on 29 December, to be followed by a second performance on 7 January. Rode completely misjudged the occasion, perhaps as Max Rostal suggests, because 'like many other [virtuosi] of that time – even, indeed, into the 1920s – [he] did not study such works really intensively, but, instead, mostly performed them *prima vista* as so-called *Hausmusik*.'[4] By contrast, the Archduke, to whom Beethoven later dedicated the sonata, had studied his part in depth and even begged Beethoven to go through it yet again a few hours before the second performance; so they were both frustrated and angry with Rode for being so casual:

As to Rode – if Your Imperial Highness will only be so gracious as to send me the [violin] part by the bearer of this letter, then I will send it on to him with a billet doux from myself. He will certainly not take it amiss that I send him the part, alas! most certainly not! Would to God that there were reasons to beg his pardon for doing so for, in that case, things would indeed be in a better state.[5]

---

[1] Brandenburg, 'Beethoven's Violin Sonatas, Cello Sonatas and Variations', p. 143. The lexicographer, Ernst Ludwig Gerber (1746–1819), had published a revised version of his *Tonkünstler-Lexicon* in 1812–14.

[2] Brandenburg, 'Beethoven's Violin Sonatas, Cello Sonatas and Variations', p. 144.

[3] Brandenburg, 'Beethoven's Violin Sonatas, Cello Sonatas and Variations', p. 144.

[4] Rostal, *Beethoven: The Sonatas for Piano and Violin*, p. 167. *Prima vista* = 'at sight'.

[5] *Letters of Beethoven*, Letter 402, January 1813: Beethoven to Archduke Rudolph.

Nonetheless, the sonata was greeted with general approval: 'it leaves behind it all other works of this nature', wrote one enthusiastic reviewer, although he was less satisfied with the performance itself: 'We must mention that the piano part was played far better, more in accordance with the spirit of the piece, and with more feeling than the violin. Herr Rode's greatness seems to lie not in his playing of this kind of music, but in his concerto performances.'[6] In a thoughtful article published some time later in the *Allgemeine musikalische Zeitung*, another reviewer explored the underlying emotions of the sonata: 'Even artists of his kind express their innermost being in whatever form this may take at a particular time, and consequently it might be concluded that the excellent Beethoven is now contented, sociable and cheerful ... This sonata helps to support that view ... Not only are the two parts consummately partnered, but when they come together, each is telling in its effect.'[7]

The musical context in which sketches for op. 96 first appeared – in the 'Petter' sketchbook (September 1811 to December 1812) just after two of Beethoven's most exuberant and optimistic works, the Seventh and Eighth symphonies – was indeed a happy one. The domestic context, however, was far more complicated and intriguing than the reviewer could have imagined, and more directly relevant to a discussion of the G major Violin Sonata.

'The Immortal Beloved', Antonie Brentano

On 6 July 1812, Beethoven began a deeply emotional letter to his 'Immortal Beloved', persuasively identified by Maynard Solomon as Antonie Brentano, née Birkenstock (1780–1869).[8] He completed it the following day. Whether or not the letter was ever sent, it shows that when Beethoven was composing his final violin sonata, he was having to come to terms with one of the greatest personal challenges of his life: a love shared with equal intensity by Antonie Brentano and himself, but one which could not be fulfilled because of her obligations to her husband and children. 'Your love', he wrote in the last part of his letter, 'has made me both the happiest and unhappiest of mortals.'[9]

Beethoven probably met Franz and Antonie Brentano in May 1810, and soon became a close friend of the family, attending soirées at Antonie's late father, Johann Melchior von Birkenstock's magnificent mansion, 'where he often gave pleasure to his friends with his wonderful playing.

---

[6] Brandenburg, *'Beethoven's Violin Sonatas, Cello Sonatas and Variations'*, pp. 143–4.

[7] Brandenburg, *'Beethoven's Violin Sonatas, Cello Sonatas and Variations'*, pp. 145–6. The article appeared on 26 March 1817.

[8] Solomon, *Beethoven*, *pp.* 207–46. See also Solomon, 'Antonie Brentano and Beethoven', p. 153.

[9] *Letters of Beethoven*, Letter 373, 6 & 7 July 1812. Beethoven's letter to his 'Immortal Beloved' was found among his papers after his death. The quotation appears near the end of the long and passionate letter.

The Brentano children sometimes brought fruit and flowers to his apartment; in return he would regale them with sweets, and he treated them
with the greatest friendliness.'[10] Franz, the head of a successful banking
house in Frankfurt, was devoted to his family but, though interested in
the arts, was the sort of man who, as his wife despairingly wrote, preferred
to go to his office 'even after supper – God, what will come of it?'[11] Like
her father, Antonie was cultured and highly intelligent. She hated Frankfurt and, although she admired her husband, she was deeply unhappy in
her marriage and, perhaps as a result, she was frequently unwell. After the
death of her father, she persuaded Franz to remain in Vienna for more than
three years (1809–12) while she supervised the sale of his immense collection of books and works of art,[12] and Franz made profitable use of their
stay to set up a branch of his bank there. By December 1811, or perhaps
earlier, Antonie and Beethoven had discovered that they were deeply in
love. Beethoven 'walks like a god among mortals' she told her half-brother
Clemens Brentano, describing him as 'guileless, straightforward, wise and
wholly benevolent', and spoke of his 'soft heart [and] ardent nature'.[13] Beethoven expressed his love in music written for her and, by association, for
her daughter, Maximiliane, a talented young pianist. When Antonie was
unwell, he would improvise in her anteroom, arriving and leaving without
seeing her but telling her all she needed to know in the music he played.
At her request, he presented her with two settings of Joseph Stoll's short
poem, *An die Geliebte*, WoO 140, one for voice and piano, the other for
voice and her own instrument, the guitar. The poem accurately reflected
their feelings and their predicament: 'O let me drink from your cheek the
tear shed from your placid eyes. It is lingering on your cheek and ardently
wishes to devote itself to fidelity; now that I receive it this way in a kiss,
now your sorrows are also mine.'

Maynard Solomon suggests that the situation was somehow resolved
in the late summer of 1812, when Beethoven met Franz and Antonie Brentano while holidaying in Karlsbad and Franzensbad: 'the trio managed to
pass through the crisis into a new stage of their relationship. Passion was
apparently undergoing sublimation into exalted friendship. Beethoven was
visibly elated during these months, as evidenced by his correspondence
and his productivity.'[14]

It seems inconceivable that an emotional crisis of such magnitude
would not have had some effect on Beethoven's music, or that ideas
from those romantic improvisations outside Antonie's sickroom, which
he perhaps recalled after the Brentanos finally left Vienna for Frankfurt

[10] Landon, *Beethoven: A Documentary Study*, p. 256.

[11] Solomon, *Beethoven*, p. 235.

[12] Antonie Brentano kept some of the finest works of art in the family, including Van
Dyck's *Descent from the Cross*, bequeathed by her to Frankfurt Cathedral, where both
she and her husband, Franz, are buried.

[13] Clive, *Beethoven and his World*, p. 50.

[14] Solomon, *Beethoven*, p. 239.

in November 1812, would not find more structured expression later. As always, Beethoven responded to their departure in the only way open to him – his music. In 1816 he composed the song cycle, *An die ferne Geliebte* (*To the distant beloved*), op. 98, a setting of six poems by Alois Jeitteles on the subject of passionate love, lived and experienced apart. Antonie would have realized, of course, that it was not possible for Beethoven to dedicate such a specific and personal work to the woman for whom it was surely written – it was dedicated to Prince Lobkowitz – but he dedicated the Piano Sonata in E major, op. 109, to her daughter, Maximiliane in 1820 and one of his greatest masterpieces, the *Diabelli* Variations, op. 120, to Antonie in 1823. There are clear signs of a more immediate response to her departure, however, in the Violin Sonata in G major, op. 96.

Sonata no. 10 in G major for violin and piano, op. 96

Allegro moderato
Adagio espressivo
Scherzo & Trio: Allegro
Poco Allegretto – Adagio espressivo – Allegro – Poco Adagio – Presto

Beethoven's last violin sonata is among the most treasured masterpieces in the repertoire of those violinists and pianists who realize that its apparent fragility conceals extraordinary spiritual and emotional depths. 'Interpreters must be able to dream, to enthuse', wrote Carl Flesch. 'The flower must blossom in their souls.'[15] The first three movements were composed before Rode arrived in Vienna in mid-December 1812, but the finale was finished only a few days before the first performance. 'Since I have been engaged on several other works, I have not hurried unduly to compose the last movement merely for the sake of being punctual', Beethoven explained to the Archduke: 'the more so, as in view of Rode's playing, I have had to give more thought to the composition of this last movement. In our finales we like to have fairly noisy passages, but R[ode] does not care for them – so I have been rather hampered.'[16] After further revision, the Sonata was published in 1816 by Steiner in Vienna and Birchall in London, together with the *Archduke* Trio.

Allegro moderato   Antonie's 'god among mortals' never revealed his 'soft heart' more intimately than in the sublime first movement. The wistful, haunting phrase with which the sonata opens (*x*), played unaccompanied by the violin and echoed by the piano, suggests that this is to be a pastoral idyll, Beethoven's metaphor for the spiritual peace he longed for and so often found in the countryside. It is soon evident, however, that more is implied: seamless lyricism in the opening melody and crystaline textures,

---

[15] Carl Flesch, *The Art of Violin Playing*, quoted in Rostal, *Beethoven: The Sonatas for Piano and Violin*, p. 168.

[16] *Letters of Beethoven*, Letter 392, late December 1812: Beethoven to Archduke Rudolph,

so different from the symphonic splendour of the *Archduke* Trio, look forward, not to the rich colours of Romantic chamber music, but to the emerging lyrical and spiritual language of Beethoven's late period. The general dynamic level is restrained and each melody, each pattern, each inflexion is meticulously shared throughout by the two voices in turn or together, like lovers in rapt conversation.

The first of three ideas in the opening group (ex. 22.1a) is wide-ranging and tender; the second, an exquisite improvisation based on the last three bars of the theme (*y*) is shared by both voices, high in register, creating mosaic-like patterns of iridescent beauty, while the third (ex. 22.1b) recalls the opening bars of another masterpiece in G major, the Fourth Piano Concerto, and also provides material for the fervent transition that follows. A quickening of movement, though not of pulse, is suggested by the arrival of triplet quavers, leading into the second group (also in three sections); and the interplay between duple and compound time adds piquancy to the first theme in the group (ex. 22.1c), a poised and enchanting minuet in D major.

Ex. 22.1

The mood deepens, however, with an unexpected modulation into B flat major, and a lyrical version (ex. 22.2a) of the opening bars of the sonata (*x*) in a language which is unmistakably 'late period'. The third theme, back in D major, is high in register and characterized by flowing, often mirrored

Ex. 22.2

phrases, which play a thoughtful part in the later bars of the development section as well (ex. 22.2b). There is heart-ache in the closing section, however (ex. 22.2c), and in the earlier bars of the development, most poignantly the inverted minor second (*z*).

The exposition is retraced melodically in the recapitulation but, after only eight bars and a sudden shift from G major to the submediant, E flat major, notice is given that tone colours are to be darker and moods less settled. The idyll returns, however, in the quiet coda – a fragrant sequence of diminished sevenths above a dialogue between the two voices, based on the opening phrase (*x*).

Adagio espressivo   The slow movement opens with a profound, hymn-like melody in E flat major (ex. 22.3), introduced by the piano above a flowing though sombre accompaniment. In Beethoven's earlier violin sonatas – the *Spring* Sonata, for instance, or the A major Sonata, op. 30 no. 1 – such expressive melodies, whether introduced by the piano or the violin, are repeated by each instrument in full. Something quite different happens here; after the piano has completed the eight-bar melody, the violin enters in the ninth bar not, as expected, with the 'hymn', but with a whispered echo (*sotto voce*) of the piano's three-note cadential phrase (*u*).

Ex. 22.3

As discussed in 'The 'Farewell" Motive' in Chapter 15, it can hardly be chance that this is the same phrase in the same key as in the outer movements of the *Harp* Quartet, and the opening two bars of the *Lebewohl* Piano Sonata, op. 81a – a phrase which would reappear later in the Cavatina, the penultimate movement in the Quartet in B flat major, op. 130. Here, on the first page of this Adagio, there are no fewer than five 'Lebewohl' phrases' (*u*) whispered *sotto voce* in turn by each instrument, and several more later. Beethoven's meaning could hardly be clearer, but it is intriguing to speculate on what Archduke Rudolph made of it all as he practised the sonata for those two early performances; to whom was Beethoven saying goodbye this time?

The extended melody (ex. 22.4a) for the violin that follows immediately after the opening theme is surely a lament, expressed in a new language already heard in the Larghetto which introduces the finale in the *Quartetto serioso*. Two bars of expressive improvisation, for example, are typical of coloratura patterns in the late quartets, and the cadence (*v*) looks ahead to cadential motives, which appear several times in the slow movement of the Ninth Symphony (ex. 22.4b).

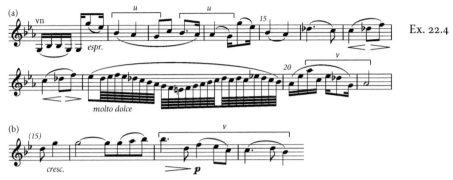

Ex. 22.4

Another more extended cadenza leads back to the opening theme, played in full this time on the violin and marked *semplice* and *mezza voce*, expressing, perhaps, the poignant intimacy of those moments of parting, while the 'lament' (ex. 22.4a) is shared by both instruments in the coda. However, there is an unexpected twist as the movement comes to an end; disquieting tremolo on the piano in place of the expected final chord of E flat major, followed by an intrusive C sharp on the violin, which raises the tension still further.

Scherzo & Trio: Allegro   The Scherzo in G minor follows without a break, and the anxious mood, though soft throughout, is further unsettled by petulant off-beat accents. The Trio, in the submediant, E flat major, is sunny and carefree – a flowing, open-air melody, played in turn by each instrument and then transformed into a canon while exploring extreme heights – another characteristic of Beethoven's late period. The carefree mood returns in the coda, now happily in G major, setting the scene for the pastoral idyll which follows.

Poco Allegretto – Adagio espressivo – Allegro – Poco Adagio – Presto
The first impression – a cheerful folk-song, which would not be out of place in light opera[17] – suggests that the finale is to be a rondo (ex. 22.5). But the theme is followed by a continuous stream of fresh, improvisatory variations – not wholly out of reach of the theme, but so adventurous that an occasional rondo-like reminder of the original folk-song is welcome.

Though very different from each other in character, the first four variations share the thirty-two-bar frame of the theme, as well as its piquant G major – B major – G major tonality, and something at least of its often concealed melodic outlines. As in the *Archduke* variations, forward momentum is maintained by quickening note-values: quavers in the

---

[17] Nottebohm noted a similar theme in J. A. Hiller's singspiel *Der Teufel ist los*, which was popular at the time; quoted in Rostal, *Beethoven: The Sonatas for Piano and Violin*, p. 180.

Ex. 22.5

expressive first variation, triplet quavers in the energetic second, semi-quavers beneath a gently syncopated and flowing dialogue in the third and powerfully assertive questions alternating with gentle, emollient answers in the fourth. Later variations are less symmetrical; the fifth, for example, marked 'Adagio espressivo', is an uneven nineteen bars long, as each voice in turn redefines the basis of the theme in an expressive and strangely remote chromatic improvisation. A short reminder of the original theme recalls the movement back from such distant, speculative regions in time for the rustic sixth variation, its exuberant *sforzandi* scattered around like confetti. Seriousness returns in the seventh variation – a secretive and chromatic fugato, marked *sempre pianissimo* – its subject closer than most to the contours of the basic theme. The final variation opens unassumingly with a simple restatement of parts of the original theme. But Beethoven cannot resist teasing Rode with at least a few of those 'fairly noisy passages [which] we like', even though the French virtuoso was known 'not to care for them'[18] – brilliant, mirrored scales and dangerously exposed unaccompanied flourishes. The second part of the theme is briefly remembered in a nostalgic Poco adagio, and the sonata ends magnificently with a suitably 'noisy', bustling Presto.

---

[18] *Letters of Beethoven*, Letter 392, late December 1812: Beethoven to Archduke Rudolph.

Two Cello Sonatas, op. 102

In spite of his mercurial temperament, Beethoven was never without friends. 'Friendship is a shade in sunlight and a shelter in a downpour of rain', he told Johannes Buel, when the tutor to Count von Browne's son left Vienna for his home in Switzerland in 1805. 'Reflect back ... and you [will realize] that we saw each other too little.'[1] Beethoven felt the loss of particular friends keenly; friends like Karl Amenda, a Lutheran pastor and talented violinist who had left Vienna for Latvia in 1799. 'A thousand times I recall you to mind and your patriarchal simplicity', he wrote in a letter to Amenda on 12 April 1815. 'How often I long to have people like yourself around me.'[2]

Countess Erdödy

Beethoven was especially sorry when he realized that he himself had caused the breakdown in his earlier friendship with Countess Erdödy (noted in Chapter 18), and that in spite of his abject apology to her, relations between them had remained cool for some years. Early in 1815, however, she decided to let bygones be bygones. 'I have read your letter with great pleasure, my beloved Countess, and also what you say about the renewal of your friendship for me', he wrote on 29 February, promising to send her manuscript copies of the *Archduke* Trio and 'everything else that has not been published ... It has long been my wish to see you and your beloved children once again. For although I have suffered a great deal, yet I have not lost my former love for children, the beauties of nature and friendship.'[3] A case or two of wine and the loan of one of her collection of pianos followed and, judging by Beethoven's jokey letters to the Countess and the no less jokey invitations he received in reply, relations between them became warmer than ever:

> From Jedlersee I've been sent to you, Sir,
> Who are next to God the greatest composer,
> Our gracious Countess Erdödy
> Invites you to take punch, you see
> And any other country fare ...[4]

'My dear and beloved Countess!', Beethoven protested with evident delight.

---

[1] Thayer, *The Life of Beethoven*, p. 366.

[2] *Letters of Beethoven*, Letter 541, 12 April 1815: Beethoven to Karl Amenda in Courland.

[3] *Letters of Beethoven*, Letter 531, March 1815: Beethoven to Countess Anna Maria Erdödy.

[4] Quoted in *Letters of Beethoven*, p. 519 n. 1.

'You are again bestowing gifts upon me and so soon too; and that is not right. For you thereby rob me of the merit of having rendered you a small service.'[5]

Joseph Linke

Countess Erdödy was living in her villa just outside Vienna at this time with her three children, their tutor, Johann Brauchle and the brilliant Silesian cellist Joseph Linke (1783–1837), whose playing Beethoven admired and whose technical advice he valued. Linke had just been pensioned off with the three other members of Prince Razumovsky's quartet when it was disbanded early in 1815,[6] and he joined the Countess's staff as 'chamber virtuoso' for a few months before taking up a new appointment as principal cellist at the Theater an der Wien. As a sensitive interpreter and powerful advocate of Beethoven's music, he would later take part in the historic premieres of most of the late string quartets in ensembles led either by Schuppanzigh or Böhm. In later years he added Schubert's chamber music to his repertoire and counted Schubert among his friends.

Whether Beethoven composed his last two cello sonatas on his own initiative to 'render a small service' to the Countess, or whether she asked him to write something that she and Linke could play together, is unclear. But according to autograph copies, the C major Sonata was completed towards the end of July 1815, and the D major Sonata early the following month. Both were dedicated to Countess Erdödy, though, perhaps wisely, she declined the honour of giving the premieres of the sonatas in favour of Carl Czerny. Certainly, Beethoven could not have wished for two more sensitive and intelligent artists than Linke and Czerny to play what Barry Cooper rightly describes as 'a new inner world of heightened sophistication – true musicians' music'.[7] Czerny had no doubt in his mind that the sonatas belonged to 'the last period of Beethoven's career, in which he no longer embellished his ideas by the ordinary effects of the pianoforte ... but ordered the structure of the work in its simple grandeur; so that the player must the more endeavour to impart to each thought, as well as to each note, its full significance.'[8]

The critics also thought that Beethoven was speaking a new language, and at least one reviewer, writing in the *Allgemeine musikalische Zeitung* in 1818, did not like it or understand it: 'most unusual and peculiar ... everything here is different, quite different from anything we have had previously, even from the same composer ... melody coarse ... harmony harsh.'[9]

---

[5] *Letters of Beethoven*, Letter 549, shortly after 20 July: Beethoven to Countess Anna Maria Erdödy.

[6] The Razumovsky palace was accidentally destroyed by fire in 1814.

[7] Cooper, *Beethoven* [Master Musicians], p. 242.

[8] Czerny quoted in Cooper, *Beethoven* [Master Musicians], p. 242.

[9] Quoted from the *Allgemeine musikalische Zeitung*, 1818, in Brandenburg, 'Beethoven's Violin Sonatas, Cello Sonatas and Variations', p. 153.

Unlike the late quartets and piano sonatas, most of which were treated by audiences and critics alike with respect and, in some cases, enthusiasm, wider appreciation of Beethoven's last two cello sonatas had to wait for several years. In 1860, Wilhelm von Lenz was among the first to write enthusiastically about them:[10] 'No instrumental duet [has] gone so far in transmitting the musical idea in abstraction from the medium. The form is raised above itself.'

Sonata no. 4 in C major for cello and piano, op. 102 no. 1

Andante
Allegro vivace
Adagio – Tempo d'Andante
Allegro vivace

Andante   Beethoven's fourth Cello Sonata is unusual in that all five movements are played without a break – the silent pause (bar 154) at the end of the first Allegro vivace is surely integral – an idea with which he had experimented fifteen years earlier in the Piano Sonata *Quasi una fantasia* in C sharp minor, op. 27 no. 2 (*Moonlight*), and which reached its apotheosis a decade later in op. 131, his penultimate string quartet in the same key. The C major Cello Sonata appears to match contemporary descriptions of Beethoven's celebrated improvisations and is also, in effect, a fantasia. All of the principal motives in the five interlinked movements can trace their origins to four phrases and cells (*x, y, z, u*) in the first two spellbinding bars (ex. 23.1), played unaccompanied by the cello. Interpretative instructions in the exquisite dialogue that follows are even more detailed than usual – *p, dolce, cantabile, teneramente* – and suggest a mood which is both tender and full of wonder, with C major unusually an introvert key, as it is in Leonore's vision of love and redeeming grace in the recitative (ex. 15.4) which leads to her great aria 'Komm Hoffnung' in *Fidelio*.[11]

Ex. 23.1

[10] Lenz's 'Critical Catalogue of all Ludwig van Beethoven's Works', quoted in Brandenburg, *'Beethoven's Violin Sonatas, Cello Sonatas and Variations'*, p. 155.
[11] See Chapter 15 below.

For all its introspective simplicity and gentleness, the Andante is structurally complex, consisting throughout of interweaving polyphonic lines created from an expressive stream of separate or shared phrases and cells. The movement ends as softly as it began, linked to the first Allegro vivace (bar 28) by a thoughtful cadenza, in which variants of the two-note cell (*u*) play a significant part.

Allegro vivace The first subject (ex. 23.2), with its minor key (A minor), *fortissimo* unisons and martial rhythms, alternating with feelings of extreme restlessness, is extended and developed from the first two opening motives in the Andante (*x, y*).

Ex. 23.2

The second subject, a variant of the third motive (*z*), is expressive, then impassioned and finally resigned in a cadence of unforgettable, wistful beauty (ex. 23.3a), before the return of martial music (risoluto) in the closing section (ex. 23.3b).

Ex. 23.3

The development section, framed by the opening bars of the first subject (ex. 23.2), is short and concentrated – dotted rhythms above a series of quietly emphatic (*fp*) minims – coming to rest eventually in one of those visionary asides which add mystery to so much of Beethoven's music. After the recapitulation and a forceful coda, the movement breaks off abruptly with a silent pause bar to ensure that there is no lessening of tension before the short Adagio begins.

Adagio Like the cadenza at the end of the first movement, this too is improvisatory in character – although an ornamental version of the third phrase (*z*) in the first two bars of the Sonata, it is more focused melodically.

Tempo d'Andante The opening bars of the first movement are then recalled (*z* in ex. 23.1), though in varied form – an inspirational, unifying idea, not without a touch of nostalgia perhaps, to which Beethoven would return the following year in the Piano Sonata in A major, op. 101.

Allegro vivace The finale, however, is pure comedy – a playful movement which Countess Erdödy's children could perhaps have enjoyed as
well. The first motive in the opening bar of the sonata (*x*) is turned on its
head and provides a template for both themes in the movement, and also
for most of the cheerful contrapuntal material which accompanies it. The
first theme (ex. 23.4) is frisky.

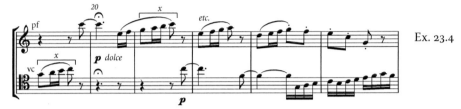

Ex. 23.4

The second, by contrast, is robust – a brisk and cheerful march (ex. 23.5)
which Schubert may well have remembered when he composed his celebrated *Marche Militaire*.

Ex. 23.5

The introduction to the short development section, repeated later just
before the coda, is still more playful and eccentric: three identical statements, each in a different key – E flat major, C major (ex. 23.6), and A flat
major – and each in three stages: the first silent, the second tense and
the third explosive; a private joke, perhaps, or a prophetic Tom and Jerry
moment, with the cat (as always) just missing the mouse so as not to upset
the Countess's children?

Ex. 23.6

What follows is a masterpiece of cheerful, closely imitative writing, still
based on the first motive (*x*), initially distant, but soon engulfed in assertive *sforzandi*. The exposition and development, though more adventurous
in matters of tonality, are fully recalled in the recapitulation, and after a
pastoral reference in the coda (triplet quavers), the sonata ends in the highest of spirits.

Sonata no. 5 in D major for cello and piano, op. 102 no. 2

Allegro con brio
Adagio con molto sentimento d'affetto
Allegro fugato

Allegro con brio   Where the C major Sonata is almost entirely created from material presented in the first two bars, the D major Sonata is expansive in character and richly varied melodically. There are no fewer than seven themes and motives in the first movement alone, and the dramatic introduction (ex. 23.7a), with its second-beat *sforzandi* and leaping intervals, provides two of the most productive ones. The first motive (*x*), which Schubert surely remembered a decade later when he composed one of the greatest of all string quartets, *Death and the Maiden* (ex. 23.7b), introduces not only the movement as a whole, but each formal paragraph as well, while the second motive (*y*) eventually brings the development section and coda to a no less dramatic end.

Ex. 23.7

Beethoven's dynamic marks are never more surprising and tantalizing than in the cello's powerful entry in the fourth bar (ex. 23.8). Marked *forte* and encompassing a span of two and a half octaves, the notes themselves suggest a *crescendo*, followed by an impassioned melody high on the A string. But the opposite happens: the thrusting arpeggio fades to *piano dolce*, suggesting that the first subject is to be played with quiet, unassuming nobility rather than dramatic intensity.

Ex. 23.8

The lyrical second subject in A major (ex. 23.9) is also quiet and restrained, and the delightful cadence with which it ends (*z*) later provides inspiration for the central theme in the Adagio (ex. 23.12).

Ex. 23.9

The cello opens the exhilarating development section with the introductory motive (*x*) alternating with a sequence of sparkling, prismatic harmonies on the piano, which would not be out of place in a Rachmaninov prelude. But it is the transition that later provides the main topic of conversation, driven forward by a sequence of increasingly muscular minims. Now doubled in length, they return in the coda, quietly recalling the interval of a tenth in the second bar of the sonata (*x*), and the movement ends in spectacular fashion with the second motive (*y*) in full cry.

Adagio con molto sentimento d'affetto　Few can doubt the late period credentials of the Adagio, the only full slow movement in Beethoven's cello sonatas. Spiritual and emotional contrasts are reflected in two themes: first, a mystical chorale (ex. 23.10) played by the cello.

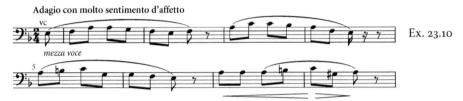

Ex. 23.10

Second, an expressive, ornamental dialogue (ex. 23.11), which seems almost operatic in its quiet intensity.

Ex. 23.11

The serenity of the middle section lifts the Adagio onto a still higher spiritual plane, as a lyrical melody (ex. 23.12) recalls a phrase (*z*) from the second subject in the first movement, and is joined in idyllic dialogue by a flowing countersubject.

Ex. 23.12

Allegro fugato　Beethoven often included fugal episodes in his instrumental music, some short and some substantial, as in the finale of the third *Razumovsky* quartet. But apart from the short Fugue for string quintet, op. 137, this is the first example in his chamber music of a movement entirely focused on fugue. As his renewed enthusiasm for Bach became, Maynard Solomon suggests, 'a veritable contrapuntal obsession during

[his] last decade',[12] other fugal movements would follow – in three of the late piano sonatas (op. 101, op. 106, op. 110), for instance, and in two of the late quartets (op. 131 and op. 133). However, with the exception of the *Grosse Fuge*, none are so uncompromising as this movement. As ever, dynamics play a vital part, not least in ensuring clarity of texture.

The first forty bars are predominantly quiet and restrained, and contain such unlikely instructions (at least in the context of such a powerful fugue) as *dolce* and *sforzando/pianissimo*. There are two very different fugue subjects in this double fugue: the first (*u*) presides over the movement as a whole, and three motives from it (*u*, *v*, *w*) act as useful signposts to guide the listener through numerous subsidiary patterns woven into the movement's intricate fabric. The scale motive (*u*), for example, provides momentum, while the other two repeatedly (*v*, *w*) challenge the rhythmic symmetry of the fugue with off-beat accents, tied-note anticipations and hemiolas. The second fugue subject (*s*), introduced softly by the cello alone and then discussed only briefly, appears much later in the movement; but when eventually the two are combined (ex. 23.13), it is clear that, for all their differences, they belong to each other in some kind of mystic union.

Ex. 23.13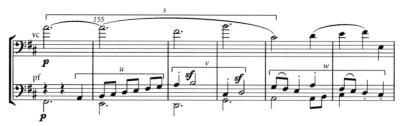

Beethoven may also have had a more personal union in mind. The second fugue subject (*s*) has a distinguished history, appearing in Handel's *Messiah* (ex. 23.14a), Bach's *Musical Offering*, Haydn's String Quartet, op. 20 no. 5, and Mozart's *Requiem* (ex. 23.14b), among other masterpieces. So it may not be too far fetched to regard its inclusion in this 'musicians music' – heralded in the powerful coda by peals of bell-like scales, celebratory trills, inversions and forceful hemiolas – as Beethoven's graceful acknowledgment of his debt to Handel, Bach, Haydn and Mozart, while at the same time laying claim to his own seat with them at the high table.

Ex. 23.14

---

[12] Solomon, *Beethoven*, p. 391.

PART SIX ⁓ 1816–27

'The imagination wishes also to assert its privileges, and today a new and really poetic element must be introduced into the old traditional form.'

Beethoven, in conversation
with Karl Holz, 1817

The Late String Quartets – Context and Background

'Beethoven now busies himself, as Papa Haydn once did, with arrangements of Scottish songs. He is apparently quite incapable of greater accomplishments.'[1] When the *Missa Solemnis* and the Ninth Symphony appeared two or three years later, the unfortunate critic who wrote those words in the *Allgemeine musikalische Zeitung* in 1821 must have thanked his lucky stars that his article had been published anonymously. But he had a point. The last decade of Beethoven's life began strangely enough. For several years after completing the two cello sonatas, op. 102, discussed in the previous chapter, he composed no chamber music of importance apart from a fine arrangement for string quintet of the Piano Trio in C minor, op. 1 no. 3, published as op. 104, and the short Fugue in D major, also for string quintet, op. 137 – both composed in 1817.

Beethoven's health, which had taken a turn for the worse in 1815, was at least partly responsible. That year, and yet again in the 1820s, he was confined to bed for several weeks at a time with serious abdominal and breathing problems. To add to his woes, by 1818 his hearing had deteriorated to such an extent that, in addition to his ear-trumpet, he increasingly had to resort to conversation books in which his many visitors and friends wrote their questions and comments. There were periods of remission, however, when Beethoven's general health improved. Between 1816 and 1820, for example, he spent many happy evenings with the cultured and musical Giannattasio family, whose school his nephew Karl attended for a time. He particularly enjoyed accompanying the Giannattasio's two daughters, Franziska (Fanny) and Anna, in performances of his own songs – evenings which, unknown to him, had at least one unsuspected consequence: 'Is it really possible', the serious Fanny wrote in her diary in 1816, 'that he has become so important, so dear to me that I should have been irritated and hurt by my sister's facetious advice not to fall in love with him?'[2]

There were some cheerful letters from Beethoven too: 'Well, thank God, I am now feeling better', he told Franz Brentano some time later; 'good health seems at last to be returning to revive my spirits, so that I may again start a new life to be devoted to my art. This I have had to renounce for almost two years, both for lack of health and also on account of many

---

[1] Quoted in Schindler, *Beethoven as I Knew Him*, p. 231.

[2] Fanny Gianattasio, quoted in Ludwig Nohl, *Eine stille Liebe zu Beethoven*: see Clive, *Beethoven and his World*, p. 129. Cajetan Giannattasio and his wife, Katharina, the parents of Franziska (Fanny) and Anna, ran a private boarding school, which Beethoven's nephew and ward, Karl, attended for a time.

other sorrows.'[3] Whether or not Franz Brentano's wife, Antonie, guessed that those 'other sorrows' still included their unfulfilled love for each other, it is clear from the letter Beethoven sent three weeks later to Maximiliane, the Brentano's nineteen-year-old daughter, with his dedication to her of the Piano Sonata in E major, op. 109, that her 'excellent and gifted mother'[4] was not forgotten.

Family responsibilities

Apart from his deteriorating health, Beethoven had much else to worry about, especially his new role as the guardian of his nephew Karl after the death of his brother, Kaspar Karl, in 1815. He took his family responsibilities seriously, but like many a fond, if inexperienced 'father', as he liked to be known, he tended either to spoil his nephew or to be unduly severe when things went wrong. A note which he sent to Czerny, who was giving the reluctant Karl some piano lessons, is typical of letters written before and since by generations of parents to music teachers the world over: 'Please be as patient as possible with our Karl, even though he may not be making as much progress as you and I would like. Treat him therefore so far as possible with affection, but *be firm with him*!'[5]

Beethoven added to his worries – worries which persisted for several years – by attempting, in a series of court appearances, to extricate Karl from the influence of his mother, Johanna, whom he described as 'an extremely depraved person ... most evil, wicked and spiteful'.[6] The 'Queen of the Night', as he called her, had earlier been convicted of embezzlement and imprisoned for four months, and later gave birth to an illegitimate daughter; so his opinion of her was not without some justification. Johann and Nanette Streicher, whose long friendship with Beethoven was particularly warm and untroubled, were quick to come to his aid. Johann was among those who helped him on matters of business and Nanette, whose talent as a pianist when young had impressed Mozart – though he made fun of her mannerisms – took charge of Beethoven's domestic arrangements for several years, on top of her own responsibilities as director of the family piano manufacturing business, 'Nanette Streicher, née Stein.'

---

[3] *Letters of Beethoven*, Letter 1059, 12 November: Beethoven to Franz Brentano in Frankfurt.

[4] *Letters of Beethoven*, Letter 1062, 6 December 1821: Beethoven to Maximiliane Brentano.

[5] *Letters of Beethoven*, Letter 878, 1817: Beethoven to Carl Czerny.

[6] *Letters of Beethoven*, Letter 1502, August 1826: Beethoven to the magistrate Ignaz von Czapka.

Commissions

Legal costs, rising inflation and the inevitable expenses involved in Karl's upbringing were both financially and emotionally draining. Apart from the regular income which he received from Archduke Rudolph and the Kinsky and Lobkowitz families, Beethoven mostly depended on commissions and on rival publishers, eager to publish everything that he wrote during his later years – Artaria, Peters, Schlesinger, Steiner and Schott among them. Only the *Hammerklavier* Sonata and the *Missa Solemnis*, with its touchingly personal dedication, 'From the heart to the heart', were unprompted gifts to Archduke Rudolph, although they too were financially productive when eventually published, as were various piano transcriptions of his other music. But he found the whole business wearisome. 'It is hard to compose entirely for the sake of earning one's daily bread',[7] he told Ferdinand Ries, who was then living in London and doing what he could to promote Beethoven's music there. Hard it may have been, but in the 1820s, his indomitable spirit reasserted itself, as he ventured further than ever in his exploration of the 'endlessness of possibility'.[8]

A series of supreme masterpieces followed one after the other, slowly at first, but then in an astonishing burst of creative energy: the last three piano sonatas (op. 109, op. 110, op. 111), the *Diabelli* Variations, op. 120, two sets of Bagatelles, op. 119 and op. 126, the *Missa Solemnis*, the Ninth Symphony and, during the last three years of his life, the five legendary string quartets: op. 127, op. 132, op. 130/op. 133, op. 131 and op. 135. Commissioned or not, Beethoven was not to be hurried, and many a promised deadline came and went before any of his later compositions were completed. Archduke Rudolph, for example, received his copy of the *Missa Solemnis* on 19 March 1823, almost exactly three years after his installation as Archbishop of Olmütz on 9 March 1820, the ceremony for which it was written.

Public support

Despite recurring ill-health, domestic worries and his 'many other sorrows', Beethoven had much to be thankful for during those difficult years. For instance, when his friends in Vienna heard that he was negotiating with Count Brühl for the premieres of the *Missa Solemnis* and the Ninth Symphony to be given in Berlin, they organized a public petition in the local press, drawn up by Count Moritz Lichnowsky in February 1824, and at the same time presented a copy personally to him. The petition took the form of an open letter, signed by leading members of the musical community,

---

[7] *Letters of Beethoven*, Letter 939, 20 March 1819: Beethoven to Ferdinand Ries in London. The *Missa Solemnis* also became profitable, when various heads of state and other grandees were persuaded to buy advance manuscript scores, among them Prince Nikolay Golitsïn and the Tzar of Russia.

[8] Capell, *Schubert's Songs*; see the Preface for the full quotation.

begging him to keep the premieres in Vienna where they belonged. Beethoven was deeply touched, not least, perhaps, because his name was specifically linked in the petition to those of his two illustrious predecessors, Mozart and Haydn. The signatories were 'conscious with joyous pride that the sacred triad in which these names and yours glow as the symbol of the highest within the spiritual realms of [music], sprang from the soil of their fatherland.'[9] Even Weber, among the last of Beethoven's leading contemporaries to appreciate his music, was full of enthusiasm when he wrote to him shortly before conducting *Fidelio* in Dresden and Prague in 1823. 'Every [performance] will be a festival day, on which I shall be privileged to offer to your exalted mind the homage which lives in my heart, where reverence and love for you struggle with each other.'[10]

The Tagebuch

Perhaps in an attempt to overcome his loneliness after Antonie Brentano returned with her family to Frankfurt, loneliness compounded by his increasing deafness, Beethoven decided to keep a 'commonplace' book. The Tagebuch (1812–18) as it is known, was partly a repository for those thoughts and feelings which could no longer be shared with his 'Immortal Beloved'; partly an *aide mémoire* of quotations which interested him in the books he was reading at the time: German poetry, philosophy, theology, studies of Eastern religions and literature, the *Iliad* and the *Odyssey*, the novels of Sir Walter Scott and the works of Shakespeare. Also included were such down-to-earth 'good resolutions'[11] as a reminder to study daily 'from half past five until breakfast.' Cathartic though this may have been, Beethoven's love for Antonie (or Toni, as she was affectionately known) remained a constant source of anguish expressed, for example, in his beautiful setting of Johann Herder's poem, *Die laute Klage* (*The Loud Lament*), WoO 135, composed in 1815: 'O turtledove, I mourn like you, and hide my mourning deep in my wounded heart ... Ah, what a cruel thing is love!' – a song, unsurprisingly in tragic C minor, which may have prompted a self-inflicted rebuke later in his Tagebuch: 'With regard to T', he wrote in 1816, 'there is nothing else but to leave it to God, never go there [Frankfurt?] where one could do wrong out of weakness; only leave this totally to Him, to Him alone, the all-knowing God!'[12] Beethoven comforted himself with other quotations, among them more verses by Herder: 'In adversity, do not despair of seeing that day which will bring you joy rather than sorrow, and pleasure rather than grief ... Therefore, be of good heart even when accidents befall. Time brings miracles to light; numberless are the graces you

---

[9] Thayer, *The Life of Beethoven*, p. 897.

[10] From one of a series of letters which Weber wrote to Beethoven: Thayer, *The Life of Beethoven*, p. 863.

[11] Beethoven's *Tagebuch* [48], quoted in Solomon, *Beethoven Essays*, p. 259

[12] *Tagebuch* [104], quoted in Solomon, *Beethoven Essays*, p. 279.

can hope for from God.'[13] As it happens, it was not long before his optimism on that occasion was rewarded: 'Just as some time ago', he noted in
1816, '[I am] again at the piano in my own improvisations, despite my hearing [deficiences].'[14]

A new polyphony and a new lyricism

No doubt stimulated by his extensive theological, philosophical and literary studies, undertaken during those weeks when he was well enough to
read but not well enough to compose, clear signs of innovation and deep-
ening spirituality in Beethoven's later years are to be found in his increasing interest in all aspects of polyphony and in new forms of lyricism. When
preparing the *Missa Solemnis*, for example, he spent many happy hours in
Archduke Rudolph's magnificent library studying ancient modes, Renaissance polyphony, Handel and, above all Bach, 'because of his infinite and
inexhaustible wealth of combinations and harmonies'.[15]

In conversation with the young violinist Karl Holz, who would later act
as his secretary and assistant, Beethoven explained his vision of the music
he planned to write in the future in what amounted to a personal manifesto: 'To make a fugue requires no particular skill. In my [student] days I
have made dozens of them. But the [imagination] wishes also to assert its
privileges, and today a new and really poetic element must be introduced
into the old traditional forms.'[16]

A beautiful example of 'poetic elements' introduced into 'old traditional
forms' is to be found in the Piano Sonata in A flat major, op. 110 (1821–2),
with its two short fugues, the first recto and the second inverso, sand-
wiched between the sad, improvisatory Arioso dolente – a contemporary
realization, perhaps, of Bach's intentions when he prefaced the forty-eight
fugues of his *Well-Tempered Clavier* with improvisatory preludes, all of
which Beethoven had studied in depth as a young pupil of Christian Gottlob Neefe in Bonn. In the *Missa Solemnis* he included some fairly traditional (though greatly expanded) fugal movements, in deference perhaps to
its sacred nature – 'In gloria Dei Patris' (Gloria), for example, and 'Et vitam
venturi' (Credo) – but he also explored polyphonic textures more generally
in the 'Christe eleison' and the joyful double fugue (ex. 24.1) in the finale of
the Ninth Symphony.

Inventive polyphonic textures, sometimes of great complexity, abound
in the late quartets too: monumental and epic in the *Grosse Fuge*, op. 133,
for instance, or meditative and 'poetic' in op. 131. Lyricism in Beethoven's
later music is either simple and profound or complex and profound. An

[13] *Tagebuch* [58], quoted in Solomon, *Beethoven Essays*, p. 261. Verses from Herder's
poem *Life's Solace*.

[14] *Tagebuch* [102], p. 278.

[15] A conversation with Karl Freudenburg, quoted in Thayer, *The Life of Beethoven*, p. 956.

[16] Beethoven in conversation with Karl Holz, quoted in Thayer, *The Life of Beethoven*,
p. 692.

Ex. 24.1

example of the first is the finale of the Piano Sonata in E major, op. 109 (1820), dedicated to the Brentano's daughter, Maximiliane – a loving, deeply tender melody (ex. 24.2) played before and after six variations. 'I have always a picture in my mind when I am composing and work up to it',[17] Beethoven told his English visitor, Charles Neate. On this occasion there can surely be little doubt that the picture he had in his mind was of Maximiliane's 'excellent and gifted' mother, not least because of the minutely detailed interpretative instructions, written in both Italian and German, which underline the heartfelt nature of the music.

Ex. 24.2

Examples of the second kind of lyricism include the prayer for peace ('Dona nobis pacem') (ex. 24.3a) in the *Missa Solemnis*, and the infinitely tender violin solo which dives and soars its way through the 'Benedictus' (ex. 24.3b). In character, shape and language both are similar to the Adagio (ex. 25.5) in the Quartet in E flat major, op. 127, discussed in the next chapter.

Ex. 24.3

Beethoven's imagination 'asserted its privileges' in other ways too, not only in matters of form in general and variation form in particular, but also in scale; those two titanic statements of religious belief and human aspiration – the *Missa Solemnis* and the Ninth Symphony – were the result. After such confident and universal proclamations, could any more be said? Well, it could be, and in the introspective, personal arena of the late string quartets, it was.

---

[17] Beethoven in conversation with Charles Neate, quoted in Thayer, *The Life of Beethoven*, p. 620.

String Quartet in E flat major, op. 127

Prince Nikolay Borisovich Golitsïn

After Prince Razumovsky's quartet was disbanded in 1814, Schuppanzigh spent some years in Russia and introduced Beethoven's more recent compositions to music lovers there. Among them was Prince Nikolay Borisovich Golitsïn (1794–1866), a keen amateur cellist and composer, who would become one of Beethoven's most enthusiastic admirers: 'Je lui ai trouvé cette Sublimité qui préside à toutes vos Compositions', he told Beethoven in a letter written in November 1823; 'et qui rendent vos œuvres inimitables.'[1] The Prince was clearly a man of action as well as words and, not content with ordering a pre-publication score of the *Missa Solemnis* and persuading the Tsar to subscribe to this 'trésor de beauté',[2] he organized the first complete performance of the Mass in St Petersburg on 7 April 1824.

However, his most enduring contribution to the history of music was the fateful letter he had written two years earlier in November 1822, asking Beethoven to compose 'one, two or three new quartets' and to name his price.[3] Beethoven, who was already considering a successor to the F minor Quartet, op. 95,[4] agreed at once, but he still had to complete the *Missa Solemnis* and was about to embark on the Ninth Symphony, which would occupy most of his time over the next two years, so suggested deadlines came and went and financial confusion of one kind or another followed.

Nonetheless, three of the highest pinnacles in music, the three string quartets dedicated to the Prince – op. 127, op. 132 and op. 130 – were eventually scaled, soon followed by arguably the greatest of them all, the Quartet in C sharp minor, op. 131, and finally by the beautiful, though underrated, Quartet in F major, op. 135. The original finale to op. 130, the *Grosse Fuge*, was published separately as op. 133 and dedicated to Archduke Rudolph. Many years after Beethoven's death, there would be a touching end to the Golitsïn–Beethoven saga, when the Prince's son, the conductor and composer Yuri Nikolayevich Golitsïn, presented a substantial donation

---

[1] Clive, *Beethoven and his World*, quoting *Corr.* B1752, 29 Nov. 1823.

[2] Clive, *Beethoven and his World*, p. 137.

[3] Clive, *Beethoven and his World*, p. 135.

[4] *Letters of Beethoven*, Letter 1079 5 June 1822: Beethoven to Carl Peters, in which he offered a number of works for publication – from the sublime *Missa Solemnis* to the humdrum 'Military Marches'; also a projected complete edition of his compositions – which never materialized – and a 'quartet ... which you could also have very soon.' There appear to be no signs of such a quartet in Beethoven's sketchbooks, apart from an introduction to a string quintet in D minor, written in 1817 (Hess 40).

to Beethoven's heirs 'as a token of the admiration which Russian musicians felt for his music'.[5]

Ignaz Schuppanzigh and Joseph Böhm

On his return from Russia in April 1823, Ignaz Schuppanzigh (1776–1830) resumed his career as conductor, organized and led the orchestra for the first two performances of the Ninth Symphony in May 1824, and relaunched his popular chamber music concert series after re-forming his quartet with two colleagues from his Razumovsky quartet days: the violist Franz Weiss and the cellist Joseph Linke – together with a former pupil, Karl Holz, as second violinist. When Schuppanzigh heard that Beethoven was writing a new quartet, the first for fourteen years, he begged him to grant his colleagues and himself the honour of giving the premiere at the inaugural concert of the new season in January the following year, adding that it would 'make a big difference to [his] present subscription'.[6] Schuppanzigh's innovatory programmes, in which he placed serious or 'difficult' compositions between popular, established works, attracted audiences of as many as 500, and on this special occasion he decided to sandwich the new quartet between Spohr's Octet and Beethoven's ever popular Septet. Beethoven had not finished it in time, however, and the F minor Quartet, op. 95, was performed in its place to great effect.

The premiere of the new quartet was then rescheduled for 6 March 1825, and morale was high when Beethoven sent the manuscript parts to Schuppanzigh and his colleagues a few days in advance, accompanied by one of his jokey letters: 'Most Excellent Fellows! Each of you is receiving herewith his part. And each of you undertakes to do his duty and, what is more, pledges himself on his word of honour to acquit himself as well as possible, to distinguish himself and to vie in excellence with the others.'[7]

Beethoven's hearing had deteriorated so much by then that he decided not to attend the concert himself, but to rely on others to tell him how it went. Several people, including one of his closest friends, the publisher Tobias Haslinger, thought that Schuppanzigh and his colleagues had played well, but Beethoven's nephew Karl and his brother Johann, neither of whom knew much about music, reported that the premiere had been a failure. Beethoven was furious and decided that a second performance should be given as soon as possible with the brilliant young Hungarian violinist Joseph Böhm (1795–1876) as leader in place of Schuppanzigh – a deeply hurtful decision, but one that the loyal Schuppanzigh reluctantly accepted.

Böhm, who later taught Joachim, was the first Professor of Violin at the newly formed Vienna Conservatoire (now the prestigious Hochschule für

---

[5] Clive, *Beethoven and his World*, p. 136.

[6] Beethoven's conversation books, quoted in Thayer, *The Life of Beethoven*, p. 938.

[7] *Letters of Beethoven*, Letter 1356, March 1825: Beethoven to Schuppanzigh, Weiss, Linke and Holz.

Musik). When Schuppanzigh went to Russia, Böhm was invited to lead the quartet, and he continued to play with Weiss, Linke and Holz from time to time after Schuppanzigh's return, focusing mainly on quartets by Mozart, Haydn, Beethoven and later Schubert. On the evidence of at least one enthusiastic reviewer, they were highly regarded for the authenticity of their playing. 'This is how Beethoven and Mozart should be played', he wrote after one of their concerts in the *Gesellschaft der Musikfreunde*;[8] so in the circumstances Beethoven's decision was perhaps understandable. Much to the alarm of the players, Beethoven attended all the rehearsals.

> Rehearsing in his presence was not easy [wrote Böhm many years later]. With close attention, his eyes followed the bows ... to judge the smallest fluctuations in tempo or rhythm and correct them immediately ... At the close of the last movement ... there occurred a meno vivace, which seemed to me to weaken the general effect. At the rehearsal, therefore, I advised that the original tempo be maintained, which was done to the betterment of the effect. Beethoven, crouched in a corner, heard nothing, but watched with strained attention. After the last stroke of the bows he said, laconically: 'Let it remain so', went to the desks and crossed out meno vivace in the four parts.[9]

When the quartet was published – the only late quartet to be published in Beethoven's lifetime – he renamed the final section of the last movement 'Allegro commodo'.

Double performances and the 'new ideal of absolute music'

To help audiences and critics alike to understand the new work more fully, the second violinist, Karl Holz, came up with the novel suggestion that they should play the quartet twice, in a concert exclusively devoted to it. Initially, Beethoven had some reservations, but soon relented and Böhm's quartet gave two double performances of op. 127 to general acclaim, the first on 23 March and the second on 7 April 1825. Several other performances followed: 'The misty veil disappeared and the splendid work of art radiated its dazzling glory',[10] wrote a critic in the *Allgemeine Theaterzeitung Wien*, while another reported that the quartet 'was worked with such genius, that the audience swooned'.[11]

The idea caught on; some double performances were small-scale affairs, but others were packed: 'The four quartet players had barely enough room for their stands and places and were thickly surrounded', wrote the poet

---

[8] Clive, *Beethoven and his World*, p. 38.

[9] Joseph Böhm, quoted in Thayer, *The Life of Beethoven*, pp. 940–1.

[10] Thayer, *The Life of Beethoven*, p. 941.

[11] Ludwig Rellstab, quoted in Adelson, 'Beethoven's String Quartet in E flat op. 127', p. 236.

Ludwig Rellstab, noting that they 'had held seventeen (or more) rehearsals before daring to give this enigmatic new composition even a semi-public performance before a number of connoisseurs.'[12]

Later generations of music lovers owe a great deal to that intelligent and persistent audience of connoisseurs in Vienna, and to such organizations as the British Quartet Society of London, founded in 1845. It became clear to them, as well as to performers and publishers more generally that, because the late quartets were so complex and challenging, scores should be published together with individual parts as a matter of course, so that each work could be studied and understood more fully – something which, in general, had not been thought necessary before. The practice was increasingly adopted from op. 127 onwards, and spread in later years to include all chamber and orchestral music. It is also clear, as Carl Dahlhaus noted, that 'it was only a matter of time before the string quartet overtook the symphony as … the new ideal of absolute music.'[13]

String Quartet no. 12 in E flat major, op. 127

Maestoso – Allegro
Adagio ma non troppo e molto cantabile
Scherzando vivace – Presto
Finale – Allegro commodo

Maestoso   The quartet opens with a grand proclamation (ex. 25.1) – not merely an introduction, but an integral thematic statement which will return twice more with increasing resonance, define the formal outlines of the movement and, at the same time, convey something, perhaps, of its meaning.

Ex. 25.1

With unevenly spaced *sforzandi*, phrasing in each successive proclamation is purposeful and powerfully asymmetric. The second Maestoso heralds the development section and the climactic third, marked *fortissimo*, in 'divine' C major (see Chapter 15), leads to a complex blend of further development, variation, extended recapitulation and coda. Beethoven used the term 'maestoso' comparatively rarely, either as a metaphor for divine justice – Don Fernando's entry in the last scene of *Fidelio*, for example: 'Our

---

[12] Ibid.

[13] Carl Dalhaus, 'The Idea of Absolute Music', quoted in Adelson, 'Beethoven's String Quartet in E flat op. 127', p. 238.

sovereign Lord, the King commands me to succour all who suffer here. To him, his subjects are his brothers'; or, as Birgit Lodes has suggested,[14] as a specific reference to 'a sacred godhead' in, among other examples, the Introduction to *Christ on the Mount of Olives*, op. 85, and the 'Quoniam tu solus sanctus' in the *Missa Solemnis*. Quoting a persuasive parallel in Beethoven's Tagebuch – 'All things flow clear and pure from God' – Birgit Lodes has also written: 'this is the message I hear in the opening Allegro ... all things flow clear and pure from the Maestoso.'[15]

Allegro   Like a butterfly emerging from its chrysalis, the tender opening theme (violin 1 in ex. 25.2), marked *sempre piano e dolce – teneramente*, emerges freely and naturally from a three-note phrase (*x*) in the Maestoso, to be welcomed by each member of the quartet in turn, creating a richly varied tapestry of interrelated patterns above a chorale-like *cantus firmus* (*y*) – a fine example of Beethoven's innovative approach to traditional polyphony discussed in the previous chapter; reason enough also for the practical suggestion made by one of Beethoven's circle that, to understand the quartet fully, it should be heard at least four times, with the listener focusing on each part in turn.

Ex. 25.2

Though deeply significant in the coda, the *cantus firmus* (*y*) remains in the background for much of the time, while the two lyrical phrases (*z*, *u*) in the first group reappear in various guises throughout; the second phrase (*u*), for example, will later bring the movement to its sweet-toned conclusion. There is energy at times in the transition and development but, for the most part, the emphasis on growth, characteristic of classical sonata form, is here replaced by a much greater emphasis on lyrical polyphony, on introspection rather than on drama, mirroring perhaps the introspection now imposed on Beethoven by his increasing deafness. After visiting Beethoven in 1825, the poet Ludwig Rellstab noted that he had 'lost nothing of that mysterious magnetic power, which so irresistibly enchains us in

[14] Lodes, *'So traumte mire, ich reiste ... nach Indien'*, p. 197.
[15] Lodes, *'So traumte mire, ich reiste ... nach Indien'*, p. 200.

the external semblance of great men', but he 'read sadness, suffering and kindness in his face ... [though] not a trace of harshness'[16] – a description which perfectly matches the changing moods in this wonderful quartet. Though no less lyrical and contrapuntal, the second group (ex. 25.3a) is more emotional and, in later bars, borrows the lyrical opening phrase from the first group (*z*), perhaps to soothe anxieties expressed in a new motive in G minor (ex. 25.3b), recalling the opening bars of Mozart's troubled Symphony no. 40 in the same key.

Ex. 25.3

Rellstab's reading of 'sadness and suffering' in Beethoven's face is also reflected in the profoundly spiritual coda, where two varants of the *cantus firmus* (ex. 25.4a, c) rise to the surface retracing, consciously or not, the first two bars of two well-known chorales – one in the St John Passion and the other in the St Matthew Passion (ex. 25.4b, d) – in both of which Bach meditates on divine acceptance of suffering, acceptance which Beethoven strove so hard to emulate in his later years.

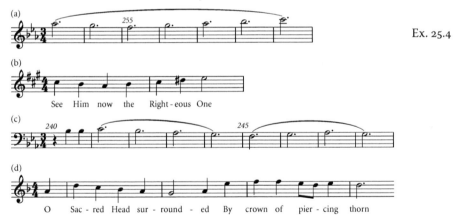

Ex. 25.4

Adagio ma non troppo e molto cantabile   The first movement ends *pianissimo* in the tonic, E flat major, with a phrase from the first group and, after a silent pause, the second movement – a theme followed by five variations and coda – opens softly in the same key with a gently syncopated introduction, so a sense of continuity, explored further by Beethoven in the Quartet in C sharp minor, is surely implied. The theme, a seamless melody

[16] Ludwig Rellstab, quoted in Sonneck, *Beethoven: Impressions by his Contemporaries*, p. 180.

of great beauty in the new tonic, A flat major (ex. 25.5), played alternately
by the first violin and cello and enriched by descants as visionary as the
theme itself, shares the same time-signature, the same melodic character
and deep spirituality with two movements in the *Missa Solemnis* discussed
in the previous chapter – 'Dona nobis pacem' (ex. 24.3a) and 'Benedictus'
(ex. 24.3b).

Ex. 25.5

In the first variation (ex. 25.6), based on the opening phrase of the
theme (*v*), Beethoven combines chromatic lyricism and rich polyphony
with swung rhythms to extraordinary effect. Ever-greater waves of emotion in later bars, heightened dynamics and an increasingly extended tessitura reach a level of intensity unsurpassed in chamber music, with the
cello plumbing the depths and the violin reaching for the stars five octaves
above.

Ex. 25.6

Though still chromatic and technically complex, the second variation
(Andante con moto) is cooler in mood and lighter in texture – a cheerful,
improvisatory dialogue shared antiphonally by the two violins, focusing
in particular on variants and inversions of the short motive which introduced the theme (*v*), above a crisp accompaniment. But perhaps the heart
of the movement is to be found in the third variation, Adagio molto espressivo (ex. 25.7), with its magical slide from A flat major to unrelated E major
within the space of two quavers. As discussed in Chapter 15, E major for
Beethoven is the key of divine hope, expressed, for instance, in Leonore's
aria 'Komm Hoffnung'. The rising phrase, reflecting her determination and
courage, is remembered here in the third variation's underlying contours
and glowing aura, not merely transforming the original theme, but trans-
figuring it.

Ex. 25.7

Light textures and delicate, rising arpeggios provide the framework for parts of the theme in the fourth variation, safely back in A flat major and in 12/8 time, played in turn by the first violin and cello, then shared by the second violin, viola and cello in a richly harmonized melodic sequence of 6-3 chords. Simplicity and economy of line, characteristic of the original theme, return in the fifth variation (ex. 25.8) – another vision of hope in E major in the form of an exquisite, almost Elgarian meditation on a variant (*w*) of the opening phrase (*v*) involving mirrored polyphony– a reminder, incidentally, of similar passages in the slow movement of the Ninth Symphony.

Ex. 25.8

After a few moments' silence, the coda is heard as if in the distance, and the movement ends with a fragile, vulnerable cadence, the final pause on one of the weakest beats of the bar. Philip Radcliffe's comment on this magical moment is typically succinct: 'Very unceremonious, but totally convincing.'[17]

Scherzando vivace An attractive feature of the quartet as a whole is that each movement has its own introduction, and each is very different in character. The introduction to the Scherzando is the shortest: four piz-zicato chords borrowed, as so often in the late quartets, from Beethoven's earlier music – in this case, the important four-note motive, also in E flat major, which unites the outer movements of the Septet (ex. 9.11–13, 17). The principal motive, a variant of *v*, borrowed from the theme and the fifth variation in the previous movement, dominates the Scherzando. In the first section (ex. 25.9a), the mood is playful, though soon called to order by authoritative (though no less sparkling) off-beat crotchets, marked *Ritmo di tre battute*. The much extended second section is again dominated by similar rhythms, played alternately in relentless unison or in cheerful, mir-rored counterpoint – though brought to a halt by a further variant unex-pectedly in duple time (ex. 25.9b).

Although many performers play this Allegro at the same tempo as the Scherzando vivace (i.e. crotchet = crotchet), Robert Simpson has provided

---

[17] Radcliffe, *Beethoven's String Quartets*, p. 105.

Ex. 25.9

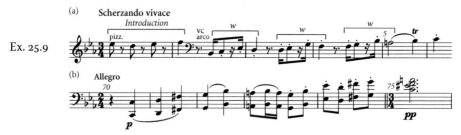

an alternative explanation of Beethoven's intentions in this strangely ambiguous passage (ex. 25.9b):

> With Beethoven *allegro* is always slower than *vivace* (the main indication for the scherzo); what he requires here is two crotchets in the time of the previous three ... If he wanted no change of tempo, why add 'Allegro'? the crotchets are usually allowed to go marching on at the same pace, with a complete loss of the mystery the composer intends.[18]

Presto   A short transition unleashes the Presto, a movement as unlike a traditional Trio as it could possibly be. The distant sound of a 'rushing, mighty wind' seems threatening, even overwhelming, as it approaches, picking up fragments of earlier motives on the way. But when it arrives, it proves to be wholly benevolent – a joyful celebration of life in one of Beethoven's most exuberant dances, kept on its toes by off-beat *sforzando* chords, repeated three times (D flat major – G flat major – B flat major) and briefly remembered later when the recapitulation makes way for a mischievous coda.

Finale   The finale is in two related, though very different, parts: the first a complete movement in sonata form, warm and appealing; the second much shorter, but on a higher spiritual plane.

Ex. 25.10

Most unusually, Beethoven provides no indication of tempo for the first section, perhaps because he thought that it would be obvious in such an accessible movement; certainly the pastoral opening melody (ex. 25.10) and the robust second group suggest a leisurely tempo. Forward momentum is established by the *sforzando* placed on the second (weak) beat in the first bar of the short introduction and maintained by unassertive second-beat stresses. The five-note motive (*t*) plays a prominent part in various guises

---

[18] Simpson, 'The Chamber Music for Strings', pp. 266–7.

throughout the movement, initially in the secretive transition, leading to a festive march, followed by a rousing, bucolic dance. All the thematic ideas, including the introduction, are explored in some depth and motives from both groups are combined from time to time in co-operative polyphony.

Allegro commodo   However, exuberance makes way for wonder as the recapitulation draws serenely to a close (ex. 25.11). The pastoral and bucolic may be beautiful, but they are no match for heaven glimpsed, if only for a few spellbinding bars in 'divine' C major, at the start of the Allegro commodo. Though structurally correct, the term 'coda' is far too prosaic a word for this celestial dance and its graceful version of the five-note motive (*t*). The overarching shape of the quartet comes gradually into focus, with divine power in the majestic opening bars of the work (ex. 25.1) balanced and illuminated by divine grace at its close (ex. 25.11) – an exquisite meditation in sounds and textures never heard before and rarely heard since, except perhaps in the subtly muted tone-colours of Fauré, Debussy and Ravel. So it is hardly surprising that members of the audience 'swooned' at that concert given by Böhm and his colleagues on 6 April 1825, when the 'misty veil [finally] disappeared and the splendid work of art radiated its dazzling glory.'[19]

Ex. 25.11

---

[19] Ludwig Rellstab, quoted in Adelson, 'Beethoven's String Quartet in E flat op. 127', p. 236.

String Quartet in A minor, op. 132

A few days after the concert mentioned in the last chapter, Beethoven again became seriously ill. Dr Anton Braunhofer, one of Vienna's leading physicians, did not mince his words: 'No wine, no coffee, no spices of any kind. I'll arrange matters with the cook', he wrote in Beethoven's conversation book on 18 April 1825; 'then I will guarantee you a full recovery, which understandably means a lot to me, as your admirer and friend ... You must do some work in the daytime so that you can sleep at night. If you want to get entirely well and live a long time, you must live according to nature.'[1] Beethoven was already sketching the A minor Quartet – early sketches for it had appeared the previous year – but, for three or four anxious and frustrating weeks, he was too ill to do any creative work. By the end of May, however, he was composing again and had decided to replace his original plan for a slow movement with a 'Hymn of Thanksgiving to God of an Invalid on his Convalescence', a title he noted in his current sketchbook.

The quartet was finished in July and two private performances took place on 9 and 11 September at the Zum Wilden Mann in Baden. Schuppanzigh had been forgiven for the mixed reception of the premiere of op. 127, described in the previous chapter, and Holz, Weiss and Linke joined him. It can be assumed that there were plenty of rehearsals this time, some attended by Beethoven's closest friends. Among them, for instance, was one of his 'most discreet and supportive benefactors', Johann Wolfmayer, the senior partner in a firm of cloth-merchants, who 'wept like a child' as he listened to the slow movement.[2]

Sir George Smart

Also present at both of the private performances was the leading English conductor of the time, Sir George Smart (1776–1867), organist at the Chapel Royal, Windsor, and violinist, who promoted Beethoven and his music unstintingly in Britain. As a young man, he had had the (perhaps unique) distinction of being given a timpani lesson by Haydn when the timpanist failed to turn up for a rehearsal; though a member of the violin section, he bravely volunteered to do what he could to help. Among the many Beethoven concerts which he directed over the years was a series of ten hugely successful performances in London and Liverpool of *Christ on the Mount of Olives*, op. 85, and the *Battle* Symphony, op. 91, to raise

---

[1] Beethoven's conversation books, 18 April 1825, quoted in Thayer, *The Life of Beethoven*, p. 945.

[2] Karl Holz, quoted in Clive, *Beethoven and his World*, p. 401.

money for the widows of soldiers killed at the Battle of Waterloo. As a leading member of the Philharmonic Society of London, he was among those responsible for commissioning the Ninth Symphony, and it was he who conducted the English premiere in the Argyll Rooms on 21 March 1825. A few months later, he travelled to Vienna, determined to meet Beethoven – partly, no doubt, as an act of *pietas*, but also because he wanted to hear the composer's definitive views on tempi and other practical matters in the symphonies, the Ninth Symphony in particular.[3]

Sir George had heard plenty of stories about Beethoven's unpredictable behaviour, so he must have been relieved as well as gratified to be welcomed by the composer 'in a most flattering manner', and invited to join the 'select audience of professors' at what were effectively open rehearsals of the A minor Quartet. On both occasions, Beethoven directed the performers more by eye than by ear, keenly aware of every detail. He even borrowed Karl Holz's violin at one point to demonstrate the precise articulation that he wanted; a pretty rough demonstration, though effective enough to be understood by the players, two of whom, Schuppanzigh and Weiss, had known him for thirty years.

Later, when discussing with Beethoven the recitative for cellos and basses in the last movement of the Ninth Symphony, Sir George was taken aback to be told that it should be played 'in strict time'. He boldly argued that it could not therefore be a true recitative; but Beethoven told him firmly that he had 'called it so', and finally closed the discussion with 'I wish it to go in strict time.' 'This from the composer', Sir George added wryly, 'was of course decisive.'[4] No doubt, Beethoven's response would have been different if their discussion had turned to the recitative in the A minor Quartet, with its two *ritardandi*, one *accelerando* and three distinct changes of tempo – Più allegro, Presto and Poco adagio – within the space of twenty-two bars.

When the quartet was heard for the first time, the 'select audience of professors' might have been forgiven for thinking that Beethoven, the composer, had been replaced to an even greater extent by Beethoven, the master of improvisation – mastery demonstrated later that day when he improvised 'in an extraordinary manner' on a theme suggested by Sir George Smart. What the connection was between the polyphonic Assai sostenuto (ex. 26.1a) in the opening bars of the quartet, the impetuous violin cadenza (ex. 26.1b) and the melodic fragments that follow, must have been (and still is) hard to grasp at first hearing. Even the enthusiastic Sir George wisely confined his comments on the music in his diary to two words only, 'most chromatic'. No doubt, he felt on safer ground when describing Beethoven,

---

[3] In his capacity as conductor at Covent Garden, Sir George Smart travelled to Europe with the General Manager, Charles Kemble, hoping to persuade Weber to compose an opera for London; *Oberon* was the result. Sir George then travelled alone to Vienna for his rewarding meetings with Beethoven.

[4] Sir George Smart in conversation with Beethoven, quoted in Thayer, *The Life of Beethoven*, p. 963.

the man – 'no-one could be more agreeable than he was', and the convivial party after the concert – 'plenty of jokes we all wrote to him by turns.'[5]

Those generally familiar with Beethoven's chamber music may have noticed, and even felt reassured by, thematic links between the opening bars of the Quartet and semitone motives in the *Kreutzer* Sonata, for example (ex. 14.4–8), or the C minor String Trio (ex. 8.15a) – a motive which resurfaced in Beethoven's mind from time to time throughout his creative life and would reappear a few months later, after a shake or two of the kaleidoscope, in the *Grosse Fuge* (ex. 28.1b–d) and the outer movements of the Quartet in C sharp minor (ex. 29.1). Interesting though such thematic links may be, the fact that the outcome in every case is totally different is, of course, still more interesting.

The 'professors' would surely have been intrigued and surprised by Beethoven's unprecedented decision to explain the Molto Adagio in such a personal, self-revealing way, something he had never done before: 'Hymn of Thanksgiving to God for recovery from illness – in the Lydian mode', he wrote, followed in the Andante by 'feelings of renewed strength'. Beethoven sometimes made notes in his sketchbooks as an *aide-mémoire* of the emotional or literary background of a new composition – the slow movement of the F major String Quartet, op. 18 no. 1, for instance, inspired by the vault scene in Shakespeare's *Romeo and Juliet*. But he rarely included them in his published scores, though the *Pastoral* Symphony, with its detailed description of each movement, is an exception, as are the few notable compositions with one-word titles: *Pathètique*, for example, or *Eroica*.

This occasion was different; Beethoven must have accepted that Dr Braunhofer was right and that his recent illness was far more serious than before – perhaps even life-threatening. Like his English contemporary, the poet and artist William Blake, however, Beethoven was not one to 'cease from mental fight.'[6] He had always accepted, as he told Countess Erdödy in an earlier letter, that 'as finite beings, who are the embodiment of an infinite spirit [we] are born to suffer both pain and joy; one might almost say that the best of us [attain] joy through suffering.'[7] So perhaps he wanted his listeners to understand that the attainment of 'joy through suffering' is what the magnificent A minor Quartet, op. 132, is all about.

The first public performance took place on 6 November, a fact that Prince Golitsïn picked up a few weeks later in St Petersburg, when reading a report in the Leipzig Gazette: 'I am so impatient to get acquainted with this new masterpiece', he told Beethoven in a letter written on 14

[5] Ibid.

[6] William Blake: *Jerusalem*, verse 2: 'Bring me my bow of burning gold! Bring me my arrows of desire! Bring me my spear! O clouds, unfold! Bring me my chariot of fire! I will not cease from mental fight …'. Like Beethoven, Blake died in 1827.

[7] *Letters of Beethoven*, Letter 563, 19 October 1815: Beethoven to Countess Anna Maria Erdödy.

January, 'that I beg you to send it to me … without further delay.'[8] For once, Beethoven responded quickly, and a manuscript copy of the quartet duly arrived the following month confirming, no doubt, Golitsïn's prophetic view of Beethoven's genius, expressed in an earlier letter written soon after the premiere of the *Missa Solemnis*: 'It can be said that your genius has anticipated the centuries.'[9]

String Quartet no. 13 in A minor, op. 132

Assai sostenuto – Allegro
Allegro ma non tanto
Molto adagio – Andante
Alla Marcia, assai vivace – Più allegro – Presto – Allegro appassionato –
Presto

Assai sostenuto – Allegro Sir George Smart's succinct comment, 'most chromatic', is undoubtedly correct. Semitones pervade almost every cell, motive, phrase and melody in the troubled first movement, recreating the extreme tensions which Beethoven must have experienced during those worrying and frustrating weeks in the summer of 1825. In character and mood, the dark, introspective introduction (ex. 26.1a) – created from two pairs of semitones a sixth apart, with the second an inversion of the first (*x*), and played *pianissimo* by each instrument in turn – could hardly be

Ex. 26.1

---

[8] Prince Nikolay Golitsïn to Beethoven, 14 January 1826, quoted in Thayer, *The Life of Beethoven*, p. 978. When published, together with the Quartet in F major, op. 135, by Adolph Schlezinger in Paris and his son Maurice in Berlin in September, 1827, the A minor Quartet, op. 132, was misplaced chronologically; op. 130, op. 131 and op. 133 had already been published that year.

[9] Prince Nikolay Golitsïn to Beethoven, 8 April 1824, quoted in Thayer, *The Life of Beethoven*, p. 925.

more different from the majestic certainties expressed in the opening
bars of op. 127. Tensions are heightened still further by the first violin's
unexpected – even subversive and shocking – cadenza at the start of the
Allegro (ex. 26.1b), as Beethoven's imagination, in his own words, 'asserts
its privileges' violently by introducing 'a new poetic element into the old
traditional forms:'[10] The chromatic motive (*x*) has an additional structural
and unifying part to play, characterizing and shaping the first subject in the
Allegro which, like the introduction, is shared in turn by each instrument
in tense and anxious discussion, and reappears in different guises in every
subsequent movement.

The opening motive (*x*) also defines the formal boundaries of the movement; the quiet though muscular transition, for example, and the reflective
bars at the start of an unusually short development section. In addition, it
introduces the two recapitulations. The first, though more ornamental, is
similar to the exposition while the second (ex. 26.2) is more contrapuntal
and dramatic.

Ex. 26.2

The combination of emotional extremes and structural freedom in the
quartet was picked up approvingly by a critic in the *Allgemeine musikalische Zeitung* soon afterwards. Like E. T. A. Hoffmann in his review of
the op. 70 piano trios, published in 1812,[11] the critic took it for granted that
Beethoven was one of the new romantics, identifying him with the influential romantic writer Jean Paul Richter: 'What our musical Jean Paul has
offered here is indeed great, marvellous, unusual, surprising and original;
it must, however, not only be heard often, but really studied.'[12] Only the
sweet-toned second subject (ex. 26.3a) is more independent, though even
here emotional pressure is brought to bear, with intervals in the first violin's lyrical solo – a variant of *y* – squeezed out of shape chromatically (*z*).

[10] Beethoven in conversation with Karl Holz, quoted in Thayer, *The Life of Beethoven*,
     p. 692.

[11] Concerning E. T. A. Hoffmann's celebrated article on the op. 70 piano trios, see
     Chapter 18 above.

[12] Quoted from *Ludwig van Beethoven: Die Werke im Spiegel seiner Zeit*, ed. Stefan
     Kunze, in Kinderman, *The String Quartets of Beethoven*, p. 321 n. 68.

Ex. 26.3

Nor is relief to be found in the coda (ex. 26.3b), with its flurry of discordant semitones beneath a curt, march-like version of the first subject's opening bar (*y*).

Allegro ma non tanto   If the first movement is an expression of the suffering which Ludwig Rellstab read in Beethoven's face when they met in 1825,[13] kindness, which he also detected, is surely evident in the Allegro ma non tanto – a gentle scherzo and trio in form, if not in name. There are only two themes in the 'scherzo' section (ex. 26.4a). The first, based on a three-note cell (*u*), introduces the movement, but otherwise has a subsidiary role. The second (*v*) is more extended in form, more melodic in spite of its curiously breathless character, and more suited to contrapuntal development. Both themes work in tandem for much of the time, especially in the first section, dominating the movement almost as comprehensively as the first subject in the F major String Quartet, op. 18 no. 1, written a quarter of a century earlier (ex. 10.1b), and for that reason the movement is best played, perhaps, in a graceful, flowing one-to-the-bar.

When composing the delicate 'trio' section, Beethoven looked even further back for inspiration, perhaps a little nostalgically as older people often do, to recall popular tunes he had heard or pieces he had composed in the 1790s. It is an exquisite musette, high in register and complete with an accompanying drone, followed by an extended solo, mostly for viola – almost identical to the Allemande for piano, WoO 81, composed in 1793, which he had already borrowed in 1795 for his Piano Trio, op. 1, no. 2 (*z* in ex. 5.9a). In the midst of this graceful and nostalgic entertainment a variant

Ex. 26.4

[13] Ludwig Rellstab in Sonneck, *Beethoven: Impressions by his Contemporaries*, p. 181.

of the principal cell *x* from the opening bars of the first movement pays an unexpected visit (ex. 26.4b) – a particularly intrusive and upsetting one when repeated in duple time (ex. 26.4c) – and then vanishes without further ado.

Molto Adagio – *Heiliger Dankgesang eines Genesenen an die Gottheit, in der lydischen Tonart*   The slow movement is in two contrasted and alternating sections, each in turn followed by a single variation, and ultimately by an extended coda. In the first section, Beethoven composed his 'Hymn of Thanksgiving to God for recovery from illness' in the style of one of the more archaic chorales that he had studied when writing the *Missa Solemnis*. Each phrase of the 'Hymn' is preceded by a short polyphonic introduction, as in Bach's chorale preludes, and the plain note-values, the simple harmonies and the ancient Lydian Mode[14] – the mode traditionally associated with healing and recovery – evoke feelings of timelessness, awe and reverence.

Andante – *Neue Kraft fühlend*   In the Andante, the change from the prayerful Lydian mode to the confident, joyful key of D major, the key of the Violin Concerto, is overwhelming, as Beethoven expresses 'feelings of renewed strength.' Striding motives, trills, grace notes, vibrant textures and off-beat stresses follow one another with vigour, and eventually unite to sing, *cantabile espressivo*, an ethereal, beautifully sculpted hymn of praise and thanksgiving (ex. 26.5).

Ex. 26.5

In spite of the greater textural complexity which both frames and accompanies the chorale variation that follows, there is still not a sharp or a flat in sight, so the purity of the Lydian mode remains intact – a rare example of self-restraint from a composer whose instinctive approach to keys in his later music was increasingly adventurous. There is complexity of another kind in the Andante variation, enriched by intricate lacework together with reminders of those semitone cells in the opening bars of the first movement (*x*). However, Beethoven reveals his most personal thoughts and feelings in the coda; some of his loveliest, most original music is to be found here in an extended fantasia based on the first phrase of the chorale. Decorated in flowing polyphony by phrases from the prelude (ex. 26.6), Beethoven expresses his gratitude to God quietly at first, but eventually with overwhelming fervour (*sforzandi* on each note of the Hymn) before returning to the reflective, prayerful mood of the opening bars.

---

[14] The Lydian mode is a major scale with its fourth degree raised by a semitone. Thus, whereas the scale of F major is F–G–A–B♭–C–D–E–F, the scale of F Lydian is F–G–A–B♮–C–D–E–F.

Ex. 26.6

Alla marcia, assai vivace Because the march and the recitative are both so short, their importance is sometimes overlooked, but Beethoven himself regarded them as separate movements: 'I am in mortal fright about the [A minor] quartet', he wrote to his nephew Karl when he had heard nothing for some days from Karl Holz, who was making a fair copy of the quartet at the time. He 'has taken away the third, fourth, fifth and sixth movements ... What a terrible misfortune if he has lost the manuscript ... Make my mind easy as quickly as possible.'[15] The Alla marcia (ex. 26.7) certainly has a spring in the step, but with fading dynamics and an underlying pulse distorted by *sforzandi* on weak beats, it is strangely unsettling, like the sinister March (no. 6) in *Fidelio*.

Ex. 26.7

Più Allegro – Presto Although similar in shape to parts of the recitative played by cellos and basses in the finale of the Ninth Symphony, the mood of this instrumental recitative is about as far removed from those confident proclamations as it is possible to be – swirling contours, a tremolo accompaniment, and a reminder of the bleak semitone motive with which the quartet began (*x*). The climax of the movement, aptly described by Joseph Kerman as a 'scream',[16] anticipates by seventy years the mental anguish expressed by the Norwegian artist Edvard Munch in his vivid portrayal of psychological terror, *The Scream*. The first violin's top F, held high above a *fortissimo* chord of the diminished seventh, swoops down almost three octaves in a cadenza (ex. 26.8) – even more dramatic than the two in the first movement (ex. 26.1b) – to settle on the dominant of A minor in the final cadential bar (Poco Adagio), unaccompanied, isolated and desolate.

[15] *Letters of Beethoven*, Letter 1410, 11 August 1825: Beethoven to his nephew, Karl.

[16] Kerman, *The Beethoven Quartets*, p. 244.

Ex. 26.8

Allegro appassionato – Presto So hopes of another 'Ode to Joy' are clearly premature, though in theory not implausible, as sketches for the principal theme in this rondo (ex. 25.9a) appeared in Beethoven's sketches for a proposed instrumental finale in the Ninth Symphony with his written comment: 'Perhaps more beautiful than the Ode to Joy?' Two opposed psychological and emotionally ambiguous states of mind are at work simultaneously in the Allegro appassionato. The last two bars of the recitative (ex. 25.8), based on the troubled cell *x* from the first movement (ex. 26.1), provides a disturbing and ultimately explosive accompaniment for the principal rondo theme (ex. 26.9) – all the more disturbing for its pulsating second-beat accents. By contrast, Beethoven's 'more beautiful' rondo theme is a free spirit, though at times an anxious one as it soars and dives this way and that, sometimes beyond the reach of dangers lurking beneath it, and at other times drawn into direct conflict with them.

Ex. 26.9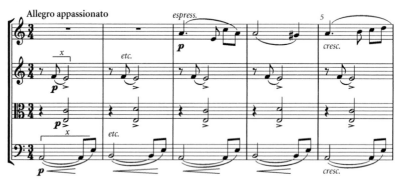

The first episode, accompanied by a flowing phrase borrowed from the cadence at the end of the rondo theme, is gentler. But it is not long before emotional storms return – an unexpectedly violent one with all four players involved in savage close combat. By contrast, the introspective transition (ex. 26.10), which leads back to the rondo theme, is a colourful, if muted, chromatic mosaic created almost entirely from variants of the opening cell (*x*).

Similar mood-swings dominate the rest of the movement. At the start of the Presto, the music is wild, even frantic, the rondo theme played by the cello with great intensity high on the A string, beneath the first violin's hysterical variant of the 'scream.'

However, there is a complete change of mood in the coda: not a fully fledged ode to joy perhaps, but a radiant variation of the rondo theme,

Ex. 26.10

followed by a comforting, ecstatic dance, swirling softly on its way with hope and youthful abandon. 'Take care', Beethoven had warned his pupil Ferdinand Ries in one of his tongue-in-cheek letters the previous year. 'You think that I am old. But I am a *youthful* old man.'[17]

---

[17] *Letters of Beethoven*, Letter 1175, April 1823: Beethoven to Ferdinand Ries.

String Quartet in B flat major, op. 130

While still at work on the Quartet in A minor, Beethoven began sketching ideas for the third and last of the Golitsïn quartets in May or June 1825. According to Karl Holz, 'new ideas streamed from [his] inexhaustible fantasy'[1] and, partly as a result perhaps, the number of movements in each successive quartet rose inexorably from four in op. 127 to five in op. 132 (if the Alla marcia and the ensuing recitative are counted as one movement rather than two); six in op. 130 (with an alternative finale added later) to seven in op. 131, dropping back to four in op. 135. Ideas were sometimes moved from one quartet to another; for instance, the beautiful Alla danza tedesca, placed originally in the A minor Quartet, was moved at quite a late stage to the Quartet in B flat major, and replaced by the Alla marcia, together with its dramatic recitative. 'Art demands of us that we shall not stand still', Beethoven told Karl Holz, adding: 'Thank God there is less lack of fantasy [in the quartets] than ever before.'[2]

Far from 'standing still', Beethoven worked with intense concentration while supposedly convalescing in Baden that summer. He had completed most of the new quartet by August, and assured Karl Holz in a letter, dated 24 August 1825, that he hoped to complete the sixth and final movement by the end of the month.[3] Two comments in the relevant sketchbook suggest that he wanted to complete the set of three Golitsïn quartets in an imposing manner: 'the last quartet with a serious and weighty introduction', he wrote; and a few pages later: 'last movement of the quartet in B flat-Fugha'.[4] He would not have forgotten that Prince Golitsïn had been responsible two years earlier for staging the world premiere in St Petersburg of the *Missa Solemnis*, with its own 'serious and weighty introduction' and magnificent fugues, and he clearly decided to treat the last of the Golitsïn quartets just as seriously. However, he became so absorbed when writing the fugal finale, the *Grosse Fuge*, that it took him four months to complete rather than the predicted week or two; by late December it had grown to a massive 741 bars, 98 bars longer than the other five movements combined.

Schuppanzigh, Holz, Weiss and Linke duly arrived for the first rehearsal of the quartet in Beethoven's new (and final) apartment in the

[1] Karl Holz, quoted in Solomon, *Beethoven*, p. 418.

[2] Beethoven in conversation with Karl Holz, quoted in Thayer, *The Life of Beethoven*, p. 982.

[3] *Letters of Beethoven*, Letter 1415, 24 August 1825: Beethoven in Baden to Karl Holz in Vienna.

[4] The *De Roda* sketchbook, quoted in Kinderman, *The String Quartets of Beethoven*, p. 295.

Schwartzpanierhaus, the romantically named 'House of the Black-Robed Spaniards', on Tuesday, 3 January 1826. Numerous rehearsals followed over the next eleven weeks, and although Holz was able to report at one stage that 'everything will go easily', he warned Beethoven that the fugue was causing so many problems that it 'must be practised at home', and that the players must therefore be allowed to take their precious manuscript parts away with them.[5] Even after further exhausting rehearsals, none of them felt that they really understood the fugue. 'Holz has fallen asleep', laughed Schuppanzigh on one occasion, 'since the last movement has made him *kaputt*.'[6]

It is not surprising then that the quartet caused such controversy after the premiere on 21 March 1826, a controversy which remains unresolved to this day. The audience greeted the first five movements warmly – the Presto, Alla danza tedesca and Cavatina in particular received 'tumultuous applause.' A critic, writing in the *Allgemeine musikalische Zeitung*, was more circumspect, describing the quartet as 'serious, dark and mysterious, and sometimes bizarre, abrupt and capricious'. Players, audience and critic alike were baffled by the massive fugue with which the new quartet ended; baffled not only by its complexity, but also by its immense length. When he described the *Grosse Fuge* as 'incomprehensible ... a sort of Chinese puzzle', the critic probably reflected what most of the audience felt that day. But he concluded his article with a thoughtful proviso: 'Yet we must not denounce the work prematurely; perhaps there will come a time when what at first glance seems to us so turbid and confused will be perceived as clear and perfectly balanced.'[7]

Contemporary for ever

That time arrived earlier perhaps than he expected: 'Finally, the sounding of both fugue themes, the one simple and the other in double counterpoint, was crowned with resounding bravos. That says a great deal', wrote a later critic in the *Neue Zeitschrift für Musik*, after a concert given by the Hellmesberger Quartet in 1859 which included op. 131, op. 130 and the *Grosse Fuge*, op. 133.[8] Schoenberg liked the *Grosse Fuge* because he and many of his friends thought that it sounded atonal;[9] and Stravinsky, not known for his admiration for Beethoven, was even more enthusiastic, describing it as 'the most perfect miracle in music ... the most absolutely contemporary piece of music I know, and contemporary for ever. The

---

[5] Karl Holz, quoted in Kinderman, *The String Quartets of Beethoven*, p. 301.

[6] Ibid.

[7] Quoted in Schindler, *Beethoven as I Knew Him*, p. 307.

[8] Kinderman, *The String Quartets of Beethoven*, p. 8.

[9] Schoenberg, 'My Evolution', in *Style and Idea*, p. 88. 'I have heard many a good musician, when listening to Beethoven's Great Fugue, cry out: "This sounds like atonal music." '

Great Fugue is, in rhythm alone, more subtle than any music of my own century ... I love it beyond anything.'[10] Beethoven never ventured further in his exploration of the 'endlessness of possibility' than in the *Grosse Fuge*. But unknown to him, a shy, miraculously talented young composer would follow him a few weeks after that historic premiere with his own apocalyptic vision of the future: the raw, terrifying opening movement of his String Quartet in G major, D887, with its foretaste of the sound world in the first movement of Bartók's Fifth String Quartet composed in 1934. Unlike Beethoven, Schubert composed what would be the last of his quartets 'as fast as he could put pen to paper' and completed it in a mere ten days – 20–30 June 1826. He included the same prophetic movement in his celebrated 'Private Concert' in March 1828, which consisted 'entirely of works composed by himself after the model of Beethoven'.[11]

The alternative finale: October–November 1826

The more perceptive members of the audience at the premiere of op. 130 refused to give up on the *Grosse Fuge* and agreed to the suggestion of the publisher Mathias Artaria that a piano version would help them to understand the work more fully. Beethoven agreed, and Anton Halm, who had recently given a fine performance of the *Emperor* Concerto, was asked to make the arrangement. He completed it in a couple of weeks, but it did not measure up to Beethoven's exacting standards and he reluctantly decided to do the job himself. Some went further and suggested that an attempt should be made to persuade Beethoven to publish the *Grosse Fuge* as an independent string quartet in its own right, and to compose a more approachable finale in its place. Those with long memories may have recalled one particularly encouraging precedent. In November 1805, a month after the failed premiere of *Fidelio*, Princess Lichnowsky and several of Beethoven's professional colleagues organized a complete play-through of the opera at the Lichnowsky palace, hoping to persuade him to make substantial cuts and changes. But 'without the prayers and entreaties of the very delicate and invalid princess, who was a second mother to Beethoven and acknowledged by himself as such, his united friends were not likely to have succeeded in this, even to themselves, very doubtful enterprise.' But by the evening three numbers had been cut and 'when we, exhausted, hungry and thirsty, went to restore ourselves by a splendid supper, then none was happier and gayer than Beethoven.'[12]

[10] Quoted in Kinderman, *The String Quartets of Beethoven*, p. 279.

[11] Einstein, *Schubert*, p. 308.

[12] Thayer, *The Life of Beethoven*, pp. 388–9. One of those involved, the singer, Joseph Röckel, described this dramatic occasion in a conversation with Alexander Thayer, which took place in Bath in 1861: 'As the whole opera was to be gone through, we went directly to work. Princess L[ichnowski] played on the grand piano the great score of the opera, and Clement' – the leader of the orchestra – 'sitting in a corner of the room, accompanied with his violin the whole opera by heart, playing all the solos of

Nonetheless, the proposed mission must have seemed 'a very doubtful enterprise', not least to 'the chosen ambassador', Karl Holz, whose judgement Beethoven was known to trust.

> I was charged with the terrible and difficult mission of persuading him to compose a new finale, which would be more accessible to the listeners as well as to the instrumentalists. I maintained that this Fugue, which departed from the ordinary and surpassed even the last quartets in originality, should be published as a separate work, and that it merited a designation as a separate opus ... Beethoven told me that he would reflect on it, but already on the next day I received a letter giving his agreement.[13]

Karl's attempted suicide

The months separating the completion of the *Grosse Fuge* and the first sketches for a new finale were quite surreal. On the positive side, Beethoven completed the Quartet in C sharp minor, op. 131, in July, and the Quartet in F major, op. 135, was mostly finished by the time he turned his attention to the new finale in October. However, at a personal level, the fears anticipated in the Cavatina's wordless recitative in op. 130 (ex. 27.8), were realized with crushing effect on 6 August 1826, when Beethoven's nephew Karl tried unsuccessfully to take his own life. Relations between guardian and ward, though affectionate at heart, had deteriorated in recent years – a situation that many parents have to face at one time or another. Karl seemed incapable of sustained effort and, after failing to complete his studies in philosophy and languages, he dropped out of university and later gave up his polytechnic course in commerce as well.

'Everything I do, apart from music, is badly done and is stupid', a frustrated Beethoven once confessed to his friend Johann Streicher,[14] so he must have known that, however well intentioned, he lacked the experience to support and encourage his nephew in a positive way. He was devastated by the attempted suicide, and all the more distressed, no doubt, when Karl told the court investigating the incident that he shot himself because of his uncle's endless, if well-intentioned, meddling. Luckily, the wound was not too serious and Karl's other uncle, Beethoven's youngest brother, Johann,

---

the different instruments ... Meyer and I made ourselves useful, by singing as well as we could, he (*basso*) the lower, I the higher parts of the opera ... But when after their united endeavours from seven till after one o'clock three numbers were sacrificed ... then none was happier or gayer than Beethoven.'

[13] Karl Holz, quoted in Solomon, *Beethoven*, pp. 422–3.

[14] *Letters of Beethoven*, p. 1154 n. 2, Letter from Johann Streicher to Peters, 5 March 1825: 'But what am I to say about Beethoven's behaviour to you and how can I endeavour to excuse it? This I can only do by letting you have his own opinion of himself which he expressed in my own home: "Everything I do apart from music is badly done and is stupid."'

decided to take matters in hand. Now retired from his successful pharmacy business in Linz and the proud owner of a small country estate at Gneixendorf, Johann invited his brother and nephew to spend a few weeks with him so that Karl could make a full recovery and relations between them restored. The visit seems to have been a success. Beethoven agreed, though with some reluctance, that Karl should be allowed to join the army and, on the recommendation of his lifelong friend Stephan von Breuning, who was an official in the war department, Karl duly signed up as a cadet in General Joseph von Stutterheim's regiment on 2 January 1827.

Beethoven spent most of his time during those weeks in Gneixendorf enjoying the countryside and composing a new finale for the last of his Golitsïn quartets; he completed it appropriately on St Cecilia's Day, 22 November 1826. The first version of op. 130, with the *Grosse Fuge* as finale, had already been engraved by Artaria in August 1826, but because of the proposed changes it was withheld from publication. The second version with the new Gneixendorf finale, rightly hailed by Schuppanzigh as 'exquisite', was published posthumously in 1827 by both Artaria in Vienna and Schlesinger in Paris. At the same time Artaria published the string and piano versions of the *Grosse Fuge* as op. 133 and op. 134 respectively, both dedicated to Archduke Rudolph.

String Quartet no. 14 in B flat major, op. 130

Adagio ma non troppo – Allegro
Presto
Andante con moto ma non troppo
Alla danza tedesca: Allegro assai
Cavatina: Adagio molto espressivo
Finale: Allegro

Adagio ma non troppo – Allegro   The introduction is in two expressive sections. As Beethoven had originally noted in his early sketches, the first (ex. 27.1a) is profoundly emotional, with its rich, deeply voiced chording, reminiscent of Russian Orthodox choirs, its frequent subito piano dynamics, its 'serious and weighty' questions and 'serious and weighty' answers. The second (ex. 27.1b), more sustained and polyphonic in character, is gentler and more searching.

Almost uniquely, when the double bar is reached at the end of the exposition, the introduction and ensuing Allegro are repeated in full. Moreover, extracts from the Adagio, thirteen in all, return unexpectedly at various times, suggesting that, as in the *Harp* Quartet, Beethoven had two parallel, though alternating, movements in mind, one slow and the other fast, with each in turn the focus of interest.

The multi-layered character of the movement is taken a stage further in the Allegro where the two principal themes in the first group appear

Ex. 27.1

together, simultaneously and contrapuntally (ex. 27.2) – one energetic (*z*) and the other a strikingly abrupt fanfare (*u*). As in the Adagio, both are repeatedly unsettled by sudden and unexpected changes in dynamics.

Ex. 27.2

True to Beethoven's claim that 'there is less lack of fantasy [here] than ever before', motives in the Adagio and in the first subject of the Allegro rise to the surface in improvisatory fashion elsewhere in the movement, recognizable thematically but wholly changed in character. The polyphonic motive (*y*) in the Adagio, for example, introduces and energizes the brilliant transition, while the bustling theme in the first group (*z*), now *sotto voce* and serious of purpose, frames the mystical second group (ex. 27.3) in the remote key of G flat major.

Ex. 27.3

Frequent changes of tempo from Adagio to Allegro and back again create uncertainty and tension in much of the movement. But the short development section at its heart – a serene dialogue between the 'fanfare' motive (*u*) and a lyrical variant of the second subject (ex. 27.3) – provides time for a few moments of reflection, soothed by a gentle, mantra-like ostinato created from the cadential cell (*x*) in the second bar of the introduction. Citing the *Hammerklavier* Sonata, the Credo in the *Missa Solemnis* and the *Grosse Fuge*, Robert Simpson has suggested that B flat major is the key that Beethoven chose 'as the vehicle of immense power struggles'[15] and

[15] Simpson, 'The Chamber Music for Strings', p. 270.

that is certainly true of the *Grosse Fuge*, whether attached to this quartet or independent of it.

The outcome in this movement, however, is anything but certain. When compared, for example, to those triumphant off-stage trumpet calls in *Fidelio*, also in B flat major, the 'fanfare' motive (*u*) is indecisive, and although muscles are flexed to great effect in the closing section and at the start of the coda, forward momentum is halted yet again by repeated questioning from phrases in the Adagio, before the movement is allowed to end.

Presto   After the first movement, in which Beethoven probed, extended and broke through nearly every pre-conceived formal boundary, the Presto – a scherzo and trio in all but name, in simple ternary form (A1–A2–B1–B2–A1–A2) – must have seemed like a breath of fresh air to the audience at the celebrated premiere. 'Thunderous applause' and demands for an encore reflected, no doubt, the audience's genuine enthusiasm, but a good measure of relief as well. Pianists would surely have recognized Beethoven's (perhaps unconscious) reference in bars 9–12 to the finale of the Fourth Piano Concerto, and violinists would have relished the brilliant violin solo which dominates the middle section with its thrusting weak-beat *sforzandi* and its almost unvaried six-note motive repeated, in Philip Radcliffe's laconic phrase, 'with a persistence worthy of a Bach Prelude'.[16] On closer examination the air is not as fresh as it appeared to be at first; the outer sections of the movement, with their secretive dynamics and lightning tempo, seem shadowy and harlequinesque and there is an uncompromising relentlessness in the central section. Most brilliant are the delicate and inventive textures in the recapitulation; most sinister, the silent bars and nightmarish chromatic gestures (ex. 27.4) which bridge the anxious gap between inner and outer sections, and hammer away viciously (*v*) at the opening phrase of the movement.

Ex. 27.4

Andante con moto ma non troppo   Over the years, Beethoven had written several slow movements which were scherzo-like in character – in the C minor Quartet, op. 18 no. 4, for example, or the A minor Violin Sonata, op. 23, and the Eighth Symphony – but this Andante, which he composed quickly in mid-August 1825, while 'intoxicated with fantasy',[17] is surely the most exquisite of them all. Beethoven's sense of humour was notoriously robust and his puns dreadful, but this movement, with its understated humour, is unusually subtle and refined. Two introductory bars, marked

---

[16] Radcliffe, *Beethoven's String Quartets*, p. 127.

[17] W. von Lenz, quoted in Marliave, *Beethoven's Quartets*, p. 257.

poco scherzando, recall with gentle irony the short-breathed, chromatic phrase with which the quartet opened and voices are seldom raised in the whimsical conversation that follows.

Melodic ideas are politely shared between all four instruments (ex. 27.5), illuminated, as in a mediæval manuscript, by delicate accompanying patterns and interweaving polyphonic lines. The movement is broadly in sonata-rondo form (A–B–A–C–A–B–A–C–coda) though with unusual proportions. For example, the transition, a single pizzicato bar leading from the principal theme to the delicate first episode, must be the shortest (and sweetest) that Beethoven ever wrote. The beautiful second episode, marked *cantabile* and *piano dolce*, introduces a more personal note into the conversation. All three themes are given a further chance to be heard and discussed – even the transition is allowed an extra bar – and accompanying textures are lighter, more feathery than ever as the movement draws to a close. However, Beethoven could not resist keeping one of his more robust jokes up his sleeve as a surprise in the last bar: a silent pause, two or three nano-seconds' worth of quiet grace notes and then – the only raised voice in the movement – a final and very decisive *forte*.

Ex. 27.5

Alla danza tedesca: Allegro assai   Beethoven sprang a further surprise on the audience at the premiere and one which never fails to delight us to this day: a pair of dances, warm, tender and appealing, in the unexpected and wholly unrelated key of G major, the key which he chose for some of his most beautiful compositions – the Fourth Piano Concerto, op. 58, for example, or the G major Violin Sonata, op. 96. The colourful and varied nature of each movement in op. 130 convinced Paul Bekker that the quartet is 'a suite, almost a potpourri, of movements without any close psychological interconnection'[18] and Barry Cooper sees it as 'a kind of narrative, rather than a canvas where the overall outline is clear from the start'.[19] It is this element of surprise as one movement follows another, each a masterpiece in its genre, yet wholly different in structure and mood, that gives op. 130 its unique character and its special appeal.

[18] Paul Bekker, quoted in Solomon, *Beethoven*, p. 421.
[19] Cooper, *Beethoven* [Master Musicians], p. 330.

When the Alla danza tedesca was first performed, further 'thunderous applause' and demands for an encore owed much, no doubt, to its openness, warmth and symmetry. As in a traditional scherzo and trio, there are two separate dances, each in two sections, followed by a repeat of the first dance, extensively varied, and finally a coda. Although in the first dance there is a delightful catching of breath in alternate bars, and a few moments of hesitation in the coda, this is a movement that breathes, but never falters. An unbroken stream of quavers accompanies the first dance, semiquavers the second, and a combination of both the *da capo*. Each section is mostly limited to multiples of eight bars and, as if relishing such self-imposed restrictions, Beethoven weaves a decorative web around each of them – none more charming than the hemiola-inspired variation in the *da capo* (ex. 27.6a), which is sure to involve some treading on toes and general confusion among less experienced dancers. Even in the final bars (ex. 27.6b) the viola and cello are still playing semiquavers and quavers respectively right up to the line, as if expecting, and perhaps hoping, that this enchanting music will go on for ever.

Ex. 27.6

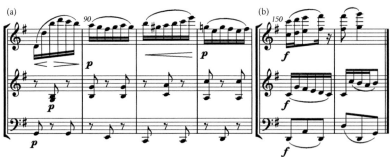

Cavatina: Adagio molto espressivo   The Cavatina is among the most personal and revealing of Beethoven's many sublime slow movements. Asked by Karl Holz which of the three Golitsïn quartets he considered the best, he replied: 'Each in its own way.' But when he was asked about this movement, he confessed that it had cost him 'tears in the writing ... nothing he had written had so moved him; in fact that merely to revive it afterwards in his thoughts and feelings brought tears to his eyes.'[20] There are three clues that may help to explain the emotional and musical context of those 'thoughts and feelings.' The first is its operatic title, 'Cavatina' a simple arioso or a short song, rare, perhaps unique in chamber music;[21] the second, the inclusion at the heart of the movement of yet another instru-

---

[20] Karl Holz, quoted in Thayer, *The Life of Beethoven*, p. 975.

[21] In literature the term *cavata* is defined as 'an epigrammatic sentence in which an important thought is expressed.' Its musical equivalent, *cavatina*, is 'a short solo song [or arioso] simpler in style than an aria.' See Apel, *Harvard Dictionary of Music*, p. 125. Beethoven would certainly have known two cavatinas in Mozart's *The Marriage of Figaro*: 'Porgi amor' and 'L'ho perduta.'

mental recitative;[22] and the third, the choice of E flat major, usually a resilient key for Beethoven, but sometimes one in which he combined warmth and affection with deeply personal feelings of loss.

Shortly after Haydn's death on 31 May 1809, for instance, he composed a poignant set of Haydn-like variations in E flat major as the finale of the *Harp* Quartet (ex. 19.7), based on a theme created almost entirely from the three-note *Le-be-wohl* ('Farewell') motive, which first appeared in *Fidelio* and later in the opening two bars of the Piano Sonata in E flat major, op. 81a (*z* in ex. 15.3),[23] and the Adagio espressivo of the Violin Sonata in G major, op. 96 (ex. 22.4a). Variants of the same 'Farewell' motive (*w* in ex. 27.7b) are heard at significant moments in the Cavatina too.

Thus the evidence appears to suggest that Beethoven conceived the movement as an operatic arioso in which the 'singer', represented by the first violin and accompanied by an obbligato string trio, expresses human sorrow and divine consolation in equal measure in the outer sections, emotions overwhelmed in the central recitative by feelings of acute anxiety. Clearly, this 'Farewell' is closer to home than ever – a reminder to Beethoven of his own mortality, perhaps, or distress over the deterioration of his relationship with his nephew, realized several months later when on 30 July 1826 Karl attempted suicide.

As in the opening bars of the quartet, accompanying textures are deep-voiced, with the viola and cello in their lowest register throughout most of the movement. Each sentence of the first violin's exquisite soliloquy (ex. 27.7a) is framed by an expressive phrase (*r*) played by the second violin, 'a curtain', in Martin Cooper's words, 'that is gradually drawn back to allow us to hear (or overhear) a melody so simple yet so

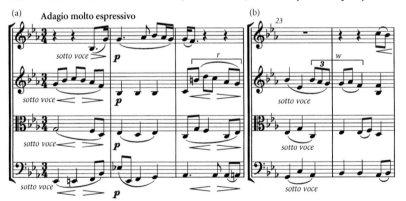

Ex. 27.7

---

[22] That is in addition to the instrumental recitatives in the A minor Quartet, op. 132, discussed in the previous chapter, and in the finale of the Ninth Symphony.

[23] Three years earlier, the same motive played a deeply emotional part in the slow movement (ex. 40h–j), also in E flat major, of the Violin Sonata in G major, op. 96, composed shortly after Antonie Brentano, Beethoven's 'Immortal Beloved', finally left Vienna for Frankfurt in 1812.

consoling.'[24] Each cadence is echoed by the obbligato string trio; after the third of those echoes, roles are reversed to reveal the most consoling melody that Beethoven ever composed – complete with its own 'Farewell' motive (*w*), played by the second violin (ex. 27.7b).

In the recitative (ex. 27.8), sorrow and consolation give way to terror in the remotest of keys, C flat major, as the 'singer', all but overcome by fear – *beklemmt* – breathlessly retraces some of the chromatic steps taken in the introduction to the first movement in halting, nightmarish asides.

Ex. 27.8

There are few changes when the soliloquy returns. However, emotions are heightened in the coda as the cello, summoned from the depths, makes a short, impassioned plea in the tenor clef, and the second violin meditates on the 'curtain' phrase with increasing intensity. The movement ends with the first violin's deeply touching *cri de cœur* – a cadential motive which may have been at the back of Mendelssohn's mind two decades later when he composed the aria 'Lord God of Abraham' in his oratorio *Elijah*. Both share the same key, the same melodic outline, the same pleading and prayerful emotions.

Finale: Allegro   Relief and reconciliation, fresh air and the countryside that Beethoven loved, even revered, are reflected in the musical and emotional landscape of this beautiful movement composed during his weeks in Gneixendorf. According to Karl Holz, Beethoven wanted the viola, with its accompaniment of sparkling quavers (*t*), to proceed to the finale without a break, so that players and audience alike might savour the sudden and extreme change of mood from darkness to light as the Cavatina ends and the finale begins. Though sometimes called the 'little finale', the Allegro, with over 600 bars (including repeats) compared with the mighty *Grosse Fuge's* 741 bars, is long enough to include two independent expositions, three principal subjects and extensive, sometimes complex, development sections. The first group, a dance in two repeated sections (ex. 27.9), is as carefree as a crisp, frosty morning and, though apparently naïve, both the theme and its chirpy accompaniment are highly productive, providing material (*t*, *n*, *p*, *q*) for numerous conversations later in the movement, some witty, some powerful, some intellectual, but none sad or tragic.

Ex. 27.9

[24] Cooper, *Beethoven: The Last Decade*, p. 312.

The opening dance includes two other motives from the first group
(*p*, *q*) both of which engage in serious and extended contrapuntal conversations (ex. 27.10) later in the development section – first *pianissimo* but
gradually becoming louder and more forceful, as views are expressed with
ever-increasing fervour.

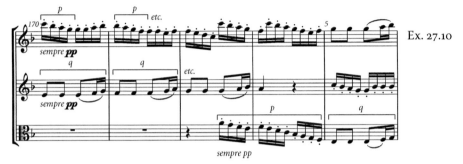

Ex. 27.10

The viola's two-note motive (*t*), for example, is given a starring role
towards the end of the movement – comedy with the lightest touch – and
the first bar of the opening dance (*n*) provides a dramatic sequence of
mirrored diminished sevenths leading, shortly before the final coda, to a
triumphant *fortissimo* celebration of the theme.

The second group is more fragmentary; sometimes vigorous and sometimes questioning, and the cadential motive (*x*), which dominates the
development section in the first movement, brings the first exposition to
a triumphant conclusion. However, the heart of the 'little finale' is to be
found in the second exposition: one of Beethoven's freshest and longest
melodies (ex. 27.11), partnered by a variant of a familiar descant (*m*) – a
rare link in this glorious 'potpourri of movements' between the opening
phrase in the A minor Quartet (ex. 26.1a) and the first of the two fugue
subjects in the *Grosse Fuge* (ex. 28.1a) which it replaced.

Ex. 27.11

Grosse Fuge, op. 133

Overtura – Fuga: Meno mosso e moderato – Allegro molto e con brio –
Meno mosso e moderato – Allegro molto e con brio

Beethoven planned the original finale for the last of his Golitsïn quartets on the grandest scale imaginable. It is a work in which emotional and musical extremes are explored to the limit – and then beyond. Like the 'little finale' which replaced it, the *Grosse Fuge* followed the Cavatina without a break, so it too can only be fully appreciated in the context of fear and sorrow, but also consolation, so hauntingly expressed in the Cavatina and its recitative. Beethoven's rare, almost unprecedented, use of block dynamics in the *Grosse Fuge* provides the clearest explanation of the powerful impact at which he was aiming. Although nuanced dynamics appear occasionally, this sequence of fugal studies is marked either by an unvarying *forte/fortissimo* or *piano/pianissimo*, so the picture which emerges is of an uncompromising and complex mental landscape, which can only be explored successfully with patience and fortitude.

While drawing technical inspiration from the past, especially the music of Bach and Handel, the *Grosse Fuge* is also a vision of the future in which fugue, canon and other contrapuntal devices – 'tantôt libre, tantôt recherché' as Beethoven put it[1] – together with variation and 'fantasy', are combined in one of the strangest, most original compositions ever written. The Gloria and Credo in the *Missa Solemnis*, completed in 1823, suggest precedents of a kind.[2] Both are similar in length to the *Grosse Fuge*, both include alternating fugal and lyrical sections performed without any significant breaks, and all three reflect Beethoven's determination, explained in an earlier conversation with Karl Holz, to create 'a new and really poetic element' in the 'old traditional forms' in which the imagination can truly 'assert its privileges.'[3] In chamber music, however, the only precedent comparable in scale to the *Grosse Fuge* is Bach's unfinished masterpiece *The Art of Fugue*.

The fact that Beethoven used the French spelling, *Ouverture*, in his original manuscript (it appeared in Italian when the *Grosse Fuge* was published posthumously in May 1827) suggests that, in addition to creating new

---

[1] From the title page of the first edition of op. 133, together with Beethoven's dedication to Archduke Rudolph.

[2] The Gloria, for example, is divided into five unbroken sections: 'Gloria' – 'Gratias agimus tibi' – 'Qui tollis peccata mundi' – 'Quoniam tu solus sanctus' – 'In gloria Dei patris'. The soloists sing in three sections, the chorus in five. Contrapuntal techniques range from immitation to full-length fugal writing, side by side with lyrical and expressive sections. The Credo includes seven interlinked sections, similarly varied.

[3] Beethoven in conversation with Karl Holz, quoted in Thayer, *The Life of Beethoven*, p. 692.

fugal forms for his time, he may also have wanted to recreate the spirit of a Baroque French overture. The trajectory of the first two bars in the overture to Handel's *Messiah* (ex. 28.1a), which Beethoven certainly knew and admired, is every bit as challenging and angular as the first fugue subject, **A**, in the *Grosse Fugue* (ex. 28.1b–d) though, of course, the outcome in each case is very different.

Moreover, the dotted rhythms characteristic of the second fugue subject, **B** (ex. 28.2a) in the ensuing Fuga are typical of similar rhythmic patterns in other Baroque overtures that Beethoven also knew and admired, such as the Overture to Handel's *Judas Maccabaeus* (ex. 6.5c). Apart from a subsidiary lyrical theme, **C** (ex. 28.1c and 28.4), the *Grosse Fuge* is created almost entirely from those two subjects and their variants. For instance, **A1**, an extended version of the mystical opening bars of the A minor Quartet, op. 132 (ex. 26.1), spawns a further three variants of its own (ex. 28.1b–d), while the second fugue subject, **B** (ex. 28.2), provides the work with much of its rhythmic energy and drive.

Overtura: Allegro – Meno mosso e moderato – Allegro (G–B flat major, bars 1–30)   Like chapter headings in a table of contents at the beginning of a book, Beethoven provides a succinct summary in the Overtura of what is in store. The first fugue subject, **A1**, proclaimed in unison *fortissimo* and *sforzando* in the opening bars (ex. 28.1b), is followed by three closely related variants, **A2**, **A3**, and **A4** (ex. 28.1b–d) each of which, though in reverse order, is given responsibilty later for individual fugues and variations. The subsidiary theme, **C** (ex. 28.1c and 28.3) suggests that gentler voices will not be neglected altogether.

Ex. 28.1

Fuga: Allegro (double fugue with three variations, bars 30–158) Under-pinned by the fourth variant, **A4**, and played *sempre fortissimo* throughout, the relentless dotted rhythms of the second fugue subject in B flat major, **B**, dominate the first of the double fugues.

In the first variation of the double fugue (ex. 28.2a), crisply martial rhythms, **B**, are challenged, though not deterred, by romping triplets to produce the rhythmic subtleties that Stravinsky admired so much. A rhyth-mic variant of the transition in the first movement of op. 130 (ex. 26.2) adds further brilliance to the second variation (ex. 28.2b), while **A4** emerges from its subsidiary role as a chaconne to dominate the climactic third.

Ex. 28.2

Meno mosso e moderato (double fugato, bars 159–232) After such relentless dynamics, rhythmic energy and fugal complexity, the gentle, introspective meno mosso in G flat major (ex. 28.3a), framed by a four-note fragment of **A2** (ex. 28.3b) is particularly welcome. The third variant, **A3**, provides the necessary foundations, sometimes played in full, some-times in canon, sometimes shortened and sometimes extended. But it is the subsidiary theme, **C**, which gives the movement its flowing, introspec-tive character.

Ex. 28.3

Allegro molto e con brio (introduction, double fugue and variation, bars 233–413) The cheerful introduction in B flat major to the next double fugue is scherzo-like in character. Based on **A2** in the Overtura, it is soon joined by a brisk and businesslike countersubject, also borrowed from the Overtura, and is decorated by the first of many extended and brilliant trills to come. **A1** is the centre of attention in the monumental double fugue that follows, assailed by three-note fragments from two other variants – one rising, **A3**, the other falling, **A2** to create extraordinary tensions and harmonic clashes, all the more overwhelming for the relentless *fortissimo*s and *sforzandi* which characterize them.

Allegro molto e con brio (double fugue and variation, bars 414–92) The second fugue subject, **B**, is now the centre of attention, similarly assailed, this time by fragments, sometimes simultaneous, of **A1, A2** and **A4**, reaching for the skies or swooping down to earth as it goes through its often discordant paces in the ensuing variation.

Meno mosso e moderato (double fugato, bars 492–510) Played triumphantly with a *sforzando* on each note and in double counterpoint – both recto and inverso (ex. 28.4) – **A3** is again joined by the flowing theme, **C**, no longer introspective, but magnificent.

Ex. 28.4

Più allegro ed accelerando – Allegro molto e con brio – coda (bars 511–741) Dynamics become more varied as the short transition and partial recapitulation lead into the coda. The music, sometimes visionary, sometimes monumental, is mostly focused on the four variants of the first fugue subject, **A1**. Tension is increased, at times almost to breaking point, by an emotionally charged discussion based on the opening subject, **A1**, the rising semitone cell and its inversion explored simultaneously, rather than in sequence (ex. 28.5a). Then after recalling the powerful opening bars of the Overtura *fortissimo*, and reflecting on them at some length *pianissimo*, the *Grosse Fuge* ends with renewed energy. The two principal themes, **A1** and **B**, accompanied by the viola's energetic quavers, are no longer in competition but fully reconciled to each other. The first fugue subject, **A1**, is extended by a further eight bars (ex. 28.5b) to become a monumental and

Ex. 28.5

complete melody, and the second, **B**, provides a radiant descant, high in register and glorious.

The two finales – Beethoven's first decision or his final one?

When performing op. 130, it is not unusual nowadays for quartets to replace the 'little finale' with the *Grosse Fuge* on the grounds that to do so is in line with the composer's original intentions. There is equally persuasive evidence, however, to suggest that Beethoven genuinely changed his mind and that the decision to replace the *Grosse Fuge* with a new finale was his definitive one. Indeed, he seems to have been on the point of doing so when Karl Holz visited him, as he agreed 'on the next day'[4] to both of Holz's suggestions: first, to publish the *Grosse Fuge* as a separate work; and secondly, to compose a more 'appropriate' finale for op. 130.

There are other sound reasons for agreeing with Holz. If, as Paul Bekker has written, the Quartet is a 'suite of movements without any close psychological interconnection'[5] – and little motivic interconnection, for that matter – is not the 'little finale' more in keeping with such a varied and diverse

[4] Karl Holz, quoted in Solomon, *Beethoven*, pp. 422–3.

[5] Paul Bekker, quoted in Solomon, *Beethoven*, p. 421.

composition? Some have argued that the *Grosse Fuge* needs op. 130; but does op. 130 need the *Grosse Fuge*? There is no doubt that it can stand on its own as an independent composition, but can the 'little fugue' do so? If not, would it not be a tragedy to discard such a colourful and lyrical finale, the last completed movement that Beethoven composed?

As his many sketchbooks show, Beethoven revised his music endlessly, and often made significant changes to a work at the last possible moment, as in the F major Quartet, op. 18 no. 1, for instance, or the A major Cello Sonata, op. 69. In both cases, there is no doubt that he considered his final thoughts preferable to his earlier ones. 'Be sure not to hand on to anybody your quartet', he begged Karl Amenda, to whom he had sent the first version of the F major Quartet, 'as I have made some drastic alterations. For only now have I learnt how to write quartets, and this you will notice, I fancy, when you receive them.'[6] So should not Beethoven's final decision here be similarly respected? After all, as John Daverio has pointed out, if he 'had wished to retain the *Grosse Fuge* as an integral part of op. 130 (or had he wished to issue two separate quartets), nothing would have prevented him from doing so ... In short, Beethoven realized that the *Grosse Fuge* threatened to upset the balance of power in the quartet, dwarfing what had gone before.'[7]

Barry Cooper has contributed an equally convincing dose of common sense to the discussion: 'When Beethoven improvised at the piano it was not unknown for him to become somewhat "carried away" and to develop a theme at great length during a single sitting. Similarly, the sketches suggest that his compositions tended to grow beyond their originally planned size ... This is what seems to have happened here.'[8] Whether quartet players decide to honour Beethoven's first or his final decision, all would agree, however, that the choice which they make affects not only the eventual outcome of the quartet but the nature of the entire work and the way in which it is perceived and experienced by players and audience alike.

[6] *Letters of Beethoven*, Letter 53, 1 July 1801: Beethoven to Karl Amenda in Courland.

[7] Daverio, 'Manner, Tone and Tendency in Beethoven's Chamber Music for Strings', pp. 162, 163.

[8] Cooper, *Beethoven and the Creative Process*, p. 214.

String Quartet in C sharp minor, op. 131

Full circle

'a kind of community life with the von Breuning family'[1]

In contrast to Beethoven's frequent bouts of illness and worries over Karl, his domestic circumstances were remarkably settled when composing his last two string quartets. Quite by chance, his move in October 1825 to a splendid set of rooms in the Schwarzspanierhaus brought him to within a stone's throw of the apartment of his old friend Stephan von Breuning. Beethoven was twelve years old when he first met 'his guardian angels' as he described the von Breuning family. Their widowed mother, Helene, had asked him to give piano lessons to her two youngest children, and it was not long before he was treated as a member of the family – Eleonore, 'his first serious love', Stephan, Julie and Lorenz – spending 'not only the major part of the day, but even many nights there'.[2]

In the mid-1790s, Stephan moved from Bonn to Vienna and spent his entire professional life as a lawyer there in the war ministry. He wrote poetry in his spare time and it was he who revised the original libretto for the 1806 revival of *Fidelio*. Beethoven dedicated the Violin Concerto to Stephan and the piano version of the concerto to his first wife, Julie, with whom he often played piano duets; as described in Chapter 17, he was distraught when Julie died after only a year of marriage. There were quarrels from time to time, some bitter and prolonged, but they were all forgotten when Stephan, with his second wife, Constanze, and their children, Gerhard and Marie, met Beethoven by chance just before he moved into his new lodgings. Gerhard, who later became a doctor, was an observant twelve-year-old and recalled the meeting fifty years later in his *Memories of Beethoven: From the House of the Black-Robed Spaniards*, a book which he was inspired to write after attending various Beethoven centenary celebrations in 1870.

> No sooner had we caught sight of one another, than there were the most joyful greetings on both sides. [Beethoven] was powerful looking, of medium height, vigorous in his gait and in his lively movements, his clothes far from elegant or conventional; and there was something about him overall that did not fit into any classification. He spoke almost without a pause, asking how we were, what we were doing.[3]

[1] Breuning, *Memories of Beethoven*, p. 59.
[2] Franz Wegeler, quoted in Clive, *Beethoven and his World*, p. 52.
[3] Breuning, *Memories of Beethoven*, p. 19.

Just as Stephan's mother had done four decades earlier in Bonn, Stephan and Constanze welcomed Beethoven warmly to their home, invited him to meals, put up with his many eccentricities and often shared their family walks with him. Though taken in good part, those walks must have been an ordeal for them because Beethoven talked very loudly without, of course, realizing that he was doing so, and also because of the frequent, though necessary, pauses during which written questions were asked and answered in Beethoven's current conversation book. Constanze kept a watchful eye on his domestic arrangements and found him the best cook he had ever had, known simply as Sali, who 'turned out to be so devoted and reliable a person that as a faithful housekeeper and later also as a nurse, she made Beethoven's house liveable from then on to the end of his days.' Constanze never forgot his distraught visit to her just after Karl's attempted suicide on 6 August 1826. 'No, he only grazed himself', Beethoven told her. 'But the disgrace he has caused me', adding poignantly: 'I loved him so much!'[4]

As children do, Gerhard remembered particular events that had made an impression on him, among them Beethoven's relief one day when he managed to hear Marie's piercing screams – after all, hearing anything was better than hearing nothing; also his intense dislike of the pleached trees at Schönbrunn, expressed (very loudly no doubt) during a family visit there: 'All frippery, tricked up like old crinolines. I am only at ease when I am in *unspoiled* nature'[5] – a reminder that the spirit of Romanticism contributed far more to Beethoven's thoughts and his music than is generally realized. 'In a word', Gerhard summed up, 'our life was now a closely-linked neighbourly one, filled with unfailing friendship and esteem ... a kind of community life.'[6]

There was a significant difference between the two projected quartets, op. 131 and op. 135, and the three composed for Prince Golitsïn in that they were not written in response to a commission, so there would be no pestering this time over completion dates and other such real or imagined irritations. Publishers were increasingly prepared to offer Beethoven high fees. Bernhard Schott of Mainz, for example, who had recently published the Ninth Symphony and the Quartet in E flat major, op. 127, agreed to pay him 80 gold ducats in two instalments for the Quartet in C sharp minor – 20 more than the 60 agreed with Prince Golitsïn for op. 127, op. 132 and op. 130 combined. A not untypical awkwardness occurred when Beethoven finally sent the manuscript of op. 131 to Schott in July 1826, with a partly tetchy and partly humorous comment on the score, to the effect that it had been 'put together from pilferings from one thing and another',[7] a remark which, not unreasonably perhaps, rattled them. 'You said in your letter',

---

[4] Breuning, *Memories of Beethoven*, p. 66.

[5] Breuning, *Memories of Beethoven*, p. 79.

[6] Breuning, *Memories of Beethoven*, pp. 83, 59.

[7] Thayer, *The Life of Beethoven*, p. 983.

he explained a week later in response to their anxious enquiries, 'that it should be an original quartet. I felt rather hurt; so as a joke I wrote beside the address that it was a bit of a patchwork. But it is really *brand new*.'[8]

After Karl's attempted suicide, Beethoven decided to dedicate the quartet to Field-Marshal Baron von Stutterheim, 'to whom I am indebted for many kindnesses',[9] in gratitude for accepting Karl as an officer-cadet in his regiment. The parts and score, together with the *Missa Solemnis*, were published 'with pride' by Bernhard Schott and 'forwarded to all warehouses of note'[10] shortly after Beethoven's death on 26 March 1827.

Although there were no public performances in Beethoven's lifetime, the Quartet in C sharp minor is known to have been rehearsed by Joseph Böhm and heard by the usual 'small circle of connoisseurs', including Schubert, who asked Karl Holz and three of his colleagues to play it again for him during his final illness in November 1828 – a distressing and poignant occasion because Schubert 'fell into such a state of excitement and enthusiasm that we were all frightened for him'.[11] The first public performance was also given in 1828 by an up-and-coming quartet from Brunswick – the Müller brothers, Karl, Georg, Gustav and Theodor – who later made it their mission to perform Beethoven's quartets during their extensive concert tours. 'The Müller brothers represent the ideal of Beethoven quartet-playing', wrote Berlioz in his *Memoirs*. 'Nowhere else have precision of ensemble, unanimity of feeling, depth of expression, purity of style, grandeur, power, vitality and passion been brought to such a pitch. Their interpretation of those sublime works gives us, I believe, an exact idea of what Beethoven thought and felt in writing them. It is like an echo of the original inspiration, a by-product of the creative act.'[12]

In 1856, inspired by 'the progressive features of Beethoven's later musical language [which] were seen as urgently relevant to new developments in composition', Wagner arranged a performance of op. 131 in Zurich, wrote an analysis of the quartet and coached the players himself.[13] Over the years a succession of performers, composers and listeners have found inspiration in the late quartets and many have come to agree with Beethoven's own judgement that the Quartet in C sharp minor is perhaps the finest of them all, evoking as it does, in Martin Cooper's words, 'a kind of

---

[8] *Letters of Beethoven*, Letter 1498, 19 August 1826: Beethoven to Schotts. Beethoven had originally intended to dedicate op. 131 to Johann Wolfmayer, but after Karl's attempted suicide he changed his mind and dedicated the quartet to General von Stutterheim in gratitude for accepting Karl as a cadet in his regiment. During his final illness, however, Beethoven is thought to have left instructions that the Quartet in F major, op. 135, was to be dedicated to Wolfmayer.

[9] *Letters of Beethoven*, Letter 1561, 10 March 1827: Beethoven to Schotts.

[10] Quoted from the *Intelligengezblatt der Caecilia* in the introduction to the score, published by Edition Eulenburg, No. 2.

[11] Solomon, *Beethoven*, p. 417.

[12] Berlioz, *Memoirs*, trans. Cairns, p. 309.

[13] Kinderman, *The Quartets of Beethoven*, p. 9.

awe, that sense of wonder that he shares with the great poets and mystics and never lost to the end of his life'.[14]

It is one of the many miracles of Beethoven's music that, after completing op. 130, he could adopt a wholly different approach when composing op. 131 without affecting the integrity of either work. Inspiration for the outer movements of the new quartet was drawn from a personal *idée fixe* (*x* in ex. 29.1), variants of which had resurfaced from time to time throughout his life, from the G minor Cello Sonata (ex. 6.6b) and the C minor String Trio (ex. 8.15a) to the Quartet in A minor (ex. 26.1) and the *Grosse Fuge* (ex. 28.1b–d). However, that is just about all that these great masterpieces have in common with each other.

Op. 131 is made up of seven movements of uneven length, each carefully numbered by Beethoven himself – three before and three after the central theme and variations which lie at the exquisite heart of the work. Each movement flows naturally into the next without any significant break and 'yields up part of its autonomy', William Kinderman suggests, 'in the interest of the work as a whole.'[15] Beethoven had earlier written three important compositions along similar interlinked lines: the Piano Sonata *Quasi una fantasia*, op. 27 no. 2 (*Moonlight*), also in C sharp minor (1801), the Cello Sonata in C major, op. 102 no. 1 (1815), and the first of all song-cycles, *An die ferne Geliebte*, op. 98 (1816). By doing so, he created an overarching sense of unity within a free, improvisatory context, in line with the 'manifesto' which he had earlier discussed with Karl Holz: 'The imagination wishes also to assert its privileges, and today a new and really poetic element must be introduced into the old traditional form.'[16]

Like most of Beethoven's contemporaries – and like most musicians today – Holz wanted to understand more fully what Beethoven was getting at: 'I always ask myself, when I listen to something, what does it mean?', he wrote in Beethoven's conversation book in January 1826. 'I would explain the difference between Mozart's and your instrumental works in this way', he continued. 'For one of your works a poet could only write one poem; while to a Mozart work he could write three or four analogous ones.'[17] Tantalizingly, of course, we will never know what Beethoven, who was already at work on op. 131, said in reply as the conversation developed, but that his music has a meaning, however it is interpreted, there can be little doubt.

---

[14] Cooper, *Beethoven: The Last Decade*, p. 392.

[15] Kinderman, *The Quartets of Beethoven*, p. 310.

[16] Beethoven in conversation with Karl Holz, quoted in Thayer, *The Life of Beethoven*, p. 692.

[17] Lockwood, *Beethoven: The Music and the Life*, p. 350; Karl Holz quoted in one of Beethoven's conversation books, dated 16–22 January 1826.

String Quartet no. 15 in C sharp minor, op. 131

I Adagio, ma non troppo e molto espressivo
II Allegro molto vivace
III Allegro moderato
IV Andante, ma non troppo e molto cantabile – Più mosso –
Andante moderato e lusinghiero – Adagio – Allegretto –
Adagio ma non troppo e semplice – Allegretto
V Presto
VI Adagio quasi un poco andante
VII Allegro

I Adagio, ma non troppo e molto espressivo The fugue subject
(ex. 29.1) in the opening bars of the quartet consists of two contrasting
phrases (*x*, *y*), each with a very different meaning. The first (*x*) is surely a
metaphor for despair or spiritual exhaustion, feelings with which Beethoven was all too familiar; the second, a metaphor for serenity and divine
consolation. In addition to setting the agenda for the first movement and
arguably for much of the quartet, the two phrases also provide more than
enough material between them to sustain the exquisite structure of the
entire fugue.

Ex. 29.1

There are comparatively few appearances of the complete fugue subject:
four in the exposition and three in the final stretto (ex. 29.2), where the
first violin plays a modified version of the subject and the cello presents it
in augmented form (*x*): while the second violin and viola weave variants of
the serene motive (*y*) in the background.

Ex. 29.2

Tensions between the two phrases are never wholly resolved but, significantly, there is no break in the onward flow of the 'serene motive' (*y*), shared in turn by all four instruments and recalling similar flowing motives and language in the *Missa Solemnis*, such as the 'Dona nobis pacem' (ex. 24.3a) and the 'Benedictus' (ex. 24.3b) – gentle, interconnected phrases which, like pilgrims on a spiritual journey, continue on their way uninterrupted from the second bar of the movement to its end 118 bars later. Two modified versions of the fugue subject also appear in the course of the movement, the first played by the viola and the second high on the first violin. But the focus is mainly on smaller cells (*z*) rather than on the subject itself, and each cell is capable of creating extended polyphonic episodes of great beauty. A duet (ex. 29.3a) for the two violins, and later for viola and cello, for example, is truly exquisite, not least the motive (*z*) remembered by Elgar as the Angel bids farewell to Gerontius in the final moments of *The Dream of Gerontius* (ex. 29.3b).

Ex. 29.3

II Allegro molto vivace Beethoven took as much care over the all-important hand-over from one movement to the next as an athlete does in a relay race, arousing expectations and resolving them in unexpected ways. The sustained chord of C sharp major, with which the fugue ends, melts into a unison C sharp pause – a fine example, Martin Cooper suggests, of 'the life-enhancing beauty of contemplative art'[18] – and is held long enough to reinvent itself as the leading note of D major, the key of the second movement; an 'impossible' modulation, of course, but a magical one. Complexity makes way for apparent simplicity in the Allegro, a round-dance (*v*) in both shape and character, and a descendant of such free-spirited dances in the opening movement of the A major Quartet, op. 18 no. 5 (ex. 10.24). The secretive principal theme is shared in turn by the first violin and

---

[18] Cooper, *Beethoven: The Last Decade*, p. 392.

viola, and reappears in various guises – initially beguiling, but later more serious.

Serious too are the first and second violins' aspirational phrases in the first episode (ex. 29.4a) and especially the first violin's fervent counter-subject (*u*), which intriguingly appears only once in the movement – a quotation, conscious or not, of the monumental Credo motive (ex. 29.4b) in the *Missa Solemnis*.

Ex. 29.4

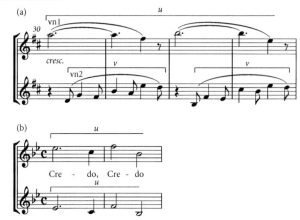

There is a strong sense of forward momentum in the second episode with its insistent off-beat *sforzandi* and clearly defined dynamic contrasts, and the movement ends powerfully with the first *fortissimos* in the quartet, followed by complete silence as the dancers slip away and the stage is left empty.

III Allegro moderato   That Beethoven was thinking here in dramatic terms is also suggested by this short linking movement, the last of his wordless recitatives, and one which begins and ends with much the same rhetorical flourishes that herald and later conclude the introduction to the 'Ode to Joy'.

IV Andante, ma non troppo e molto cantabile   However, Beethoven had something more introspective and personal in mind than the universal acclamations of the 'Ode' when he composed this transcendent movement – a 'sweet song of rest',[19] as he described it in one of his sketchbooks – a song on which he pondered at length and with ever increasing 'fantasy', in six continuous variations and an extended coda. The theme (ex. 29.5), described by Wagner as 'the incarnation of innocence',[20] opens with yet another variant (*x*) of the *idée fixe*, shared in friendly, antiphonal dialogue between the two violins:[21]

---

[19] Klein, *Autographe*, quoted in Cooper, *Beethoven* [Master Musicians], p. 340 n. 84.

[20] Quoted in Marliave, *Beethoven's Quartets*, p. 305.

[21] Beethoven's antiphonal treatment of the theme, with each bar played alternately by the two violins, raises the practical question of string quartet seating arrangements. A similar question also arises in orchestral string sections in, for example, the finale

Andante ma non troppo e molto cantabile

Ex. 29.5

Beethoven's plan was to restrict the first five variations to the same key, A major, and to two repeated, though differently embellished, sections similar in length to the theme, as if, in Lewis Lockwood's words, he viewed 'the process of variation as a kind of formal counterpart to what the fugal first movement does'.[22] Certainly, the technical processes involved in this spellbinding music are every bit as challenging.

(1) Questions are straightforward enough at the start of the first variation, but answers are increasingly elaborate as darker tone colours make way for lighter ones, the interweaving polyphony increasingly complex and the eventual outcome sublime.

(2) *Più mosso* Crisp drum-beats – a martial four-to-the-bar – are heard in the distance throughout much of the second variation and provide a disciplined, though strangely remote background to the graceful dialogue shared between the high first violin and low cello. Conversation becomes more general later, and all four instruments eventually join together in triumphant, if angular, unison.

(3) *Andante moderato e lusinghiero* The third variation is in two clearly defined contrapuntal sections. The first is a quiet conversation between cello and viola, later shared by the two violins – introspective in mood; the second, a fugato (ex. 29.6a), is also introduced by the cello and viola.

Ex. 29.6

of Tchaikowsky's *Pathétique* Symphony, in which the tragic opening theme is played alternately, one note at a time, by first and second violins, and is only fully effective if the second violins are seated opposite to the firsts, as was common practice until the mid-twentieth century. Certainly, the theme in this movement is still more enchanting if played antiphonally as Beethoven perhaps intended.

[22] Lockwood, *Beethoven: The Music and the Life*, p. 477.

Its sturdy, purposeful character, a scale rising to an accented fortepiano on the weak fourth beat of the bar, shares the majestic outlines and the same fourth-beat stresses as two similar fugues in Bach's Mass in B minor – the imposing choruses, 'Gratias agimus tibi' (ex. 29.6b) and 'Dona nobis pacem'.

(4) *Adagio* Timeless polyphony makes way for wonder in the fourth variation, as Beethoven creates a scene of pure enchantment, rich in varied tone-colours, contrapuntal detail and unexpected surprises; a limpid dream-like waltz, in which the dancers become so wrapped up in themselves, their thoughts and feelings that they scarcely notice the two-note pizzicatos at the end of each phrase. The first phrase is polite, but the second, marked *sforzando*, is distinctly ill-mannered, though soon forgotten as graceful, interweaving lines take matters in hand in the second part of the movement.

(5) *Allegretto* The fifth variation is among Beethoven's strangest: a delicate, topsy-turvy movement, in which broken chords, played softly throughout, unfold gently from top to bottom rather than the more usual bottom to top. Rhythms are consistently swung – so much so that the first beat of the bar is rarely felt, let alone marked.

(6) *Adagio ma non troppo e semplice* Perhaps as a counterbalance to the wordless recitative in the Allegro moderato (III) the sixth variation is a wordless duet played quietly by the two violins in expressive, romantic thirds, and framed by a breathless, gossamer-like accompaniment, in which fragments of the original theme are just discernible. But all is not as it seems in this innocent world. Like William Blake's 'invisible worm',[23] a troubled, niggling five-note motive, played by the cello, appears unexpectedly and at irregular intervals, as if determined to upset, or at least to question, the simplicity and wonder evoked in this exquisite idyll. Whispered cadenzas played by each instrument in turn, followed by sustained trills, replace the self-imposed restrictions in earlier variations, and lead into the coda (*Allegretto*), where the original theme is reclaimed from its ventures into remoter regions in a sequence of four mini-variations, two richly decorated and two as plain and simple as when they first appeared.

V Presto Momentarily held apart by the most fragile of silent pauses, there is little time to reflect on the beauty of the coda before the cello's hearty wake-up call heralds a complete change of mood. In character and form the Presto is a 'scherzo', though in duple rather than in traditional triple time – a particularly engaging one too, with an equally engaging 'trio' as additional proof of its credentials.[24] The cheerful theme, seemingly

---

[23] William Blake: 'O rose, thou art sick: / The invisible worm / That flies in the night In the howling storm, / Has found thy bed / Of crimson joy, / And his dark secret love / Does thy life destroy.'

[24] Examples of duple time scherzos or trios in Beethoven's music include two piano sonatas, op. 31 no. 3 and op. 110, the Quartet in B flat major, op. 130, the Sixth Symphony and the Ninth Symphony.

'found in the street, but transformed into the liveliest music imaginable'[25] (ex. 29.7a) dances and chatters away excitedly with few pauses for breath, like children in a playground, and contains enough material, including frequent hunting calls (*w*) to provide the 'trio' – a sunny, open air folksong (ex. 29.7c) – with chatty companions as well (viola and cello). Other delights in the 'trio' include an undulating landscape beautifully imagined by Beethoven in one of his most beguiling melodies (ex. 29.7d) – a much extended variant of (ex. 29.7c).

Ex. 29.7

Varied tone colours and subtle dynamics, especially harlequinesque pizzicatos – one note per instrument per bar – eventually lead back to the Scherzo. Most original of all, however, is Beethoven's use for the first time in his chamber music of *sul ponticello* (bow contact as near the bridge as possible) played softly high on all four instruments and sounding – most appropriately in this rustic setting – like a nest of fieldmice or twittering sparrows. The movement ends as heartily as it began with a widely spaced and decisive chord of E major, played *fortissimo*, followed by three incisive unison G sharps, their full significance revealed only twenty-eight bars later in their role as the dominant of C sharp minor, the key of the pugnacious opening bars of the finale (ex. 29.8).

VI Adagio quasi un poco andante   In the meantime, the simple pleasures of the countryside are forgotten as thoughts turn to the sorrows that beset mankind – a poignant and reflective elegy in G sharp minor, played in turn by the viola and first violin, in some of Beethoven's most heartfelt music.

VII Allegro   Gloves are off, fists are clenched and emotions run high in the five introductory bars of the apocalyptic finale (ex. 29.8), as challenges are offered (*s*) – all the more intimidating because of those resonant open C (B♯) strings on the viola and cello – and accepted with crisp, stiff upperlip determination (*t*). The momentum of the disciplined theme that follows in the wake of those challenges is maintained by relentless martial rhythms, angry dynamics and basic harmonies which, in their ruthlessness, recall the second fugue subject in the *Grosse Fuge*.

---

[25] Quoted in Marliave, *Beethoven's Quartets*, p. 315.

Ex. 29.8

Shared by the two violins and cello above the viola's martial rhythms, the anxious second theme (ex. 29.9) in the first group is a variant in rhythmic and melodic outline of the fugue subject with which the first movement began (ex. 29.1), and recalls a similar phrase in the opening bars of the Quartet in A minor (ex. 26.1).

Ex. 29.9

Cells and motives from these two themes, one ruthless (ex. 29.8) and the other tense and anxious (ex. 29.9), dominate most of the movement and provide material for extensive development. However, as in op. 127 and op. 132, the finale is on two levels, human and divine, reflecting Beethoven's personal philosophy expressed some years earlier in a letter to his friend Johann Nepomuk Kanka: 'I much prefer the empire of the mind, and I regard it as the highest of all spiritual and worldly monarchies.'[26]

Although the visionary second group (ex. 29.10) appears in full only twice, its beauty – basic sustained harmonies, flowing scales and slow, aspiring arpeggios – challenges the pervasive violence of the first theme and, for a time at least, stills the fears of the second.

Nonetheless, the eventual outcome of the movement – and of the whole quartet – hangs in the balance. Softly at first and almost unnoticed, however, fists are gradually unclenched, martial rhythms tamed and fears allayed as C sharp minor merges unobtrusively into C sharp major. Time is found for further reflection in the Poco Adagio – marked simultaneously *semplice* and *espressivo* – as the music consoles and persuades, finally overcoming every obstacle to proclaim victory for the 'empire of the mind' in one of the greatest of all string quartets.

---

[26] *Letters of Beethoven*, Letter 502, Autumn 1814: Beethoven to J. N. Kanka, Prague.

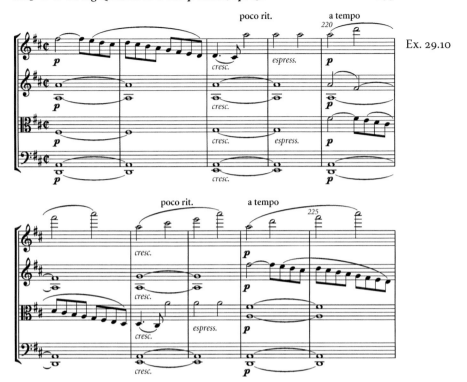

Ex. 29.10

String Quartet in F major, op. 135

'Here, my dear friend, is my last quartet', Beethoven told the Paris publisher Moritz Schlesinger in a letter written in October 1826, during his two-month visit to his brother Johann in Gneixendorf.

> It will be the last; and indeed it has given me much trouble, because I could not bring myself to compose the last movement. But as your letters were reminding me of it, in the end I decided to compose it. And that is the reason why I have written the motto: 'Der schwer gefasste Entschluss – Muß es sein? – Es muß sein!' (The decision taken with difficulty – Must it be? – It must be!) I am an unfortunate fellow, for I have failed to find a copyist who could write out the parts from the score ... so I had to write it out myself ... in the hope that the engraver will be able to read my scrawl.[1]

As it happens, op. 135 would not be Beethoven's last contribution to string quartet literature; that honour belongs to the beautiful new finale for op. 130 – the so-called 'little finale', discussed in Chapter 27 – which Beethoven completed a month later as an alternative to the *Grosse Fuge*. Ideas for several orchestral projects had appeared in Beethoven's sketchbooks during the previous two or three years, suggesting that he wanted to return to large-scale compositions as soon as possible. But after completing op. 135 and the 'little finale', his attention was further diverted to include an entirely new project, a String Quintet in C major, WoO 62, commissioned by Anton Diabelli.[2] Before much progress could be made with the quintet, however, Beethoven became seriously ill again and, after undergoing a number of painful operations, died on 26 March 1827.

'A year of awful happenings and most grievous blows'

In spite of the help and support of his friends, particularly Karl Holz and the von Breuning family, 1826 was, in Alexander Thayer's moving words, 'a year of awful happenings' and 'most grievous blows', countered in the last two quartets and in the 'little finale', 'by a display of creative energy which was amazing not only in its puissance but also in its exposition of

---

[1] *Letters of Beethoven*, Letter 1538a, October 1826: Beethoven to Moritz Schlesinger in Paris.

[2] The ultimate fate of Beethoven's unfinished string quintet was extraordinary – even shocking. Diabelli bought the almost complete sketch of the first movement after Beethoven's death and published arrangements of it for piano and piano duet. Then in an inexplicable act of vandalism he destroyed the original manuscript. Other projects which Beethoven was considering shortly before he died included a Requiem and a setting of Goethe's *Faust*.

transfigured emotion and imagination'.[3] Beethoven first mentioned the new quartet in an earlier letter to Schlesinger, written on 22 April 1826, in which he stated, with his customary blend of wishful thinking and optimism, that it would 'be finished in two or three weeks at the latest'[4] – although he had yet to complete op. 131 and serious work on op. 135 would have to wait for another two or three months.

'The highest tragedy and subtlest comedy'

The fact that Beethoven drew inspiration for the new quartet from the same surge of creative energy and the same 'transfigured emotion and imagination' as the sublime Quartet in C sharp minor suggests that, for all their many differences, they were connected to each other in Beethoven's mind in some kind of symbiotic relationship, as were, for instance, the two piano trios, op. 70, discussed in Chapter 18, the one a celebration of the supernatural, the other of the natural world. 'If we regard the last two [quartets] as a complementary pair', Lewis Lockwood has persuasively argued, 'they embody the highest tragedy and subtlest comedy that he ever achieved.'[5] Comedy, however defined, is rarely free from moments of anxiety; indeed, the greater the anxiety, the happier and more convincing the eventual outcome will be. It is inconceivable that the 'awful happenings' mentioned by Thayer would not evoke a response from Beethoven at some level; indeed, we have Constanze von Breuning's testimony, noted in the previous chapter, that he was utterly distraught when he visited her after Karl's attempted suicide on 6 August 1826 – and later by Karl's refusal to meet him for several weeks.

Relations between uncle and nephew were more or less restored, however, during their joint visit to Gneixendorf from late September to early December, and walks in the surrounding countryside must have raised Beethoven's spirits still further: 'The district where I am now staying reminds me to a certain extent of the Rhine country which I so ardently desire to revisit', he told Bernhard Schott in a letter written on 13 October 1826, adding poignantly: 'for I left it long ago when I was young.'[6] Moreover, his sense of inadequacy as Karl's guardian, a responsibility now shared jointly with Stephan von Breuning, must have been mitigated when his sister-in-law, Johann Beethoven's wife Therese, wrote reassuringly in his current conversation book that she had 'not found [Karl] angry. It is you that he loves, to the point of veneration.'[7]

---

[3] Thayer, *The Life of Beethoven*, p. 973

[4] *Letters of Beethoven*, Letter 1481, 22 April 1826: Beethoven to Moritz Schlesinger.

[5] Lockwood, *Beethoven: The Music and the Life*, p. 488.

[6] *Letters of Beethoven*, Letter 1535, 13 October 1826: Beethoven in Gneixendorf to Bernhard Schott.

[7] Therese van Beethoven, quoted in Solomon, *Beethoven*, p. 370.

Muß es sein? – Es muß sein!

Beethoven's 'subtlest comedy' began life hilariously with one of his humorous canons, *Es muß sein!*, WoO 196, composed in April 1826, for the amateur cellist Ignaz Dembscher, a wealthy bachelor who regularly played quartets with one of Schuppanzigh's pupils, Joseph Mayseder. Dembscher had missed the premiere of op. 130 in March, the controversial highlight of Schuppanzigh's current series of chamber music concerts, and he asked Beethoven to lend him the parts so that the new quartet could be rehearsed and performed in his home. Beethoven agreed on condition that he sent Schuppanzigh the 50-florin subscription he would have paid if he had been at the premiere. Karl Holz, as so often the go-between for such delicate missions, reported that Dembscher thought Beethoven was joking – 'Muß es sein?' (must it be?) – only to be firmly rebuffed by the canon – 'Es muß sein!' (It must be! Yes, yes, yes, yes! Out with your wallet!) – followed by a good deal of merriment on all sides, including Dembscher himself. Of much greater significance was Beethoven's decision to include the words for the two 'motto themes' in the score – the question, 'Must it be?', and the incisive answer (*x*), 'It must be!' – together with the heading 'Der schwer gefasste Entschluss' ('The Difficult Decision') (ex. 30.1).

Ex. 30.1

His explanation, noted at the beginning of this chapter, that he wrote the motto 'because he could not bring himself to compose the last movement', is surely disingenuous and, even if partly true, conceals what he really meant to convey. In the slow movement of op. 132, he had revealed in a surprisingly personal way that matters of life and death were much on his mind. In op. 131 he had explored the tensions between human tragedy and divine grace. So perhaps he decided that it was high time for him to reflect more deeply on the meaning of Dembscher's question and on its relevance for him personally in the divine comedy of human existence – reflections[8] which were still on his mind the day before he died.

---

[8] Gerhard von Breuning, his father, Stephan, and Schindler were all present the day before Beethoven died, when, after receiving the last sacraments, he said: 'Applaud, my friends, the comedy is over ...' 'In his favourite sarcastic, comic manner in order to convey that nothing can be done; the doctor's work is finished ... my life is over. I feel called upon to stress this clear recollection', wrote Gerhard von Breuning many years later, 'because I have had the experience of hearing the overly devout denounce Beethoven as a mocker of religion, when in fact he had an ideal faith in God.' Breuning, *Memories of Beethoven*, pp. 101–2

A 'subtle and prophetic work'

As in all of the late quartets, ideas from Beethoven's earlier years surface from time to time in op. 135. His choice of the pastoral key of F major, for instance, must have stirred many memories – the first cello sonata, the first of the op. 18 and the *Razumovsky* quartets, the *Spring* Sonata, the *Pastoral* Symphony and the Eighth Symphony. But the suggestion, often made, that in op. 135 he turned the clock back by two or three decades, is surely wide of the mark. On the contrary, as Philip Radcliffe has written, 'to underrate so subtle and prophetic a work as this would be grossly unfair';[9] while Robert Simpson finds in it 'the most sensitively coloured quartet writing in existence'.[10]

Moreover, Beethoven draws on much the same late period vocabulary and turns of phrase in op. 135 as are to be found in the *Missa Solemnis*, the Ninth Symphony and the other late quartets – a vocabulary created by him from a variety of sources from Renaissance polyphony to Bach and Handel, and on to the 'new and really poetic elements', discussed in Chapter 24, which he had himself 'introduced into the old traditional forms'.[11]

Composing the last of his quartets was a matter of conscience for Beethoven, a matter so urgent that he felt bound to address it as quickly as he could. When the Paris publisher Moritz Schlesinger bought the rights of the A minor Quartet, op. 132, after attending two private performances of the work with Sir George Smart and others in September 1825, he agreed at the same time to purchase the next quartet as soon as it was written. Beethoven seems to have forgotten their agreement, however, and sold the next two quartets to other publishers – op. 130 to Mathias Artaria and op. 131 to Bernhard Schott. However, when in April 1826, he received a courteous reminder from Schlesinger referring to their earlier agreement, he answered 'with all speed, so that our relations which suffered a rupture may be restored … as to the other quartets and quintets you would like to have, I will try to finish them as quickly as possible … with all my heart I thank you for your friendly sentiments.'[12] As always, Karl Holz was robustly helpful: 'You will not punish [Schlesinger] if it is short', he wrote encouragingly in the current conversation book before Beethoven left Vienna for Gneixendorf. 'Even if it should have only three movements, it would still be a quartet by Beethoven, and it would not cost so much to print it.'[13]

---

[9] Radcliffe, *Beethoven's String Quartets*, p. 173.

[10] Simpson, 'The Chamber Music for Strings', p. 276.

[11] Beethoven in conversation with Karl Holz, 1817.

[12] *Letters of Beethoven*, Letter 1481, 22 April 1826: Beethoven to Moritz Schlesinger.

[13] Thayer, *The Life of Beethoven*, p. 1009.

Johann Wolfmayer

That Beethoven dedicated his first string quartets to a prince and his last to a cloth merchant is a particularly apposite symbol of changing times in post-Napoleonic Europe. Johann Wolfmayer (1768–1841), to whom Beethoven dedicated op. 135, was a cultured and wealthy business man and a friend of long standing. 'Wolfmayer is happy that he championed your compositions as long as twenty-five years ago', Karl Holz noted in Beethoven's conversation book during a sociable visit in 1826. 'Now the public is beginning to appreciate them too.'[14] Throughout their long friendship together, Wolfmayer had unobtrusively helped Beethoven in a number of practical ways, most touchingly when, from time to time and unnoticed by Beethoven, he replaced his scruffy, worn-out coats with new ones. Wolfmayer was one of the last of Beethoven's friends to visit him during his final illness and came away with tears in his eyes, exclaiming: 'The great man. Alas! Alas!'[15] Appropriately, he was one of the many torch-bearers at Beethoven's funeral.

String Quartet no. 16 in F major, op. 135

Allegretto
Vivace
Lento assai, cantante e tranquillo
Grave ma non troppo tratto – Allegro

Allegretto   The first movement is an exquisitely scripted conversation of the kind which Beethoven enjoyed so much on his country walks with friends, especially in those early years before his hearing deteriorated. The viola opens the conversation in a short, though significant, introduction (ex. 30.2a) with the first of many variants of the 'It must be!' motive – a descending fourth (*x*) – which threads its way in various guises through

Ex. 30.2

[14] Quoted in Clive, *Beethoven and his World*, p. 401. Wolfmayer was a torch-bearer at Beethoven's funeral. See also Chapter 29, n. 8.

[15] Clive, *Beethoven and his World*, p. 401.

the first and third movements and dominates much of the finale as well. The Allegretto is particularly rich in melodic ideas; there are three engaging, if elusive, themes in the first group, each asking a question and receiving a prompt reply – the first (ex. 30.2b) created from fragmentary phrases shared in turn by the viola and the two violins.

The second theme (*y* in ex. 30.4) is played by all four instruments in companionable octaves, laying an expressive stress on the weaker second beat of each bar, and the third is a spritely extension of the first. The second group is no less varied, sometimes eloquent, sometimes flirtatious. Two motives appear simultaneously (ex. 30.3a) – one striding manfully uphill (*v*), the other (*z*) recalling cheerful peasants in the *Pastoral* Symphony (ex. 30.3b).

Ex. 30.3

There is wit and complexity in the development too (ex. 30.4) with, at one stage, two themes from the first group (*x*, *v*) combined with a motive from the second (*y*); all three discussed simultaneously in effortless, clear-textured polyphony.

Ex. 30.4

Vivace   The Vivace is as unlike the scherzos, let alone the minuets and trios, of Beethoven's earlier chamber music as it is possible to be, although the Presto in the *Harp* Quartet shares its momentum and energy. It is broadly in F major, though repeatedly challenged by intrusive and unsettling off-beat E flats. There are two themes (ex. 30.5), played simultaneously above or below a musette-like drone – a spritely folk-dance (*w*), tangled up in a mesmerizing, syncopated motive (*s*), from which it eventually escapes to dance freely on its own.

Ex. 30.5

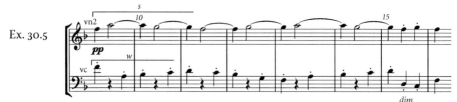

Apart from one sustained and dramatic *crescendo* and *diminuendo*, the movement is predominantly quiet; indeed there are times when the music needs to be whispered rather than played. There are four sections in the 'trio', the first three increasingly tense with a series of upward-sliding key-changes – F major to G major and then to A major – and with aspiring scales, each launched like a rocket into the sky. The first violin's boisterous fiddle tune in the fourth section, authentically rustic with its grace notes and high tessitura, must be among the roughest that Beethoven ever composed. It is accompanied by a petulant, wasp-like drone – the same phrase played by the rest of the quartet three octaves apart and repeated unchanged an awesome fifty times regardless of inevitable harmonic clashes. Beethoven had explored the effectiveness of such repeated motives before – twenty-four repeats of a double motive (duplets against triplets), for example, in the first movement of the *Pastoral* Symphony – as a metaphor, in his own words, for 'cheerful impressions awakened by arrival in the countryside'. But here the metaphor evoked is much more down-to-earth: good cheer among friends, perhaps, with plenty of frothy, overflowing steins of home-brewed beer at the end of one of those country walks?

Lento assai, cantante e tranquillo   The sense of urgency which Beethoven felt when composing his final quartet may account for the comparative brevity of this beautiful movement – a theme (ex. 30.6) and variations. The wistful, introspective theme, played *sotto voce*, is framed by a simple two-bar introduction – the chord of D flat major gradually unfurled (F–A♭–D♭) – and a two-bar refrain (bars 11–12) echoing the last two bars of the theme, as if to express profound agreement with what has just been said.

Ex. 30.6

The stepwise nature of the theme recalls both the syncopated phrase in the previous movement (*s*) and the second phrase in the fugue subject at the beginning of op. 131 (*z* in ex. 29.2), confirming that the relationship between the two quartets is indeed a close one. However, the low register and the dark, sustained harmonies here evoke human sorrow rather than divine serenity. The mood is more intense in the first variation; higher in register, with the theme partly veiled, though implied in the first violin's increasingly impassioned descant. Tears can no longer be held back in the heartbroken second variation (ex. 30.7).

Ex. 30.7

The theme emerges more clearly in the exquisite third variation, shared initially in canon by the cello and first violin. The mood is meditative throughout, the texture enriched by expressive and closely related melodic lines – the sustained viola a third above the cello. But the theme fades into the background again in the final variation (ex. 30.8) – a silent presence concealed behind a veil of tears, expressed in the first violin's fragmentary, desolate song – and the movement ends with an introspective two-bar coda to balance the two introductory bars with which it began.

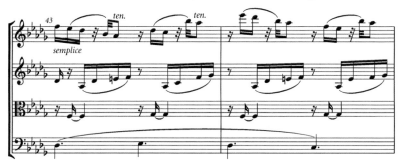

Ex. 30.8

Grave ma non troppo tratto As Beethoven contemplated his self-imposed 'Difficult Decision' – 'Der schwer gefasste Entschluss', the motto inscribed above this movement – trivial matters such as unpaid concert tickets and jokey canons seem far from his mind. The 'Must it be?' motive (ex. 30.1), may be calmed for a time by soothing, canonic polyphony, but the mood overall is serious – so serious that only the dark key of F minor, the key of the *Quartetto serioso*, op. 95, will do. Moreover, when the Grave returns at the end of the development section, it does so with terrible ferocity and with the wildest harmonies – a rare early appearance of an augmented triad (ex. 30.9) played *fortissimo* and tremolo by the violins

Ex. 30.9

high above the 'Must it be?' motive, recalling in extended form the 'scream' leading into the finale of the A minor Quartet, op. 132 (ex. 26.8). As if this were not enough, the combined development and recapitulation sections are repeated, so the question is posed yet again with still greater insistence.

Allegro The first subject in the Allegro could hardly be more different, however; a cheerful, breezy reply, 'It must be!' (*x* in ex. 30.10), alternating with a variant of the canonic phrase in the Grave (*t*), a soothing presence which reappears at various moments later in the movement when kindness is most needed. Both recall similar phrases in other comparatively recent works – the 'Dona nobis pacem' (ex. 24.3a) or the 'Benedictus' (ex. 24.3b) in the *Missa Solemnis*, for example – further evidence of the quartet's late period credentials.

Ex. 30.10

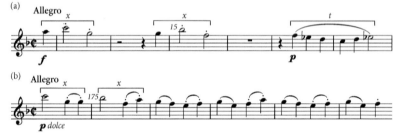

Such serious precedents for quintessentially cheerful music are typical of Beethoven, as E. T. A. Hoffmann had pointed out in his article on the op. 70 piano trios, written in 1813: 'It is as though the master thought that … even when the spirit feels itself joyously and gladly uplifted, one may not use an ordinary language; only a sublime and glorious one.'[16] There are further cheerful variants of the 'It must be!' motive in the finale. The first introduces the development in a confident, even belligerent mood, while the second (ex. 30.10, bars 109–16) is carefree and will later bring the quartet to an end in a bright and appropriately positive fashion.

However, the jewel at the heart of the movement is the second subject (ex. 30.11a), an additional variation on the principal theme in the Lento assai. Careful preparations are made for its quiet, unassuming appearances. Prefaced by a variant of the flowing canonic phrase (*t* in ex. 30.10),

[16] E. T. A. Hoffmann, quoted in Strunk, *Source Readings in Music History*, pp. 778–80.

Ex. 30.11

and accompanied by yet another variant of the 'It must be!' motive (*x*), this innocent, childlike song (*u* in ex. 30.11) surely meant something of deep significance to Beethoven.

Postscript

Gradual reconciliation with his nephew Karl, and those country walks in and around Gneixendorf, which reminded him of his childhood, provide the context for Beethoven's last two completed compositions, op. 135 and the 'little finale' in op. 130, discussed in Chapter 27. As he had done so often before, he sketched them during those walks, waving his arms around and humming loudly to himself, to the bemusement of the local peasantry and also, no doubt, the embarrassment of his relations; so it is hardly surprising that both the quartet and the 'little finale' are essentially pastoral in character. That they turned out to be Beethoven's last two completed compositions was fortuitous, however, as he had several large-scale projects in mind at the time, including a new symphony, already sketched, which had been commissioned by the Philharmonic Society of London. But there is a certain charm, even a certain rightness that, during the last few months of his life, Beethoven should have faced up to his own 'difficult decision', and found a way forward, not in powerful and heroic argument, but in some of the sweetest, most touching music that he had ever composed. There are precedents in each of his creative periods for such inspired simplicity: the opening Allegro in the Quartet in D major, op. 18 no. 3, for example, or the exquisite Adagio in the Violin Sonata in A major, op. 30 no. 1, the Allegretto in the Piano Trio in E flat major, op. 70 no. 2, and the Alla danza tedesca in op. 130. But Beethoven never composed anything sweeter or more childlike than the final pages of his Quartet in F major, op. 135.

> The setting sun, and music at the close,
> As the last taste of sweets, is sweetest last,
> Writ in remembrance more than things long past.[17]

---

[17] Spoken by John of Gaunt in Act 2, Scene 1 of Shakespeare's *King Richard II*.

Early Chamber Music for Strings and Piano

Throughout his life, Beethoven liked to keep his unpublished manuscripts and old sketchbooks by him, including chamber music which he had composed in Bonn or during his early years in Vienna; from time to time, he borrowed ideas from them.[1] Although some manuscripts were lost, a few complete and incomplete compositions were discovered after his death and published posthumously. Among them was a sedate teenage Allegretto in E flat major, Hess 48, for piano trio, composed in Bonn in 1784, and three piano quartets, WoO 36, composed the following year. Beethoven may have sensed that, like a boy's newly broken voice, his ambitious and experimental piano quartets were too raw for wider circulation, but he made good use of them in some of his later music. The opening bars of the slow movement in the Piano Sonata in F minor, op. 2 no. 1, for instance, are almost the same as the opening bars of the slow movement in the third piano quartet and share its expressive mood. Less experimental, though more appealing and 'presentable' was the graceful Piano Trio in E flat major, WoO 38, composed in Bonn in 1790–1, in which Beethoven proved to himself that he could speak the polite and civilized musical language of his contemporaries to perfection, before embarking on what he would later describe as his 'more important works'.

---

[1] Beethoven remembered a theme in the Allemande for piano, WoO 81 (1793), when composing his second Piano Trio in 1795 and – much later – the Allegro ma non tanto in op. 132. He also jokingly confessed to using 'pilferings from this and that' in op. 131.

APPENDIX 2

Variations

Variations for violin and piano

Two modest precursors of Beethoven's ten magnificent violin sonatas also pre-date those 'more important works': the suave Rondo in G major, WoO 41, and the popular Variations in F for violin and piano on 'Se vuol ballare' from Mozart's *The Marriage of Figaro*, WoO 40, which he touchingly dedicated to his 'first love' in Bonn, Eleanore von Breuning. Suspecting that other composers were appropriating ideas from the *Figaro* Variations and also from his celebrated improvisations, Beethoven reluctantly agreed to their publication by Matthias Artaria as his opus 1 in 1793. He soon regretted his decision, however, and the *Figaro* Variations, today listed as WoO 40, were downgraded to 'no. 1' in time for the 'official' relaunch of his career in Vienna on 20 August 1795, with his three historic piano trios, op. 1, discussed in Chapter 5. However, there is at least one important sign pointing to the future in the *Figaro* Variations: both instruments are equally involved. 'First of all', Beethoven noted crossly, 'there is a mistake on the title page where it is stated "avec un violon ad libitum". Since the violin is inseparably connected with the pianoforte part, and since it is not possible to perform the v[ariations] without the violin, this should be worded "*avec un violon obligate*" – exactly as I corrected it moreover in one [proof] copy!'[1] Whatever their strengths and weaknesses, however, most of those early works seem rather unadventurous when compared to the freshness and originality of the three op. 1 piano trios, and this must surely explain the almost tangible sense of excitement which the trios induced among Beethoven's new patrons and friends in Vienna.

Variations for cello and piano

Two of Beethoven's three sets of variations for cello and piano were written during his fruitful visit to Berlin in 1796 at much the same time as his two seminal cello sonatas, op. 5, discussed in Chapter 6. The first set, WoO 45, was based on the celebrated march and chorus, 'See the conqu'ring hero comes' from Handel's oratorio *Judas Maccabaeus*, which was performed in Berlin during his visit; the second, op. 66, was based on Papageno's comic aria with glockenspiel in Mozart's *The Magic Flute* – 'Ein Mädchen oder Weibchen', one of King Friedrich Wilhelm II's favourite operas by his favourite composer. The third more thoughtful set of variations on Pamina and Papageno's beautiful duet in the same opera, 'Bei Männern, welche

---

[1] *Letters of Beethoven*, Letter 5, August 1793: Beethoven to ?Zmeskall, also quoted in full in Chapter 7.

Liebe fühlen', WoO 46, was composed in 1801 and dedicated to Count von Browne. In all three sets, Beethoven created a richly diverse tapestry of contrasting emotions and technical challenges – no doubt with expert advice from Jean-Louis Duport – advice which must have contributed greatly to his confidence when writing the virtuoso cello part in the Triple Concerto in 1804–5 and his three mature cello sonatas, op. 69 and op. 102 nos. 1 and 2, discussed in Chapters 17 and 23.

Variations for piano trio

Beethoven also wrote two sets of variations for piano trio. The delightful Introduction and Ten Variations on a popular song 'Ich bin der Schneider Kakadu', from Wenzel Müller's singspiel *Die Schwestern von Prag*, was originally composed in 1803. But when Beethoven was particularly short of funds in 1816 he revised it, hoping to persuade Gottfried Härtel to publish it. In his covering letter, dated July that year, he described the trio as 'one of my early works', but assured Härtel that it was 'not poor stuff'.[2] With its solemn, chromatic introduction in G minor followed by ten entertaining variations mostly in G major on what, after all, is a pretty humdrum tune, it is anything but 'poor stuff'. Nonetheless, Gottfried Härtel turned it down – perhaps it seemed rather dated by then – and when it was eventually published in 1824 by Sigmund Steiner, two decades after it had been written, it was listed awkwardly as op. 121a between two of Beethoven's greatest masterpieces, the Diabelli Variations, op. 120, and the *Missa Solemnis*, op. 123. The Variations in E flat major, op. 44, on a hilarious theme by Carl Dittersdorf, was probably written in 1792, but not published until 1804. It is among the wittiest of Beethoven's earlier compositions, especially when in mock solemn mood.

---

[2] *Letters of Beethoven*, Letter 642, 19 July 1816: Beethoven to Gottfried Härtel.

Chamber Music for Wind

There were several interesting, though domestic and unpublished, examples of Beethoven's wind chamber music among his papers when he died. The Trio in G major for flute, bassoon and cembalo, WoO 37 (1786), for example, was probably written for the Westerholt-Giesenberg family. Friedrich 'played the bassoon and maintained a fair band among his servants, particularly players of wind instruments;' one of his sons was a 'master of the flute' and his oldest daughter, Maria Anna Wilhelmine, one of the many passing loves of Beethoven's life in Bonn, was a 'fiery' pianist, able to play 'with a rapidity and accuracy that were marvellous'.[1] As in the *Figaro* Variations, material is shared equally, with brilliant virtuoso passages for all three instruments in turn, not least in the finale, a theme and variations – a most engaging party piece. The Duo in two movements for two flutes, WoO 26, is a more modest affair; before he finally left Bonn for Vienna in 1792, Beethoven composed it for Johann Degenhart, who had presented him with a farewell album containing the good wishes of his many friends there.

The history of the Wind Octet in E flat major, op. 103 (1792), is extraordinary. Soon after his arrival in Vienna Beethoven recomposed it as a string quintet (see Chapter 12), and included it among his 'more important works' as op. 4. He then seems to have forgotten the original Octet, which was published posthumously as op. 103.[2] The principal chamber works for wind – the Quintet for Piano and Wind, op. 16, the Clarinet Trio, op. 11, the Septet, op. 20, and the Serenade for flute, violin and viola, op. 25 – are discussed in detail in Chapter 9.

After completing the Serenade in 1801, however, Beethoven gave up composing chamber music for wind altogether, offering some of his earlier compositions to publishers only when he was short of funds. As a result they appear with confusingly high opus numbers; the Wind Sextet, op. 71, for example, was probably composed in 1796, but published by Breitkopf & Härtel in 1810. 'It is one of my early works', Beethoven explained apologetically. 'What is more, it was composed in one night. All that one can really say about it is that it was written by a composer who has produced at any rate a few better works.'[3] The delightful Trio in C major for two oboes and cor anglais, op. 87, composed in ?1795 – and sometimes borrowed surreptitiously by violinists and viola players – was likewise withheld for several years, though eventually published in 1806. Curiously the colourful set of

---

[1] Thayer, *The Life of Beethoven*, pp. 110–11.

[2] Also found was a Rondo, WoO 25, originally written as the finale for the Octet; an incomplete Quintet, Hess 19 (?1793), a March for wind sextet and a (perhaps spurious) Flute Sonata, Anh. 4.

[3] *Letters of Beethoven*, Letter 224, 8 August 1809: Beethoven to Breitkopf & Härtel.

Variations on 'Là ci darem la mano' from Mozart's *Don Giovanni*, WoO 28, also composed for two oboes and cor anglais, remained unattached and forgotten.

If Beethoven had a favourite wind or brass instrument, it was surely the horn, not only because of its range and tonal variety but also, no doubt, because of the metaphors it conjures up in his music: grandeur, heroism, mystery, magic, the countryside, the hunt. The imposing Sonata for Horn and Piano, op. 17 (1800), published in 1801 by Mollo, together with an alternative arrangement for cello and piano, is the only solo sonata which Beethoven composed for either a wind or a brass instrument, and the colourful Sextet for two horns and string quartet, op. 81b (1795), the only concerto-like work. Both are classical in form, language, gesture and purpose, so by the time the horn-playing publisher in Bonn, Nikolaus Simrock, got round to publishing the Sextet in 1810 Beethoven was, of course, speaking a new and completely different language.

Beethoven composed only one work for brass ensemble – three sombre Equali for Four Trombones, WoO 30, written during a visit to Linz in 1812 as a thank-offering to Franz Glöggl, Kapellmeister at the cathedral, for the warm welcome he had received there: 'We now have the long-desired pleasure of welcoming to our city the Orpheus and greatest composer of our time', Glöggl wrote on 5 October 1812, in the *Linzer Musik-Zeitung*.[4] Later the conductor, composer and writer Ignaz Seyfried arranged two of the Equali for male voices[5] to be sung on 29 March 1827 at Beethoven's funeral, at which he, together with Schubert and a large number of Beethoven's friends, were torch or pallbearers.

---

[4] Thayer, *The Life of Beethoven*, p. 540.

[5] Clive, *Beethoven and his World*, p. 335.

APPENDIX 4

Arrangements

Arrangements of every kind were popular throughout the nineteenth century and, although Beethoven regarded them for the most part as distractions, he himself rescored several of his own compositions, among them the six noted earlier in Chapters 9, 12 and 27.[1] Other compositions arranged or approved by him include three for piano trio: op. 36, based on the Second Symphony; op. 38 (for clarinet or violin, cello and piano), based on the Septet and written for the musical family of his doctor, Johann Schmidt; and op. 63, based on the String Quintet, op. 4, which, it may be recalled, was itself a transcription of the Wind Octet, op. 103, found among Beethoven's papers when he died. To these he added or approved two additional cello sonatas: op. 17, an arrangement of the Horn Sonata, and op. 64, an arrangement of the String Trio, op. 3.

Not surprisingly, Beethoven was outraged when Hoffmeister in Leipzig and Mollo in Vienna published string quintet arrangements of the Septet and the First Symphony without acknowledgement. As he wrote in the *Wiener Zeitung* of 20 October 1802:

> The making of transcriptions is on the whole a thing against which ... in our prolific age of transcriptions ... a composer would merely struggle in vain; but at least he is entitled to demand that the publishers shall mention the fact on the title-page, so that his honour as a composer shall not be infringed nor the public deceived – this is in order to prevent cases of this kind arising in future. At the same time I am informing the public that a new and original quintet which I have composed in C major, op. 29, will be published very soon by Breitkopf & Härtel at Leipzig.[2]

The most intriguing of Beethoven's own arrangements, however, is the String Quartet in F major (Hess 34), based on his Piano Sonata in E major, op. 14 no. 1; intriguing because, on his own admission, he disapproved of the practice, but wanted nevertheless to prove to himself and to others that he could do the job as well as his two great forebears: 'I firmly maintain

---

[1] The Notturno in D major, op. 42, for viola and piano, is a transcription of the Serenade for violin, viola and cello, op. 8. The Piano Quartet, op. 16, is a transcription of the Quintet for piano, oboe, clarinet, bassoon and horn, op. 16. The Serenade for flute (or violin) and piano, op. 41, is a transcription of the Serenade for flute, violin and viola, op. 25. The String Quintet in E flat major, op. 4, is a transcription of the Wind Octet, op. 103. The String Quintet in C minor, op. 104, is a transcription of the Piano Trio in C minor, op. 1 no. 3. The *Grosse Fuge*, op. 134, for piano duet, is a transcription of the *Grosse* Fuge, op. 133, for string quartet. For a full list of other arrangements and miscellaneous works, see Coldicott, 'Arrangements of His Own Music', pp. 272–5. For unfinished and projected works, see Cooper, *The Beethoven Compendium*, pp. 275–8.

[2] *Letters of Beethoven*, Appendix H (1), p. 1434.

that only Mozart could arrange for other instruments the works he composed for the pianoforte; and Haydn could do this too – and without wishing to force my company on those two great men, I make the same statement about my own pianoforte sonatas. I have only arranged one for string quartet because I was earnestly implored to do so.'[3]

[3] *Letters of Beethoven*, Letter 59, 13 July 1802: Beethoven to Breitkopf & Härtel.

Bibliography

Abraham, Gerald, *Beethoven's Second-Period Quartets* (London: Oxford University Press, 1942)

Adelson, Robert, 'Beethoven's String Quartet in E flat op. 127: A Study of the First Performances', *Music & Letters*, vol. 79 (1998), pp. 219–43

Apel, Willi, ed., *Harvard Dictionary of Music* (London: Routledge & Kegan Paul, 1951)

Arnold, Denis, and Nigel Fortune, ed., *The Beethoven Companion* (London: Faber & Faber, 1971)

Beethoven, Ludwig van, *The Letters of Beethoven*, trans. Emily Anderson, 3 vols. (London: Macmillan, 1961)

Berlioz, Hector, *The Memoirs of Hector Berlioz*, trans. David Cairns (London: Victor Gollancz, 1969)

Brandenburg, Sieghard, 'Beethoven's opus 12 Violin Sonatas: On the Path to his Personal Style', in *The Beethoven Violin Sonatas*, ed. Lewis Lockwood and Mark Kroll (Urbana: University of Illinois Press, 2004)

—— 'Beethoven's Violin Sonatas, Cello Sonatas and Variations', in *Beethoven Bicentennial, 1770–1970*, ed. Joseph Schmidt-Görg and Hans Schmidt (Bonn: Beethoven-Archiv; Hamburg: Polydor International, 1970)

Breuning, Gerhard von, *Memories of Beethoven: From the House of the Black-Robed Spaniards,* ed. Maynard Solomon (Cambridge: Cambridge University Press, 1992)

Brown, Clive, 'Ferdinand David's Editions of Beethoven', in *Performing Beethoven,* ed. Robin Stowell (Cambridge: Cambridge University Press, 1994)

Cairns, David, *Berlioz*, vol. 1: *The Making of an Artist, 1803–1832* (London: André Deutch, 1989)

—— *Berlioz*, vol. 2: *Servitude and Greatness, 1832–1869* (London: Allen Lane, 1999)

Capell, Richard, *Schubert's Songs* (London: Pan Books, 1957)

Clarke, Rebecca, 'The Beethoven Quartets as a Player Sees Them', *Music & Letters*, vol. 8 (1927), pp. 178–90

Clive, Peter, *Beethoven and his World* (Oxford: Oxford University Press, 2001)

Cobbett's Cyclopedic Survey of Chamber Music, 2nd edn, 3 vols. (London: Oxford University Press, 1963)

Coldicott, Anne-Louise, 'Arrangements of His Own Music', in *The Beethoven Compendium*, ed. Barry Cooper (London: Thames & Hudson, 1991)

Cooper, Barry, *Beethoven and the Creative Process* (Oxford: Clarendon Press, 1990)

—— ed., *The Beethoven Compendium* (London: Thames & Hudson, 1991)

—— *Beethoven*, The Master Musicians (Oxford: Oxford University Press, 2000)

—— 'The Compositional Act', in *The Cambridge Companion to Beethoven* ed. Glenn Stanley (Cambridge: Cambridge University Press, 2000)

Cooper, Martin, *Beethoven: The Last Decade, 1817–1827* (London: Oxford University Press, 1970)

Daschner, Hubert, 'Music for the Stage', in *Beethoven Bicentennial, 1770–1970*, ed. Joseph Schmidt-Görg and Hans Schmidt (Bonn: Beethoven-Archiv; Hamburg: Polydor International, 1970)

Daverio, John, 'Manner, Tone and Tendency in Beethoven's Chamber Music for Strings', in *The Cambridge Companion to Beethoven* ed. Glenn Stanley (Cambridge: Cambridge University Press, 2000)

Davies, Norman, *Europe: A History* (Oxford: Oxford University Press, 1996)

Einstein, Alfred, *Mozart: His Character, His Work*, trans. A. Mendel and N. Broder (London: Cassell, 1946)

—— *Schubert*, trans. David Ascoli (London: Cassell, 1951)

Eliot, T. S., *Collected Poems, 1909–1962* (London: Faber & Faber, 1963)

Fiske, Roger, 'String Quintets', in *Chamber Music*, ed. Alec Robertson (Harmondsworth: Penguin, 1957)

Forbes, Elliot, rev. and ed., *Thayer's Life of Beethoven* (Princeton, NJ: Princeton University Press, 1967)

Fortune, Nigel, 'The Chamber Music with Piano', *The Beethoven Companion*, ed. Denis Arnold and Nigel Fortune (London: Faber & Faber, 1971), pp. 197–240

Kaplan, Mark, 'Beethoven's Chamber Music with Piano', in *The Cambridge Companion to Beethoven*, ed. Glenn Stanley (Cambridge: Cambridge University Press, 2000)

Kerman, Joseph, *The Beethoven Quartets* (London: Oxford University Press, 1967)

Kinderman, William, ed., *The String Quartets of Beethoven* (Urbana: University of Illinois Press, 2006)

Klugmann, Friedhelm, 'Piano Trios and Piano Quartets', in *Beethoven Bicentennial, 1770–1970*, ed. Joseph Schmidt-Görg and Hans Schmidt (Bonn: Beethoven-Archiv; Hamburg: Polydor International, 1970)

Komlós, Katalin, 'The Viennese Keyboard Trio in the 1780s: Sociological Background and Contemporary Reception', in *Music and Letters*, vol. 68 (1987), pp. 222–34

Kramer, Richard, '"Sonate, que me veux-tu?": Opus 30, opus 31, and the Anxieties of Genre', in *The Beethoven Violin Sonatas*, ed. Lewis Lockwood and Mark Kroll (Urbana: University of Illinois Press, 2004)

Kroll, Mark, '"As if stroked with a bow": Beethoven's Keyboard Legato and the Sonatas for Violin and Piano', in *The Beethoven Violin Sonatas*, ed. Lewis Lockwood and Mark Kroll (Urbana: University of Illinois Press, 2004)

Kurth, Sabine, ed., *Beethoven Streichquintette* (Munich: G. Henle-Verlag, 2001)

Landon, H. C. Robbins, *Beethoven: A Documentary Study* (London: Thames & Hudson, 1970)

—— *Haydn: Chronicle and Works: The Years of the 'Creation', 1796–1800* (London: Thames & Hudson, 1977)

—— *Haydn: Chronicle and Works: The Late Years, 1801–1809* (London: Thames & Hudson, 1977)

Lawson, Colin, 'The Development of Wind Instruments', in *Performing Beethoven*, ed. Robin Stowell (Cambridge: Cambridge University Press, 1996)

Lockwood, Lewis, *Beethoven: The Music and the Life* (New York: W. W. Norton, 2003)

—— '"On the Beautiful in Music": Beethoven's "Spring" Sonata for Violin and Piano, opus 24', in *The Beethoven Violin Sonatas: History, Criticism, Performance*, ed. Lewis Lockwood and Mark Kroll (Urbana: University of Illinois Press, 2004)

Lodes, Birgit, '"So traumte mire, ich reiste ... nach Indien': Temporality and Mythology in op.127', in *The String Quartets of Beethoven*, ed. William Kinderman (Urbana: University of Illinois Press, 2006)

Marliave, Joseph de, *Beethoven's Quartets* (New York: Dover Publications, 1961)

Marston, Nicholas, '"Haydns Geist aus Beethovens Handen"?: Fantasy and Farewell in the Quartet in E♭ major, op. 74', in *The String Quartets of Beethoven*, ed. William Kinderman (Urbana: University of Illinois Press, 2006)

—— 'Chamber Music with Wind', 'Chamber Music for Piano and Strings', 'Chamber Music for Strings', in *The Beethoven Compendium*, ed. Barry Cooper (London: Thames & Hudson, 1991)

Mason, Daniel, *The Quartets of Beethoven* (New York: Oxford University Press, 1947)

Novello, Vincent and Mary, *A Mozart Pilgrimage*, ed. Nerina Medici di Marignano and Rosemary Hughes (London: Ernst Eulenberg, 1975)

Ong, Seow-Chin, 'Aspects of the Genesis of Beethoven's String Quartet in F minor, op.95', in *The String Quartets of Beethoven*, ed. William Kinderman (Urbana: University of Illinois Press, 2006)

—— 'The Autograph of Beethoven's "Archduke" Trio, op.97', in *Beethoven Forum*, vol. 11 (2007), pp. 181–208

Platen, Emil, 'The String Trios', in *Beethoven Bicentennial, 1770–1970*, ed. Joseph Schmidt-Görg and Hans Schmidt (Bonn: Beethoven-Archiv; Hamburg: Polydor International, 1970)

Radcliffe, Philip, *Beethoven's String Quartets* (London: Hutchinson, 1965)

Rosen, Charles, *The Classical Style* (London: Faber & Faber, 1976)

Rostal, Max, *Beethoven: The Sonatas for Piano and Violin: Thoughts on Their Interpretation* (London: Toccata Press, 1985)

Sadie, Stanley, 'Boccherini, Luigi', in *The New Grove Dictionary*, ed. Stanley Sadie (London: Macmillan, 1980)

Schindler, Anton, *Beethoven as I Knew Him*, ed. and rev. Donald MacArdle (New York: Dover Publications, 1996)

Schmidt-Görg, Joseph, and Hans Schmidt, ed., *Beethoven Bicentennial, 1770–1970* (Bonn: Beethoven-Archiv; Hamburg: Polydor International, 1970)

Schoenberg, Arnold, *Style and Idea: Selected Writings*, ed. Leonard Stein (London: Faber & Faber, 1975)

Schumann, Robert and Clara, *The Marriage Diaries*, ed. Gerd Nauhaus, trans. Peter Ostwald (London: Robson Books, 1993)

Schwager, Myron, 'A Fresh Look at Beethoven's Arrangements', *Music & Letters*, vol. 54 (1973), pp. 142–60

Simpson, Robert., 'The Chamber Music for Strings', in *The Beethoven Companion*, ed. Denis Arnold and Nigel Fortune (London: Faber & Faber, 1973)

Sisman, Elaine, 'Beethoven's Musical Inheritance', in *The Cambridge Companion to Beethoven*, ed. Glenn Stanley (Cambridge: Cambridge University Press, 2000)

Solomon, Maynard, *Beethoven*, 2nd edn (New York: Schirmer Books, 1998)

—— *Beethoven Essays* (Cambridge, MA: Harvard University Press, 1997)

—— 'Antonie Brentano and Beethoven', *Music & Letters*, vol. 58 (1977), pp.153–69.

Sonneck, O. G., ed., *Beethoven: Impressions by his Contemporaries* (New York: Dover Publications, 1954)

Stanley, Glenn, ed., *The Cambridge Companion to Beethoven* (Cambridge: Cambridge University Press, 2000)

Steblin, Rita, and Frederick Stocken, 'Reminiscences about Schubert by his Forgotten Friend', *Music & Letters*, vol. 88 (2007), pp. 226–65

Stich, Norbert, 'String Quartets', in *Beethoven Bicentennial, 1770–1970*, ed. Joseph Schmidt-Görg and Hans Schmidt (Bonn: Beethoven-Archiv; Hamburg: Polydor International, 1970)

Stowell, Robin, ed., *Performing Beethoven* (Cambridge: Cambridge University Press, 1994)

Strunk, Oliver, *Source Readings in Music History* (London: Faber & Faber, 1952)

Thayer, Alexander, *The Life of Beethoven*, ed. Elliott Forbes (Princeton, NJ: Princeton University Press, 1967)

Tolstoy, Leo, *The Kreutzer Sonata*, trans. David McDuff (Harmondsworth: Penguin, 2007)

Tovey, Donald, *Beethoven*, ed. Hubert Foss (London: Oxford University Press, 1944)

Truscott, Harold, 'The Piano Music', in *The Beethoven Companion*, ed. Denis Arnold and Nigel Fortune (London: Faber & Faber, 1971)

Watkin, David, 'Beethoven's Sonatas for Piano and Cello', in *Performing Beethoven*, ed. Robin Stowell (Cambridge: Cambridge University Press, 1994)

Index of Beethoven's Music by Opus Number

Beethoven Index

General Index